PAI
POWER

Also by Paul Collins

God's Earth
No Set Agenda
Mixed Blessings

PAPAL POWER

A proposal for change in Catholicism's third millennium

Paul Collins

Fount
An Imprint of HarperCollins*Publishers*

Fount Paperbacks is an Imprint of
HarperCollins*Religious*
Part of HarperCollins*Publishers*
77–85 Fulham Palace Road, London W6 8JB

First published in Australia in 1997 by
HarperCollins*Religious*, an Imprint of
HarperCollins*Publishers* (Australia) Pty Limited Group
First published in Great Britain in 1997 by
Fount Paperbacks

1 3 5 7 9 10 8 6 4 2

A catalogue record for this book is
available from the British Library

000 6280390

Printed and bound in Hong Kong

The author and publishers wish to thank and acknowledge the following for the use of
copyright material: Cuthbert Butler, *The Vatican Council*, Collins/Fontana, London © 1962;
Robert Blair Kaiser, *The Politics of Sex and Religion: A Case History in the Development of Doctrine
1962–1985*, National Catholic Reporter Publishing, Kansas City © 1985; Colman J Barry,
Readings in Church History, Paulist Press © 1965; pp.128–9 John Meyendoerff (ed.) *The
Primacy of Peter: Essays in Ecclesiology and the Early Church*, St Vladimir's Seminary Press,
Crestwood © 1992; Brian Tierney, *Origins of Papal Infallibility 1150–1350*, Scribner, NY
© 1995; Denis Minns, *Irenaes*, Geoffrey Chapman, London © 1994; Yves Congar, *Lay People
in the Church*, Geoffrey Chapman, London © 1957; Giuseppe Alberigo, *History of the Vatican II
Vol. 1*, Orbis Books, Maryknoll NY, © 1995; James Broderick, *Robert Bellarmine, Saint and
Scholar*, Burns and Oates, London © 1961; Peter Hebblethwaite, *Paul VI: The First Modern
Pope*, HarperCollins, London © 1993; Reprinted from the *Ratzinger Report*, by Joseph
Cardinal Ratzinger and Vittorio Messori, p.59 © 1995 Ignatius Press, San Francisco. All
rights reserved; reprinted with permission of Ignatius Press. From *Peter in Rome: The Literary,
Liturgical and Archaelogical Evidence* by Daniel Wm. O'Connor Copyright © 1969 by Columbia
University Press. Reprinted with the permission of the publisher; Luis M Bermejo,
Infallibility on Trial: Church, Conciliarity and Communion, Christian Classics, Westminster,
Maryland © 1992.

For my Canberra friends:
Fran and Peter,
Graeme and Pam,
Marilyn and the sadly missed Greg.

Jesus called them to him and said,
'You know that the rulers of the Gentiles lord it over them,
and their great ones are tyrants over them.
It will not be so among you;
but whoever wishes to be great among you must be your servant,
and whoever wishes to be first among you must be your slave;
just as the Son of Man came not to be served but to serve …'
Matthew 20:25–28

Acknowledgments

My special thanks are due to Dr. Lawrence McIntosh and to the staff of the Joint Theological Library at Ormond College in the University of Melbourne. They showed unstinting kindness and good humor to my many, often arcane, requests. Without such a resource an unattached researcher like myself would be at a real disadvantage. Dr. McIntosh, in particular, made many suggestions and often pointed me in the right direction.

Anyone working in English in the area of papal history is in the debt of Canon J. N. D. Kelly and his urbane, reliable, and enormously useful *The Oxford Dictionary of Popes* (1986). My many other sources and guides are acknowledged in the notes and bibliography. Equally indispensable is Norman P. Tanner's *Decrees of the Ecumenical Councils*, which is the source of most of my quotations from the general councils.

My thanks also to Kevin Mark, who has made many useful suggestions and has acted as my ever-reliable editor.

Contents

Introduction

This is a book about power and the way it has been used to govern the Catholic Church. In a more ideal world it would be about service and Christ-like leadership. But this is not the reality of contemporary Catholicism. The second millennium of Catholic history has been characterized by the evolution of an ideology of papal power that has increasingly centralized all authority in the pope and his curial bureaucracy. Often in the process of asserting its authority papal intentions were laudable and honorable: centralization came as a result of reform of the Church and society, struggles to guard the Church from secular rulers invading the spiritual realm for their own ends, the protection of local communities from petty episcopal tyrants, and the coordination of the missionary work of the Church and the proclamation of the message of Christ. This process of the centralization of power has been going on for a little less than a thousand years and most people have forgotten that a highly centralized papacy is by no means normative for the entire history of the Church. The long tradition of Catholicism offers other models of governance and ways of relating to the Bishop of Rome.

My purpose in this book is not primarily historical, but I have used Church history as a way of approaching other models of papacy that might be developed as the Church confronts the third millennium of its existence. By 'Church' I primarily mean the Roman Catholic Church, but the importance of the role of the papacy in the ecumenical Church of the future is a major consideration in this book. The power of the pope, as presently constituted, is simply and totally unacceptable to the Orthodox, Anglican, or Protestant churches. But their views cannot be ignored by Rome. Despite many advances this century, the tragedy of Christian division still plagues us and the contemporary form of the papacy is an enormous stumbling block to the process of Christian unity.

But the power-focused Roman agenda has also become an obstacle for Catholicism itself. The centralized and absolutist operation of Rome has brought modern Catholicism to a grinding halt. Among the mainstream majority of Catholics in the Western world there is a pervasive sense that the Church has failed them, that it has not listened to their experience and their needs, and that the doctrinal and moral guidance that it offers in many areas is irrelevant to their lives. The Church hierarchy seems to offer little guidance or inspiration in the search for a contemporary spirituality and an ethical basis for living. The protection of papal power seems to be the constant underlying leitmotif of most papal decisions. To the outsider, the Vatican seems an extraordinarily conceited and self-absorbed institution.

Yet Catholicism cannot simply jettison the papacy. Catholics recognize that it is one of several defining elements of their faith. The Bishop of Rome has been part of Church history from very early in the formation of Christianity. The office has certainly developed and evolved over the centuries and its influence has ebbed and flowed in the Church, but it has been present since the Church's origins. The very fact that it has changed means that it can change again. This book is fundamentally about how that change might occur.

The core of the problem is how an institution so focused on and preoccupied with medieval, monarchical, and absolutist notions of *sacra potestas* (sacred power) can transmute into one concerned with genuine notions of leadership, especially the style of servant leadership modeled by Jesus in the Gospel of John and discussed by Peter in his First Epistle. As a model of abject service, Jesus washed his disciples' feet at the Last Supper (John 13:2–17) and Peter expands on this by saying that Church leaders should not 'lord it over those in your charge, but be examples … all of you must clothe yourselves with humility in your dealings with one another' (1 Peter 5:3–5). This is a far cry from a papal superstar who claims it as his right to regulate the most intimate details of human existence.

I am not questioning the sincerity of modern popes as they assert their right to act out the role and authority that they have inherited and have themselves helped to develop. They are as much the victims of history as the rest of Catholicism. But I do want to question the nature and limit of that role and to suggest that it can no longer be couched in terms of 'power over' people. The papacy must begin to learn the humility of genuine Christian leadership. In short, what I have tried to do in this book is to draw on the long tradition of Catholicism to suggest some alternative models that may be more acceptable ecumenically, more inspiring to Catholic people, and less destructive to the Catholic Church of today and tomorrow.

CHAPTER 1

Does the Church equal the pope, and the pope equal the Church?

The problem of papalism: the identification of Church and pope

I have lost count of the number of times I have been told, both in private and in the media, that if I cannot agree with what the pope says 'I should get out of the Church.' A year or so ago the host of a radio program, who sees himself as *very* well informed, told me during a discussion about the ethics of contraception that if I 'could not keep the rules of the club as voiced by the pope' then I should leave the Church. It was useless trying to explain that the parallel between club and Church was spurious—it is amazing how fundamentalist secular sophisticates can be! Recently a rather serious Protestant journalist told me that she could not understand how Catholics who disagreed with the pope could remain in the Church 'in good faith.'

It is exceptionally difficult to move people, from both within and outside the Church, beyond this naive identification of the pope and Catholicism. The two have become so intertwined in the popular mind that every papal statement is seen to be absolute law for every Catholic. Papal statements, from mere speeches to encyclicals, have taken on oracular status; ordinary, day-to-day magisterium (teaching) and infallibility have become conflated in the popular mind. Indeed, the very thing that the minority of bishops feared at the First Vatican Council (1869–1870)—which defined papal infallibility—has become reality: everything that the pope says is infallible and to remain a loyal Catholic you must accept it all. Pope and Church are one and the same, and the Bishop of Rome has become a papal oracle. The fact is that, as we approach the third millennium of Christianity, the papacy has emerged as the Catholic Church's major internal structural problem. It has become a stumbling block to many, both inside and outside the Church.

The papacy is one of the greatest historical institutions, and is certainly the most enduring in the European experience. Yet in the course of its long history, the papacy has become increasing problematic for the very institution in which it has such a pivotal role—the Church itself. Instead of being the center of the Church's unity and communion, it has become a divisive force that cuts Catholic off from Catholic. Instead of being the locus where different cultures interact and learn from each other as they draw on a common tradition and history that reaches back two millennia, it has become more self-engrossed and culturally circumscribed than ever. The irony is that there is multicultural window-dressing, such as the employment of clergymen of varying nationalities (and abilities) in the Roman curia, but these people are often more Roman than the Romans. And they would not be in the Vatican if they did not follow the curial line fully.

Instead of drawing its teaching on faith and morality from the deep and broad Catholic tradition, the papacy has increasingly espoused a parochial moralism and a historically superficial scholastic theology that draws little from the contemporary world and has scarcely anything to say to it. Recent papal and curial utterances sound increasingly sectarian and apocalyptic, couched in a language and rhetoric that is simply meaningless to most people. Instead of being the institution that crosses cultural divides, the papacy has lost the sense of being a bridge builder. The pope is often called 'Pontiff,' which is derived from *pontifex* which, in turn, comes from *pons facere*— to build a bridge.[1] But the modern papacy has become the mouthpiece of an increasingly narrow orthodoxy. The sad thing is that this has happened at the very time when the majority of Catholics live in the developing world.

The whole ecclesiastical malaise can be summed up in one word: *papalism*. This neologism describes the constant movement toward centralization, bureaucratic control, and a narrow orthodoxy that has characterized the activities of the papacy and the Roman curia over the last two centuries, especially since the definition of papal infallibility and primacy at the First Vatican Council in 1870. Following this Council there has been an ever-escalating tendency to conflate what Vatican I called 'ordinary magisterium'—the day-to-day teaching and advice of the pope on belief and morals—with infallibility. In fact, the Italian historian Giuseppe Alberigo argues that the papacy unconsciously compensated itself for the final loss of the Papal States to a unified Italy in 1870 by transferring its energy into the business of the daily moral and religious government of the lives of Catholics:

> [The Roman authorities] were pursuing a fundamentally consistent decision ... to transfer the axis of church government to the doctrinal domain by using [their] delicate and highly sensitive authority to determine conformity to the doctrinal content of the Gospel as an everyday instrument of regulating the life of the ecclesial community.[2]

In the process of doing this the papacy gradually attempted to muzzle all other magisterial (or teaching) sources in the Church and to subsume the entire theological function to itself. As a result the papacy since 1870 has come to act as a kind of ecclesiastical oracle, the assumed source of all wisdom and truth in the Church. This is a distortion of the true Catholic tradition.

I define papalism as the conflation of all teaching authority, with an exaggerated notion of primacy. In this context primacy is defined as the notion that the papacy owns and totally controls all the practical aspects of the Church. This book is fundamentally about how Catholicism can escape from papalism and how the Bishop of Rome can find his true role as the heart of the Church and the center of its communion. But in order to jettison papalism the pope is going to have to rediscover another of his titles: *servus servorum Dei*—the servant of the servants of God. As long as the pope and the Vatican see themselves in an authoritarian manner as the 'owners' of the Church, 'lock, stock, and barrel,' they are going to reinforce papalism. To achieve any reform in the papacy, the papacy itself will have to rediscover the notion of servant leadership that is so strong in the New Testament. According to John's Gospel, at the last supper Jesus took the drastic step of washing his disciples' feet to remind them of the central importance of service (13:1–20). So, too, the papacy needs to rediscover that its leadership is one of service, not of domination. It needs to take to heart the advice of the first pope, Peter, who told Church leaders not to 'lord it over' those in care, but to act with 'humility' (1 Peter 5:3–5). Humility must be sorely tried when you are a papal superstar!

In the process of the papacy recovering the New Testament idea of servant leadership, the Roman curia will have to be either radically recast, or abolished. It is simply not structured to act in a collegial way. Pope Paul VI tinkered with reform in the 1970s and attempted to internationalize its personnel, but this has done nothing to change its attitudes. In its present form the curia seems to be now beyond reformation. Views like this were stated as long ago as the second session (1963) of the Second Vatican Council; we will explore this further later in the book (pp. 74–85).

The need to distribute power throughout the Church

I have always believed in honestly putting my own cards on the table. This book is directed against papalism and what I believe is an increasing abuse of papal authority in the Church. In my view the present-day Catholic Church is quite unbalanced. In the contemporary Church there is the overwhelming authority of the pope, with, in practical terms, no compensating or balancing centers of power. This papal dominance is enhanced by the superstar status of Pope John Paul II. This unbalanced state is not John Paul's invention; it goes back immediately to the nineteenth century and remotely well beyond that. For the health and future of the Church, this lack of balance must be addressed. Those who should be confronting this issue—the bishops and theologians—have failed. So it is left to people like me to tackle the issue.

Theology provides many insights to help us, but I have become increasingly disillusioned by the timid approach taken by most theologians to the present state of the Church. After he left the priesthood in 1967, Charles Davis made a comment that I think remains true:

> Our age ... is characterised by an escape into theology ... [Today we] are dazzled by what is fundamentally an uncommitted theology, deluged with a spate of theological ideas that are not thought through consistently to their ecclesiastical, social and political consequences.[3]

All of the scriptural, historical, and theological approaches needed for a new approach to authority in the Church have already been articulated, but theologians seem hesitant to draw the 'ecclesiastical, social and political consequences' from the material they articulate. Part of this is an understandable academic reticence, but there is also a sense in which the intellectual leadership of the Church has let us down. So it is left to non-theologians such as myself to attempt to spell out the results of the historical and theological material that is readily available.

My training is in history and I approach all of the issues canvassed in this book from a historical and practical perspective. My questions are: How will this or that insight help us deal with the pressing contemporary crisis of authority and leadership in the Church? And what are the consequences for the Church in the real world? The whole purpose of a historical approach is to broaden our perspectives so that we do not become the prisoners of the present. History helps us see how we got to where we are now, and it frees us to make our own choices, just as people did in the past. The fundamental questions that confront us in the Church today center on leadership, authority, and power. These are all volatile issues and they will not be solved easily.

I have the impression that right now the Church in many Western countries is floundering, without any sense of direction for the future. So someone needs to suggest some priorities, however tentative, for the coming decade. At present there is also a palpable sense of fear abroad in Catholicism that is very debilitating. The superstar status of the present pope so dominates the Catholic stage that others with leadership roles or potential are either hidden or keeping their heads down. To speak out requires courage, and so perhaps it is best that those of us with nothing to lose in terms of theological reputation are the ones to do it. Our present state of fearful inertia is in sharp contrast to the outspokenness of many at Vatican II. There is a real sense in which we need to be reinvigorated by the straight-talk of many at that Council.

The attack on papalism at Vatican II

There was deep suspicion of the Roman curia and its minions at Vatican II (1962–1965), as they tried to manipulate the Council and limit its freedom. There were calls from very senior members of the Church, such as the Melchite Patriarch, Maximos IV Saigh of Antioch, and Cardinal Josef Frings of Cologne, for a thoroughgoing reform of the curia. The context of the call for reform was the discussion of the role of bishops during debate on the schema on the Church, prepared under the control of the Holy Office (formerly the Roman Inquisition and now called the Congregation for the Doctrine of the Faith or CDF) and the curial cardinal, Alfredo Ottaviani. This schema reflected the absolute unwillingness of the curalists and their allies to entertain any idea of collegiality in the government of the Church. Speaking in French, rather than Latin, on 6 November 1963, Patriarch Maximos called for the establishment of a permanent synod (which he called a 'supreme Sacred College') that would represent the whole Church. In calling his proposed synod a 'supreme Sacred College' he was being ironic: the Holy Office was the only 'supreme' congregation in the curia, and the college of cardinals (which Maximos, as an Eastern Patriarch, had three times refused to join) saw itself as a kind of papal senate. He said bluntly:

> All the Roman offices should be subjected to this supreme Sacred College. These [Roman] ministries have no right to block all progress in a uniform and sometimes niggling manner. Moreover, the problems proper to each country should be resolved in those countries. The pope cannot rule the Church with the advice of his familiars alone. The Church was given to Peter and the apostles, not to the Curia. These reforms are urgent. Otherwise we will be courting catastrophe.[4]

Speaking in the same debate, Cardinal Frings of Cologne, in what seemed like a throwaway remark, said:

> Let us not confuse administrative and juridical procedures. This distinction holds for the Holy Office, whose methods are out of harmony with modern times and are a cause of scandal in the world … No one ought to be judged and condemned without having been heard, without knowing what he is accused of, and without the opportunity of correcting his views.[5]

Naturally enough there was a strong reply from Ottaviani, who said that to attack the Holy Office was a direct insult to the pope. Support for the curial opposition to collegiality came also from Archbishop Marcel Lefebvre who, as the leader of the extreme reactionaries, was later to break with Rome and die an excommunicated schismatic.

Two things are significant in this discussion at Vatican II. Firstly, the Holy Office may have changed its name, but the ideology underpinning it has survived. It has certainly not changed its methods. It still accepts anonymous accusations, hardly ever deals directly with the person accused, demands retractions and imposes silences, and continues to employ third-rate theologians as its assessors. This body has no place in the contemporary Church. It is irreformable and therefore should be abolished. I highlight it not because it is significant in itself, but because it is symptomatic of much of the Roman curia. This body exists to prop up papalism. The curia shows little or no consciousness of the wider Church, and no understanding of contemporary reality of the world, and is blindly but profoundly self-interested. It exists to serve papal power, not the ministry of the Church.

Secondly, and more importantly, the notion of the collegiality of the bishops with the pope in governing the Church was quickly quashed after Vatican II. Richard McBrien defines collegiality as:

> The principle that the Church is a communion (college) of local churches which together constitute the Church universal. In practice, collegiality introduces a mode of decision-making in the Church which emphasizes coresponsibility among the bishops expressed in ecumenical councils, synods, and episcopal conferences.[6]

Although it is set out clearly as part of the constitution of the Church in the Vatican II document *Lumen Gentium* (nn. 22–23), collegiality was only half-heartedly supported by Paul VI and strongly opposed by many in the curia. Yet the doctrine of collegiality is the revival of a Church teaching with profound traditional and historical roots. Interestingly, the curia (and specifically the CDF) has no such traditional historical roots, as both the present-day curia and the Inquisition are products of sixteenth-century rejigging of the Roman bureaucracy. This is very recent by Roman standards!

Little has changed in the attitudes of the curia in the thirty years since Vatican II. Under John Paul II the Synod of Bishops has simply become a rubber stamp for his own views. Also, the present head of the CDF, the German Cardinal Josef Ratzinger, has consistently questioned the theological status of local and national episcopal conferences. He maintains that Rome wants to deal with individual bishops. Of course it does; a single bishop facing the curia on his own has much less clout than a national episcopal conference. But it is these conferences that make collegiality a reality. We need to consider seriously if there is any real need for the cumbersome curial bureaucracy that, as we shall see, has developed extraordinarily since the 1960s. It simply reinforces papalism. The most that the pope really needs is a small secretariat.

Besides radically reordering the curia, papalism could also be challenged if the electoral constituency for papal appointments was widened from the college of cardinals, as now constituted, to elected representatives of bishops, priests, and laity, so that a broader cross-section of the Church would have a say in who is pope. But, above all, papal attitudes will have to change so that the pope sees himself, and is seen by others, not as the Church incorporated, but as its servant, its leader, and the focus of its unity.

The need to confront papalism

The time has come, I believe, for those of us who have a deep belief in the genuine Catholic tradition to speak out about the distortions of theology and belief that are found in contemporary papalism. This is not an expression of disloyalty or a lack of faith in the Church, but a reassertion of the genuine

Catholic tradition, a determination to draw on as much of the rich and multifaceted past as is possible. It is only when Catholics have integrated the wealth of their history that they will be able, with confidence, to face the actual reality of the present and the possibility of the future with creative confidence and flexibility. Those who take refuge in the past keep repeating it. At the end of the twentieth century the papalist ideology still lives on, drawing its inspiration largely from the ideas and faith-formulas of the world of the nineteenth century. In the words of Marshall McLuhan, it drives into the future looking through the rear-view mirror! And still more worrying is that the rear-view mirror gives such a circumscribed vision of what actually went on in the past.

By definition the person who lives in the past is a reactionary. Reactionaries should not be confused with genuine conservatives, who actually believe in the conservation of all that has value from the past. Papalism is not a conservative movement; it is essentially reactionary. To speak against such a powerful institution is, of course, a risky undertaking for a Catholic. The Vatican is notoriously self-protective and vindictive toward those who criticize it and, as we shall see, many in the recent past have suffered at its hands. But for those of us who value the breadth, complexity, and subtlety of the Catholic tradition there is increasingly no other option but to speak out. Of course, the papacy is an important part of the tradition that we value, but in recent history papalism has pushed itself so much into the foreground that it has almost totally obscured the broad experience of faith that lies behind it.

For many today, both inside and outside the Church, the simple equation that the pope equals the Church is truth. But the Church historian, especially, has a peculiar responsibility to confront the historical amnesia embedded in this view. As a Catholic it seems to me that I have an obligation to speak against papalism, both on my own behalf and for that large number of Catholics who instinctively and intuitively identify with the long experience of the Church, with its symbols and sacraments, with its tradition of belief in the transcendent presence of God in the world, and its broad appreciation of the value of thought and reason as it struggles to understand and articulate the meaning of our human existence and of our relationship to the natural world. It is sad to see that so many Catholics of good will are alienated and marginalized as a result of the narrow scholasticism and the repressive moralism that characterizes so much papal teaching. Many Catholics, other Christians, and people interested in basic human issues are repelled by the cult of the papal personality, the secretive viciousness of the Roman curia, and the fear and toadyism that characterizes so many in the ecclesiastical hierarchy today.

The origins of the problem

Problems with the papacy are not new for Catholicism. In one form or another they have troubled the Church for the last thousand years. But the highly centralized structure of the contemporary papacy has no real historical precedent. As we shall see, it is only since the early nineteenth century that all of the usual limitations on papal power in the Church have been eliminated or have disappeared. This is why the pressure on contemporary theologians is so great; they are the last group— if one can call them a 'group'—who act as independent thinkers. I am not asserting that there has been some conscious decision on the part of the papacy to impose itself completely on the Church. Rather, I am saying that it has been part of the historical process, especially since that low point in papal history, the French Revolution of 1789 and the Napoleonic Wars that followed.

Peace returned to Europe in 1815 after twenty-six years of turmoil. But the actual state of Europe in 1815 was very different from what it was in 1789. The ideas of liberty, equality, and fraternity were abroad and what was later in the century to be summed up as 'liberalism' had gained the ascendancy with the bourgeoisie. While many of the kings and traditional rulers returned, and while some pretended that the clock could be turned back to the days before 1789, the reality was different. The tide had turned toward liberalism and the rulers of Europe were going to have to adjust. However, a different view was held in the papal court. Here, partly as a result of Popes Pius VI and Pius VII and a number of cardinals having been imprisoned by the forces of the Revolution and Napoleon, an intransigent and reactionary attitude prevailed. This did not happen without a struggle, but eventually the

'Zelanti' cardinals carried the day. These were the religious zealots who were to turn the papacy back in on itself. To what purpose? Basically in order to protect the Church's power in the Papal States.[7]

So papalism is not the fault of any one pope. As I said, it has been developing for many centuries and is an inevitable consequence of the 'hierarchicalization' of the Church. Its contemporary expression has been evolving over the last one hundred and eighty years. Since 1815, papal centralism has grown apace, and modern transportation and communication have made it possible for papal pretensions about centralized power to become a reality. The result is that John Paul II is, in fact, the most powerful pope in history. This is as much the result of what has happened in the Church since 1815 as it is the consequence of his personal style, travel, and theological agenda, and the fact that, as one of the most well-known people alive, he is a media superstar. It is precisely at this peak point of papal power that the ideology underpinning it needs to be challenged. Church history provides us with a way to do this.

I am a firm believer in the power of understanding. If we know how we got to where we are, we will have the potential to move forward in a creative and imaginative way. We will be able to see our experience and beliefs in perspective. History is ultimately liberating. However, the ideology that at present underpins contemporary papalism is profoundly suspicious of history. The paradox is that while this ideology pretends to be traditional, it is actually deeply ambivalent about history. Tradition is the living expression of history; it makes sense only within a historical context. But papalism has no sense of history. It holds the view that there are permanent and never-changing absolutes, and such a mindset stymies its ability to comprehend the evolution and development not just of the Church's belief, but also of its structure and experience.

The actual authority and influence of the papacy in the Church—and in the world—has ebbed and flowed throughout its two-thousand-year history. The greatest of the medieval popes, such as Gregory VII (1073–1085)[8] in the *Dictatus Papae* of 1075, Innocent III (1198–1216), and Boniface VIII (1294–1303) in the bull *Unam sanctam* (1302), claimed that papal power was divine in origin and was superior to any other power in the world. In fact, Innocent thought he was the spiritual monarch of Europe and king of the world, although his actual power was circumscribed by the difficulty of projecting papal power beyond his immediate geographical circumstances. Because of the limitations of transport and communication, medieval papal pretensions had to be squared with geopolitical reality.

John Paul II and modern papalism

No such geographical limits constrain John Paul II. The papacy now seems omnipresent, and the dominant and powerful personality of the Polish pope has stamped the institutional Church in a way that no other pope has managed to achieve for many centuries.[9] This has been reinforced by the length of his pontificate (he was elected in 1978). In both his longevity and his influence he very much resembles Pius IX (1846–1878). John Paul's personality and agenda gives the equation 'pope equals Church' wide credibility. The fact that it is a gross distortion does not prevent this papalist ideology spreading even among those in the Church who should know better.

An entirely new phenomenon has arisen in the Church—the omnipresent papacy. This has been created by the speed of modern travel and by the media, especially television. John Paul II has exploited these possibilities to the full. Previous popes have claimed a universal jurisdiction and pastorate; John Paul II has made it a reality. This can be expressed in simple geographic terms: for instance, between late 1978 and the beginning of 1994, he had made sixty-two foreign 'pastoral visits,' nearly all of them taking in a number of countries. It is hard to find a country that John Paul has not visited, and he has been to most major countries several times.[10] What is the purpose of these visits? The pope has said that they are to strengthen the faith of the local church and to be a visible symbol of the unity of the Church. They are also part of his view of his ministry as a kind of 'universal catechist.'

There are clear differences between trips to developed countries and those to the third world: in the former the emphasis is on both large crowds and the media, particularly television. In the latter the stress is on mass gatherings of people. But the core agenda is always the same: the pope must be at center stage.

It is he who has the message to be proclaimed and it is clear that Rome thinks that he has nothing to learn from the local church.

The peripatetic John Paul II leaves me with a deep sense of uneasiness. This is not because I think that these pastoral visits will particularly change the local churches, or local people. But the tours and the constant highlighting of the pope on television effect a shift at a deeper level of perception: they change the image of the papacy by making the pope *seem* to be personally present. People see him, especially on television, as an accessible, human figure, no longer remote like the 'quasi-divine' Pius XII, but a man of the people. The illusion is that you can reach out to touch him. Because of his ability to communicate, many participants in papal ceremonies, or viewers of the pope on television, feel an intimacy with John Paul. As well as creating a false sense of intimacy, television also creates a situation in which images are more important than reality. A critical regression occurs in which complex realities are reduced to simplistic images and slogans. Television evangelists trade on this constantly. An unreality creeps in wherein viewers believe that the image conveys the truth; so as long as the pope is the only face of the Church on the screen, the equation that the pope equals the Church gains ground. Papalism is reinforced by the relationship between a high-profile papacy and the media. The pope is present in a way that the bishop and other local church leadership is not. Also television thrives on the personality, the lively, animated person who keeps the show moving. So the focus is on John Paul alone. National church leadership, the bishops, and local communities disappear from view.

John Paul II has given a new lease of life to the papal monarchy. In times of uncertainty and shifting values many people search for the simple answer and authoritative certainty. A papal monarch can provide this. Because of his role, it is always the pope who is highlighted; he is the world evangelist. The ministries of others pale into insignificance beside his. As he is a populist leader, his lifeblood seems to be enormous crowds. But there is a danger built into this style. It can so easily create a messianic personality cult, a form of manipulative demagoguery. It is precisely for this reason that Jesus seems so careful to avoid allowing himself to be called messiah. While he was surrounded by crowds, he was constantly on his guard against the cult of personality. He always pointed beyond himself to the God who sent him.

In all of this, collegiality has been pushed into the background. It is the world captain, not the local team, that is highlighted. Local bishops look like papal acolytes in purple. A strong focus on Roman leadership inevitably weakens local leadership. If these pastoral visits of the pope were more low-key and less expensive, they might be very helpful to the local church. This would be especially true if John Paul came, listened critically to the local leadership, and, after dialogue, reinforced the efforts of Catholics to confront local realities. This would be, in the truest sense, a ministry of unity as the center strengthened and confirmed the work of the local church. But that is not the way it happens. Rather, the powerful figure of John Paul jets in from outside to dominate center stage for a brief time, delivers his message (frequently developed with some local consultation), and then leaves. The way in which the tours are organized actually prevents the possibility of input during the visit. Any local participation is vetted well in advance. The sheer length and speed of the trips does not allow any time for discussion, let alone a chance to stop and experience the indigenous church, environment, and culture. One can admire the pope's stamina, but the purpose of the speed must be questioned. Is it to avoid having to hear the local people, to prevent the expression of agendas different from those of the Vatican? Moreover, national bishops' conferences are ignored.

Who will oppose papalism?

Even though bishops are the successors of the apostles, they in fact owe their appointment to the pope, or at least to that section of the Roman curia (the Congregation for Bishops) that makes episcopal appointments. By right their jurisdiction may be personal ('ordinary,' as the jargon of canon law terms it), but *de facto* they are still very much the pope's men, and, because of the types of candidates appointed by Rome, this has become increasingly so during the pontificate of John Paul II. *The Code of Canon Law* says that 'A diocesan bishop ... possesses the ordinary, proper, and immediate power which is required for the exercise of his pastoral office' (can. 381.1).[11] However, it also makes it clear that Rome can limit this power and that it is exercised '*ad nutum Sanctae Sedis*'—subject to the nod of the Holy See.

Canons 375–380 of the Code set out the process by which bishops are appointed. Although it is not spelled out in canon law, the role of Rome and its nuncios and delegates in each country is absolutely central in the process of appointing bishops. They are the ones who draw up lists of possible candidates for episcopal office and submit names to Rome. Even where there is a surviving practice that the canons (the senior priests) of the cathedral chapter have a right to nominate the list of possible candidates to be submitted to Rome (as is the case in Switzerland and Austria), this has often been ignored and reactionary bishops, such as Bishop Wolfgang Hass in Chur (which takes in Zurich), and Cardinal Hans Hermann Groer in Vienna, have been forced on dioceses with disastrous results. (Cardinal Groer has since been forced to resign amid allegations of sexual misconduct.) And Rome can depose bishops, as the outspoken Bishop Jacques Gaillot of Evreux in France recently found out. With some courageous exceptions, one cannot expect much opposition to papalism from the ranks of the bishops.

That is why the role of theologians is so important. For the fact is that they have some independence, especially if they work within the context of state universities that are not dependent on the Roman curia. Also, if they are members of religious orders and have the support of their superiors, they can take advantage of the fact that they belong to semi-independent units within the Church. If they are laypeople they have even more independence. In fact, one of the most creative and important developments of recent times has been the training of an increasing number of lay theologians.

Because of their apparent independence there has been enormous pressure put on theologians by the Vatican during the present pontificate. In fact, as we shall see, a considerable number have been isolated, and then in an attempt to destroy their influence they are removed from any official role, such as teaching, and pushed to the margins of the Church. This is generally done in ways that lack even basic charity and respect. In the papalist ideology theologians are not the explorers at the interface between contemporary culture and the transcendent, but their task is apologetic: that is, to be apologists for the official line proposed by pope and curia.

Traditionally, there have been three magisteria (or teaching authorities) in the Church. In historical order, the episcopal magisterium developed first. It is exercised at its highest level by bishops acting together in a synod or an ecumenical council. Almost coterminous with the development of the episcopal magisterium was the role of theologians. The task of the theologian is to contribute to the teaching mission of the Church by scholarly competence. Historically, the papal magisterium developed somewhat later. The context of all teaching authority is the *sensus fidelium*. This 'sense of the faithful' is difficult to define precisely, but it refers to the actual acceptance of beliefs by Christians down through the centuries. It is linked to the doctrine of reception, which holds that if the Christian community accepts a teaching *then* that teaching is confirmed. If the teaching is not received, then it can be said that it is not the teaching of the Church. Yet in recent Church history—with the exception of the periods of the two most recent councils, Vatican I (1869–1870) and Vatican II (1962–1965)—the papal magisterium has seemingly tried to subsume the roles of both bishops and theologians. One of the characteristics of papalism is to conflate all the magisteria, to subsume them into the papal magisterium, and to extend to the Roman curia itself a share in the pope's teaching authority.

The attempt to destroy traditional speculative theology

The relationship between the Vatican and speculative theology over the last one hundred and eighty years has usually been a fraught one. This is especially true of those theologians who have tried to move the Church beyond accepted establishment positions. The reason for this is quite simple: the papacy has been determined to bring theology under its control and the best way to achieve this is to maintain the status quo. There have, of course, been discussions and statements throughout this period by both the official magisterium and theologians about their respective roles and the relationship of the papacy to theology. The most recent of these is the *Instruction on the*

Ecclesial Vocation of the Theologian (24 May 1990),[12] signed by Cardinal Josef Ratzinger, head of the Congregation for the Doctrine of the Faith (CDF). It is significant that it is signed by someone who himself has practiced as a theologian and who, at first sight, seems to have taken a more open-minded approach.

The Ratzinger *Instruction* appears to have much to recommend it: there is a clear acknowledgment of the cultural context (including philosophy, history, and even the 'human sciences') within which all theological work occurs, and it recommends the value of 'freedom of research':

> Freedom of research, which the academic community rightly holds most precious, means an openness to accepting the truth that emerges at the end of an investigation in which no element has intruded that is foreign to the methodology corresponding to the object under study.[13]

But this freedom is immediately limited by the obligation to present doctrine with integrity and accuracy. The *Instruction* argues that the papal magisterium alone is the source of this. And when the magisterium speaks 'in a definitive way' the theologian, despite his or her much vaunted 'freedom of research,' must firmly accept and hold these teachings, even if they 'are not divinely revealed [but] are nevertheless strictly and intimately connected with revelation.' They must respond with 'religious submission of will and intellect' even when the magisterium does not act 'definitively.'[14] In case the theologian thought that they might get away with an outward show of submission, Ratzinger's *Instruction* insists that the response 'cannot be simply exterior or disciplinary.' The consequence of this is that even when the papal magisterium (that is, pope and curia) is not teaching infallibly, or even when the teaching is clearly an exercise of the *ordinary magisterium*, 'submission of will and intellect' is required.

So much for freedom of research! 'Truth,' according to Ratzinger, is the final arbiter, but it is 'truth' as defined by the papal magisterium. He admits that the Vatican's 'truth' can reflect a particular school of theology, but anything the magisterium says has 'a validity beyond its argumentation.' Seemingly this means that whatever the pope or curia says is the 'truth' (at least provisionally), no matter how badly argued or how contrary to historical fact. The *Instruction* explicitly denies that there is a theological magisterium and it comes close to denying the *sensus fidei* of believers. In the Ratzinger document there is a conflation of the papal magisterium and the curial 'magisterium' (especially that of the CDF) and both are equally binding on theologians and believers.[15]

When viewed within the broader historical context of the Church's tradition, Ratzinger's *Instruction* is a remarkable document. It expresses directly and without equivocation the papalist ideology on the role of theology and, as such, is an explicit denial of the long-held tradition in the Church of the role of the theologian and the believing community in the process of discerning and developing the Church's teaching. It also effectively destroys theology as a discipline. No longer is the theologian judged by peers and by the acceptance of the believing community. The papacy alone is the judge of theological truth. The *Instruction*'s rhetorical style is also very revealing: it is couched in a prissy style that resembles that of a headmaster lecturing his rather obtuse pupils on the subject of the 'school rules.'

The consequences of the Ratzinger *Instruction* became clear in the debate about the ordination of women, which has continued for over two decades. Given the pope's idiosyncratic personal views on the respective roles of women and men,[16] the notion of female ordination has obviously annoyed John Paul II. In order to remove all doubt on the subject, he declared in his Apostolic Letter *Ordinatio sacerdotalis* (22 May 1994) that 'the Church has no authority whatsoever to confer priestly ordination on women and that this judgment is to be definitively held by all the Church's faithful' (n. 4). This is clearly a strong statement, but is it an infallible declaration? Does it belong to the deposit of faith? According to a reply by Ratzinger's CDF (dated 28 October, 1995 and approved by the pope) to questions such as these, the teaching given in *Ordinatio sacerdotalis* 'has been set forth infallibly by the ordinary and universal magisterium.'[17] The reply here refers to Vatican II's Dogmatic Constitution on the Church, *Lumen Gentium* (n. 25). This long section situates papal infallibility within the context of the teaching authority of the bishops, but there is no reference in this section to the term 'ordinary and universal magisterium.'[18] Ratzinger also cites no evidence that the world's bishops have been consulted on this issue. Already a number of theologians have questioned both the pope and Ratzinger's grounds for claiming that this is part of the infallible magisterium. Francis A. Sullivan, author of the important study *Magisterium*,[19] has asked for evidence that the bishops and scholars of the Church have been consulted. Sullivan says that for something to be taught infallibly by the ordinary magisterium, what has 'to be clearly established is that the tradition has remained constant, and that even today the universal body of Catholic bishops is teaching the same doctrine as to be definitively held.'[20] He also says that the way in which you establish that a doctrine is taught by the ordinary magisterium is by consultation with the bishops, the establishment of the assent of theologians and acceptance of the doctrine by faithful Catholics.[21] Nicholas Lash has pointed out that there could hardly be universal consensus and common adherence since the question of the ordination of women has only been asked very recently.[22] He describes the invoking of infallibility as a 'quite scandalous abuse of power' on the part of both the pope and Ratzinger.

This whole question is a vivid illustration of papalism in action. The idea that the pope—let alone the Cardinal Prefect of the Congregation for the Doctrine of the Faith—can independently and without consultation of the bishops and the wider Church declare something to be 'infallibly' binding on Catholics simply does not square with the teaching of Vatican I. The pope and Ratzinger have turned what is simply a serious teaching of the pope (what Vatican I would call 'ordinary magisterium') into an 'infallible' teaching. This seems to me to border on heresy and be a denial of conciliar teaching.

Further, Ratzinger's *Instruction* makes it clear that the papalist ideology does not tolerate any alternative source of inspiration in the Church. In the process of controlling theology, the Vatican has not hesitated to attack some of the most intelligent and creative people in the Church, including some whose sanctity is undoubted. The treatment of theologians is in sharp contrast to that given to priests whose immoral and criminal actions have brought disgrace on the Catholic community. It is ironic that, at the same time as it censured theologians, the Vatican and the bishops did little or nothing to deal decisively with clerical child molesters, simply moving them on secretly from place to place, with hardly any disciplinary action and certainly no public rebuke for behavior that was profoundly contrary to both moral and civil law—behavior that was far more destructive than 'temerarious opinions' that were really only offensive to the Roman censors. The reason why the 'sinner' priest could be absolved is that then the institutional Church could experience itself as forgiving and generous. But the Church had to be protected from intellectual 'deviants,' because their inquiries might upset and disturb the status quo. So the same Church authorities that cosseted the child molesters did not hesitate to attack publicly, and at times viciously and destructively, the reputations of some of the Church's most creative and devoted minds as they honestly tried to grapple with the profound theological problems involved in the interface between religion and life in the contemporary world.

The 'Affaire Lamennais'

There is nothing particularly new about the destructive treatment of the Church's most creative minds by its own authorities. The first major attack on a Catholic thinker in the period after 1815 occurred on 15 August 1832, in the encyclical *Mirari vos* of Pope Gregory XVI (1831–1846).[23] In *Mirari vos* the views of a group of French Catholics who associated with the priest Félicité Robert de Lamennais (1782–1854) were condemned. The group included some of the most important French Catholics of the period, including Henri Lacordaire, Prosper Guéranger, and Charles de Montelambert. They argued that the Church must integrate into its life the principles of the French Revolution and the emerging liberal society. They argued that the essence of Christianity was freedom, which reached its fullest realization in political liberty. There are echoes of the condemnation of modern liberation theology in the Lamennais affair. Ironically, Lamennais was a strong ultramontane[24] and he looked to the pope to lead a crusade for liberty. There was something very naive about this group of French liberals. It is hard to understand how they could have expected the papacy, involved at that very time in suppressing liberalism in the Papal States, to have suddenly assumed the leadership of a crusade for freedom and liberalism.

The affair came to a head after the publication in 1829 of Lamennais' book *Des progrès de la révolution et de la guerre contre l'église*. In the book he called for the Church to free itself from the monarchy, to abandon 'the degenerate and paltry scholasticism' that was taught in French seminaries, and to abandon its privileges and its bondage to the state—especially the patronage of the restored Bourbon monarchy. Lamennais looked forward to the papacy leading a great crusade of freedom, a vain and illusory hope in the case of Gregory XVI, who was a reactionary curialist and before that a Camaldolese hermit. The papacy was strongly influenced by the French bishops, who fought a hard campaign in Rome to have Lamennais's views condemned. The irony was that many of these same French bishops were Gallicans. Expediency makes strange bedfellows: French Gallicans united in common cause with Italian curialists against French ultramontanes!

Mirari vos was Gregory XVI's response. In the encyclical, the pope condemned the 'evil-smelling spring of indifferentism' from which flowed:

> the erroneous and absurd opinion—or rather, derangement—that freedom of conscience must be asserted and vindicated for everybody. This most pestilential error opens the door to the complete and immoderate liberty of opinions, which works such widespread harm both in church and state. Some people outrageously maintain that some advantage derives from it for religion.[25]

Lamennais and his group had been very successful in the publication of a daily Catholic newspaper in Paris, *L'Avenir*. So it was natural that Gregory XVI condemned freedom of the press as a 'deleterious liberty, which can never be execrated and detested sufficiently.'[26] The pope asserted that the early Christians showed 'fidelity to their rulers' and, as a result, 'divine and human law inveigh against those who attempt by the shameful machinations of rebellion and sedition to turn away subjects from fidelity to their rulers and to snatch the government from them.'[27] This was a blow for Polish Catholics, who had revolted against the oppressive Orthodox Czarist regime in 1830–1831. The Poles were told that the Russian regime had 'legitimate authority' and that obedience to the Czar was an 'absolute precept.'

It is worth asking, in the light of Cardinal Ratzinger's *Instruction*, whether all contemporary Catholics, especially theologians, must give full 'submission of will and intellect' to these statements of Gregory XVI. This issue is made even more ironic by the fact that these teachings of Gregory XVI are the opposite of the teaching of the Second Vatican Council. The Declaration on Religious Freedom (*Dignitatis humanae*) directly contradicts *Mirari vos*.[28] Is this an example of a council correcting the papacy? Which teaching is right? How could something be so true that in 1832 Catholics such as Lamennais had to give full 'submission of will and intellect' to Gregory XVI's teaching, or else leave the Church, and yet so *un*true that the encyclical could be quietly dumped by Vatican II one hundred and thirty years later? Direct contradiction of a papal teaching little more than a century after it has been given cannot be a legitimate example of development of doctrine. Either Gregory XVI or Vatican II is right: Ratzinger cannot have it both ways. The whole problem is reinforced by the fact that Gregory's successor, Pius IX, in the *Syllabus of Errors* (8 December 1864) assured the world that the Roman Pontiff could not and ought not 'reconcile and adjust himself with progress, liberalism, and modern civilization.' *Quanta cura*, the encyclical accompanying the *Syllabus*, seemed to make the list dogmatically binding. And this occurred exactly one hundred years before Vatican II debated the issue of religious liberty!

Gregory XVI demanded absolute submission from Lamennais. French ecclesiastical intrigues in Rome and Paris against him and the other liberal Catholics were persistent. Lamennais's book *Paroles d'un croyant* (1834) argued his case brilliantly against the abuses of liberty current in the Europe of his time. In the *Paroles* he applied biblical curses and imagery to contemporary rulers. The book is doctrinally orthodox, but he uses that orthodoxy to call down God's judgment on the oppressors of liberty. The critics of his own time fixed on his identification of liberty with the name of Christ and his incitement to disobey rulers who disobeyed the law of God—a perfectly licit Catholic position held also by the Spanish Jesuit theologian of the sixteenth century, Francisco de Suárez. Sadly, Lamennais ended his life outside the Church after further condemnation in the encyclical *Singulari nos* (25 June 1834), in which Gregory XVI described the *Paroles* as a book 'small in size but immense in its perversity.' Historian E. E. Y. Hales perceptively comments that Gregory XVI condemned Lamennais fundamentally because liberal principles could not be applied in the Papal States.[29] It was not until after the popes had lost the Papal States in 1870 that Rome became more indifferent to specific forms of government.

The Lamennais affair is important because it sets the pattern for the next century and a half for the fraught relationship between the papacy and the Church's most creative thinkers. This has lasted until our own time and was really only slightly interrupted by Vatican II. The historian Giuseppe Alberigo has emphasized the programmatic significance of *Mirari vos*. Gregory XVI argued in the encyclical that the spiritual health of the age was so pathological that he must set aside Christian charity, *indulgentiam benignitatis* (the spirit of gentleness), and use the rod, *virga compescere* (the reference in the encyclical is to 1 Corinthians 4:21). In a significant explanation of the influence of this attitude on later papal policy, Alberigo points out that this negative attitude became a predominant aspect of the modern popes' approach to the world. Things were so bad that it was only through condemnation (that is, using the rod) that they could get their message across. This negative evaluation characterised papal policy for more than a century.[30]

The tension referred to here between the papacy and the modern age found its quintessential expression in attempts to control theology. The relationship between the two became especially tense after Vatican I. In this period the bureaucratic energies of the curia shifted inward toward more and more complete control of thinking in the Church. This came to a head in the so-called 'Modernist' crisis at the beginning of the twentieth century.

The Modernist crisis

Modernism is very difficult to define. But it caused terrible suffering to Catholic scholars at the beginning of the twentieth century. The papal condemnation of Modernism quickly developed into a witch-hunt. The word 'modernism' was used by Pius X (1903–1914) in the encyclical *Pascendi Dominici Gregis* (8 September 1907) to describe Catholic thinkers who, he claimed, 'present their doctrines without order and systematic arrangement, in a scattered and disjointed manner, so as to make it appear as if their minds were in doubt or hesitation, whereas in reality they are quite fixed and steadfast.'[31] These are thinkers who 'put themselves forward as reformers of the Church,' but they are, in fact, 'thoroughly imbued with the poisonous doctrines taught by the enemies of the Church.'[32] The attribution of such perverse motivation to fellow Catholics is astonishing. Two months previously, in the decree *Lamentabili*, he had called Modernism a 'synthesis of all heresies.'

The facts are that the Modernist scholars actually called for freedom of inquiry; a new historical approach to the development of theology and doctrine; liberty to use the newly developed tools of literary and historical criticism, and to apply these to the Bible and Church history, especially the early period of the Church; and a more creative approach to the philosophy of religion and apologetics. Basically, the Modernists were a group of Catholic scholars, both lay and clerical, who tried to adopt contemporary scientific methods and apply them to Catholic thought. They realized that the Neo-Scholastic intellectualism of the Roman schools was totally insufficient to confront the philosophical questions of the day, especially as expressed in the anti-rational tendencies of Schopenhauer, Nietzsche, and Bergson, and the evolutionism of Hegel, Spencer, and Darwin. They also saw that a new apologetic was needed, one derived not from Church dogma but from life itself.

The best known English-speaking Modernist was the Irish-born convert and Jesuit priest, George Tyrrell (1861–1909). His views have been seen by some as extreme, but in other ways he was a perceptive forerunner of Vatican II. While some argue that the expulsion of Tyrrell from the Jesuits in 1906 can be understood in its context,[33] the attack on other scholars was totally unjustifiable. The French Catholic historian Louis Duchesne (1843–1922) was influenced by the German liberal Protestant historian, Adolf von Harnack (1851–1930). Duchesne's *L'Histoire ancienne de L'Eglise chrétienne* (three volumes, 1906–1910) was placed on the *Index of Forbidden Books* in 1912.[34] It is here that the imprecision of the use of the term 'modernism' by Pius X becomes clear. It is a catchall word and it is difficult to see why the work of such a fine scholar as Duchesne would be seen as Modernist. It is a symptom of papal paranoia that any work that suggested the idea of 'development' of doctrine and of Church structure was under suspicion. It also shows the fear of history implicit in the papalist ideology.

The heartland of Modernism was in biblical exegesis. Among liberal Protestant scholars in Germany in the nineteenth and early-twentieth centuries a new critical approach to the Bible (especially the Old Testament) had developed. They called into question traditional and literal interpretations of scripture. The areas of particular debate were the Pentateuch,[35] the theology of inspiration and the question of the inerrancy of scripture, and issues centering on the life and miracles of Jesus. Here the key modernist scholar was Alfred Loisy (1857–1940).[36] His starting point was that the biblical scholar must prescind completely from supernatural and dogmatic considerations; he argued that the Bible must be studied like any other historical document. Thus he indirectly called for the freeing of exegesis, historiography, and, ultimately, theology from the control of the magisterium. Dogmas, he maintained, were not truths fallen from heaven but rather, like the Church and revelation itself, they were subject to evolutionary development. Loisy's views became increasingly extreme, and he was excommunicated in 1908. He is perhaps the only person who could accurately be called a 'modernist' in the sense used by Pius X. But the work of other moderate Catholic biblical scholars, such as M. J. Lagrange (1855–1938) and Giovanni Genocchi (1860–1926), got caught up in the general atmosphere of suspicion of all scripture study.

To understand the papal condemnation of Modernism and the treatment of those accused of being 'modernists,' it is important to realize that from the time of the election of Pius X to the papacy the situation quickly polarized. Roger Aubert says that Pius X 'instinctively mistrusted progressive endeavors' and that he turned away decisively from the policies of his predecessor, Leo XIII (1878–1903).[37] To understand Modernism it is important to remember the polarization that had occurred within Catholic culture on two levels: firstly the divorce between Catholicism and modern culture, and secondly the divorce between Catholic liberals and Catholic reactionaries. As early as November 1903, the French philosopher Maurice Blondel was aware of the polarization:

> With every day that passes, the conflict between tendencies which set Catholic against Catholic in every order—social, political, philosophical—is revealed as sharper and more general. One could almost say that there are now two quite incompatible 'catholic mentalities,' particularly in France.[38]

The whole thing was brought to a head by Pius X's encyclical *Pascendi* in 1907. The condemnation was reinforced by the 'Anti-modernist Oath' that all seminarians were required to take before ordination to major orders, all bishops before their ordination to the episcopate, and all priests and seminary teachers before taking up office.[39]

Modernism was seen by Rome as an insidious plot nurtured by the connections and correspondence that developed among the modernist group. This centered on the layman Baron Friedrich Von Hügel (1852–1925), who was in contact with all the leading Modernists. The condemnation led to what can only be described as a quite despicable campaign by elements in the curia to hunt down and root out all those suspected of 'modernism,' or even 'semi-modernism'! Often totally innocent scholars, such as Lagrange and Duchesne, were denounced and sacked from their teaching posts. Most of this integralist reaction centered on the shadowy figure of Monsignor Umberto Benigni (1862–1934), of the Papal Secretariat of State, and the small, secret organization that he set up, the *Sodalitium Pianum*.[40] Through a clandestine network of denunciation and the planting of articles in right-wing publications attacking anyone the *Sodalitium* disapproved of, a climate of suspicion and fear was developed right under the nose of Pius X and his Secretary of State, Cardinal Raphael Merry del Val.

Although there was a reaction against integralism and the *Sodalitium* in the pontificate of Benedict XV (1914–1922), the fear of secret condemnation had crept into theology and it remained there until the 1940s. The focus of this fear was the so-called 'Holy Office,' which ironically had dropped the term 'inquisition' from its title in 1908. This congregation has been through two metamorphoses this century: established in 1542 and reformed in 1587, it entered the twentieth century as the *Sacra Congregatio Romanae et Universalis Inquisitionis seu Sancti Offici* (Sacred Congregation of the Roman and Universal Inquisition, or Holy Office). In 1913 it became the *Supreme* Sacred Congregation of the Holy Office, and in 1965 Paul VI re-formed it under the title *Congregatio pro Doctrina Fidei* (Congregation for the Doctrine of the Faith). It imposed a narrow orthodoxy on the whole Church and its influence extended far beyond theology to a claim that it could judge every moral and religious issue considered by the Church. Alberigo argues that in setting up such a centralised bureaucracy, the papacy resembled the fascist states. It certainly reduced theological pluralism and suppressed minority opinion.[41]

Seemingly the papacy had beaten the fascists at their own game and set up a dictatorial government nine years before Mussolini. In the light of this it is significant that Monsignor Benigni ended his days as an apologist for the Italian Fascists. The influence of the Holy Office was felt most in the Church during the 1930s and 1940s; yet the oath against Modernism remained in force until late 1966.

Humani generis *and the 'new Modernism'*

Theology, both systematic and biblical, and the renewed interest in historical sources that was to form the foundation of Vatican II, only began to revive again during and after the Second World War. The roots of this revival go back further, but its celebrated names only came to prominence in theological circles in the late 1940s. Theologians like Yves Congar, Henri Bouillard, and Henri de Lubac, patristic scholars like Jean Danielou, and—behind them all—the palaeontologist and philosopher-poet, Pierre Teilhard de Chardin, were all at the height of their powers by the end of the Second World War. This period also saw the development of theological periodicals and the beginning of *Sources chrétiennes*, a series of new editions of works of patristic theology. The emphasis in this movement was on a personal assimilation of the truths of faith, the historical context in which faith is lived out, and the importance of relating belief to contemporary philosophy and culture. This was 'all lumped together under the pretty colorless designation' of *La théologie nouvelle* (the new theology).[42]

There is a real sense in which Pope Pius XII could be said to have encouraged new developments in theology by his encyclicals *Divino afflante Spiritu* (30 September 1943), which supported the use of historical and critical methods in biblical exegesis, and *Mediator Dei* (20 November 1947), which strengthened the renewal of the liturgy and emphasized lay participation in the eucharist. However, the followers of the 'new theology' were in for a rude shock if they thought Pius XII was on their side. It was all very well for the pope to be talking about the possibility of change; but it was a different matter for theologians to be talking about personal faith and historical context. Their approach raised the hackles of the hard-nosed integralists in Rome, the most important of whom was the Dominican Reginald Garrigou-Lagrange, who was quick to raise the alarm.[43] The result of this concern was Pius XII's encyclical *Humani generis* (12 August 1950).

Again we are dealing with a broad-brushstroke condemnation, directed not so much against individuals as against a movement. It was clear that it was addressed to the propounders of the *théologie nouvelle*. Alberigo notes the way in which the encyclical identifies *discordia* (dissent) and *aberratio a veritate* (aberration from the truth, or error).[44] This has become a continuing papalist theme since Vatican II: the dissenters are as bad as—perhaps even worse than—the heretics, for both disturb the status quo. So dissent is equated with heresy. Pius XII casts the whole post-war age in apocalyptic terms: unless the Church is tightly united with the hierarchy and centered on the papal magisterium, the Catholic faith will disintegrate. Those who think otherwise are acting in a destructive manner. The 'sacred magisterium' was, the pope argued, 'the proximate and universal norm of truth in matters of faith and morals.'[45] The task of the theologian is to act as a kind of magisterial catechist and source-text expert: theology's job is to show 'how the doctrine defined by the Church is contained in the sources.' Alberigo comments that *Humani generis* stifled debate and caused havoc throughout the church.[46]

Pius XII was followed by John XXIII (1958–1963). John turned decisively away from the attitudes of his predecessors and returned literally to *indulgentiam benignitatis*—benign mercy. In many ways his pontificate was in sharp contrast to everything that had gone before in papal history since the beginning of the nineteenth century. The greatest work of his papacy was the Second Vatican Council (1962–1965).

But, looked at historically, there is a sense in which John XXIII and Vatican II were mere incidents in the ongoing history of papalism. Pope John certainly changed the face of the whole Church, but he failed to change attitudes in the Roman curia. These days the faces may be different and the personnel come from many countries as well as Italy. But the assumption of superior knowledge and the possession of a monopoly on theological truth still characterizes the Vatican. Clearly papalism does not change with personnel; it is inherent in the very structure of the papacy as it is constituted today.

History versus ideology

It is for this reason that we need to return to the historical and traditional sources of authority in the Church, to try to discover clues as to other ways in which we might change the notion and practice of authority in the Church. While the actual authority of the popes has ebbed and flowed throughout history, they have never before been the absolute masters of the Church. They have certainly claimed such pretensions in the past, but they never actually achieved total power. My fundamental argument in this book is that the position of the contemporary papacy is not only unique in Christian history, it also distorts the *traditionally* understood structure of the Church.

A historical study of the evolution of the papal office does not reveal a smooth development from primitive beginnings to high papalism. It actually shows a very uneven evolution in which the papal office is sometimes powerful in the Church and at other times has only the most limited influence. But until now there has always been a check on papalism: synods, councils, the college of cardinals, theologians, emperors, kings, and Catholic governments have all provided some balance to centralized papal power. The collegial nature of authority in the Church has provided some form of balance to the monopoly of power in the hands of one person. Absolutism is not the norm in the Church. And always there has been the *sensus fidelium*, the acceptance or rejection, by the Catholic people, of the Church's teaching.

But the influence of the ideology of absolute monarchy, which first emerged in the sixteenth century with kings such as Francis I (France), Philip II (Spain), and Henry VIII, gradually permeated the Church; and the popes began to see themselves not as Italian Renaissance princelings, but as the vice-regents of God and the monarchs of the ecclesiastical kingdom. The divine right of kings has much in common with the divine right of popes. Something of this was articulated in the seventeenth century by Saint Robert Bellarmine, although its roots go back much further to the imperial Roman model of government.[47] But, paradoxically, it was only in the nineteenth century that the notion of the papal monarchy was fully realized, at the very time when it was in retreat in civil society. It is to this that I will turn when dealing with Vatican I (pp. 46–62).

But before we look at how the pope became both the absolute owner of the Church and infallible, there is an important caveat. It is important to remember that history offers a radical critique of papalism by broadening our perspectives. Papalist ideology tries to keep us fixated in the realm of doctrine, for it is there that the theoreticians of papal power can try to insulate us from the realities of papal history. The papacy has related to the Church in several different ways in its long history. There is no reason why it cannot discover a new role in the emerging century. Development is an ongoing process, and just because John Paul II is so powerful it does not mean that the Church cannot move on from here. In order to move we need firstly to draw on the long tradition of Catholicism, and secondly to feel free to use our imaginations. If Saint Robert Bellarmine felt free to apply the contemporary idea of absolute monarchy to his model of the papacy, so present-day theologians should not feel afraid to use models from our time—such as a synodal or democratic approach. Historically, no model is exhaustive or absolutely normative.

People today do have a tendency to presume that contemporary papalism goes right back to the earliest times. But this is not true; it is very recent in its development. So in order to see the contemporary papacy in perspective it is useful to reflect historically on how the extraordinary centralization of papal power that we experience today developed. Its ultimate expression came at the First Vatican Council (1869–1870), but its roots go back further.

1 Originally the term *Pontifex Maximus* was the title of the chief pagan priest of the Roman state. In *De pudicitia*, Tertullian used it satirically of Pope Callistus I (217–222), but from the fifteenth century onwards it became a regular title of honor for the popes. It was recently disavowed by Popes John Paul I and John Paul II because of its pagan overtones.

2 Giuseppe Alberigo, 'The Authority of the Church in the Documents of Vatican I and Vatican II,' in Leonard Swidler and Piet F. Fransen (eds), *Authority in the Church and the Schillebeeckx Case*, New York: Crossroad, 1982, pp. 130–1.

3 Charles Davis, *A Question of Conscience*, London: Sheed and Ward, 1967, pp. 190, 236.

4 Quoted in Henri Fesquet, *The Drama of Vatican II: The Ecumenical Council June 1962–December 1965*, New York: Random House, 1967, pp. 210–11. See also Xavier Rynne, *The Second Session*, London: Faber and Faber, 1964, pp. 180–1.

5 Quoted in Fesquet, p. 215. See also Rynne, *Second Session*, pp. 182–3.

6 Richard McBrien, *Catholicism*, new edition, Melbourne: Collins Dove, 1994, p. 1236.

7 See E. E. Y. Hales, *Revolution and Papacy 1769–1846*, Notre Dame: University of Notre Dame Press, 1966, pp. 227–95.

8 As is customary, dates given for the popes are for their papal reign.

9 See my book *Mixed Blessings: John Paul II and the Church of the Eighties*, Ringwood: Penguin, 1986, especially pp. 154–76. See also my article 'The Peripatetic Pope' in Hans Küng and Leonard Swidler (eds), *The Church in Anguish: Has the Vatican Betrayed Vatican II?*, San Francisco: Harper and Row, 1986, pp. 52–7.

10 For details see Michael Walsh, *John Paul II: A Biography*, London: HarperCollins, 1994. Refer to the index under individual countries.

11 Translations in this book from the current *Code* are from the translation by the Canon Law Society of America published as *Code of Canon Law: Latin-English Edition*, Washington: Canon Law Society of America, 1983.

12 For a translation see *Origins* 20:8 (5 July 1990), pp. 117–26.

13 Ibid., p. 120.

14 Ibid., p. 122.

15 Ibid.

16 See Collins, *Mixed Blessings*, pp. 171–2.

17 *L'Osservatore Romano*, 22 November 1995, p. 2.

18 The text can be found in Austin Flannery (ed.), *Vatican Council II: The Conciliar and Post Conciliar Documents*, Dublin: Dominican Publications, 1975, pp. 379–81.

19 Francis A. Sullivan, *Magisterium. Teaching Authority in the Catholic Church*, Dublin: Gill and Macmillan, 1983.

20 Francis A. Sullivan, 'Guideposts from Catholic Tradition,' *America*, 9 December 1995.

21 Ibid.

22 Nicholas Lash, 'On Not Inventing Doctrine,' *The Tablet*, 2 December 1995, p. 1544.

23 See Colman J. Barry (ed.), *Readings in Church History*, Westminster: Newman Press, 1965, vol. 3, pp. 37–44.

24 The word 'ultramontane' is derived from *ultra montes* ('beyond the mountains') and it refers to the tendency of the French Catholics to look beyond the Alps to papal Rome as the source of power and wisdom in the Church. It is in contrast to 'Gallicanism,' which saw the Catholic Church in France as centered there and subject to the French monarchy. 'Cisalpinism' is the literal opposite of ultramontanism.

25 Translation in Barry, vol. 3, p. 41.

26 Ibid., pp. 41–2.

27 Ibid., p. 42.

28 See Alberic Stacpoole (ed.), *Vatican II by Those Who Were There*, London: Geoffrey Chapman, 1986, pp. 283–97.

29 Hales, *Revolution*, p. 294.

30 Alberigo in Swidler and Fransen, p. 121.

31 Translation in Barry, vol. 3, p. 113.

32 Translation in ibid., p. 112.

33 For the Roman view on Tyrrell see David G. Schultenover, *A View from Rome: On the Eve of the Modernist Crisis*, New York: Fordham University Press, 1993, pp. 83–113.

34 A three-volume English translation appeared between 1909 and 1924, entitled *The Early History of the Church from its Foundation to the End of the Fifth Century*, London: John Murray.

35 The term given to the first five books of the Bible, with authorship traditionally attributed to Moses.

36 Alfred Loisy, *The Gospel and the Church*, English trans., London: Isbister, 1903. Reprinted Philadelphia: Fortress, 1976.

37 Roger Aubert in Herbert Jedin and John J. Dolan (eds): *History of the Church: The Church in the Industrial Age*, New York: Crossroad, 1981, vol. 9, p. 386.

38 Maurice Blondel, *Letter on Apologetics and History of Dogma*, trans. and edited by Alexander Dru and Illtyd Trethowan, London: Harvill Press, 1964, p. 221.

39 For the Latin text see the Motu proprio *Sacrorum antistites* (1 September 1910).

40 For the integralist reaction see Aubert in Jedin and Dolan, vol. 9, pp. 467–80.

41 Alberigo in Swidler and Fransen, p. 131.

42 Leo Scheffczyk in Jedin and Dolan, vol. 10, p. 268.

43 Karol Wojtyla (later Pope John Paul II) studied at the Angelicum University in Rome between 1946 and 1948 and he completed a thesis under Garrigou-Lagrange's direction on Saint John of the Cross in 1948.

44 Alberigo in Swidler and Fransen, pp. 132–3.

45 Quoted by Alberigo, ibid., p. 132.

46 Ibid.

47 See Patrick Granfield, *The Papacy in Transition*, Dublin: Gill and Macmillan, 1981, pp. 34–61.

CHAPTER 2

How the pope became the infallible head of the Church

The beginnings of the modern papal revival

The odd thing is that two hundred years ago, in contrast to the enormous power and influence of the contemporary papacy, things had reached rock bottom in Rome. The pope of the time, Pius VI (1775–1799), was seen as the last of the line and it was expected that he would be swept away with the rest of the detritus of the old regime by the forces of the French Revolution and Napoleon. In fact, in the latter part of the eighteenth century the papacy reached one of several nadirs in its history in terms of its influence and power. The popes of the period were not particularly bad; they were simply mediocre and inadequate. Yet 1800 was the turning point—right through the nineteenth and twentieth centuries the papacy has been rebuilding its power and influence and has gradually centralized more and more authority in Rome. In order to understand the contemporary papacy we must understand what has happened to the Church over the last two hundred years.

The clearest symbol of the weakness of the late-eighteenth-century papacy was the way in which Clement XIV (1769–1774) was forced by Catholic powers, led by the Marquis de Pombal of Portugal, to suppress the Society of Jesus (Jesuits).

The elimination of twenty-three thousand Jesuits was an enormous loss to the Church, education, and culture in Europe. However, the Society survived in parts of Germany, Prussia, and Russia, due to the support of local monarchs who appreciated their educational work, as well as in small groups in the United States and England. J. N. D. Kelly says bluntly that Clement XIV's papacy 'saw the prestige of the papacy sink to its lowest level for centuries.'[1]

Four months after Clement's death, the inadequate Pius VI was elected. From 1789 onwards he faced the challenge of the French Revolution. Again, to understand much that happened subsequently it is important to see the scarring experience that the papacy endured during the revolutionary and Napoleonic period. The first direct conflict with the revolutionary government came over the Civil Constitution of the Clergy (12 July 1790).[2] This ordinance of the French National Assembly was meant only to effect the civil aspects of the Church, but it actually went much further. Parish priests were elected by the parish. Bishops were to be elected by *citoyens actifs*. Dioceses were to conform to the borders of the new state departments. Newly elected bishops were to receive their *institutio canonica*, or episcopal installation, from their metropolitan archbishop; the pope would merely be notified. The Church was made a part of the state. Freedom of opinion and religious toleration were guaranteed in the *Declaration of the Rights of Man*. An oath of fidelity to the Civil Constitution was imposed on the clergy and this split them. Most of the bishops refused to take it and left the country. Only a minority of the clergy took the oath. Pius VI stalled for time to see what the attitude of Louis XVI (1754–1793) would be, while the king in turn was waiting for the view of the pope! The Bishop of Autun, Charles Maurice de Talleyrand, who had taken the oath, set out to consecrate an entirely new episcopate. He was soon to give up belief in Catholicism altogether. The majority of priests who took the oath did so with reservations. Those who did completely refuse (the 'non-jurors') were expelled from their appointments.

Eventually the pope condemned the Civil Constitution in March 1791. The king was unwilling to break with the papacy and from this point onward he turned away from the revolution. The government soon tired of trying to settle the religious issue, but the clerical oath had become identified with patriotism. Non-jurors were identified with emigrés and enemies abroad. The new Legislative Assembly decreed that non-jurors were to be considered under suspicion of revolt against the law and in the 1792 September Massacres, two hundred and twenty-five priests were executed. On 20 September, the National Convention assumed power. The monarchy was abolished and in January 1793 King Louis XVI was executed. The Terror became an instrument of state policy under Maximilien de Robespierre. The Convention pushed for total de-Christianization. By this time the Constitutional priests and bishops were in an invidious position. They were in schism in a state that was becoming increasingly anti-Christian. A new, pagan calendar was established. The Constitutional Church fell apart and a new revolutionary cult was introduced—the cult of Reason. On 8 June 1794, the Feast of the Supreme Being was celebrated in Notre Dame.

With the fall of Robespierre and the Termidorian Reaction of mid-1794, the Terror receded. But the principles of the Revolution had already spread to Italy. The newly emerging French general, Napoleon Bonaparte, had taken Milan in 1796 and then invaded the Papal States. In February 1797 he imposed the Peace of Tolentino on Pius VI. One year later the Roman Republic was established and the pope was deposed from his civil power. War broke out again in Italy and, after a brief stay in Florence, Pius VI was taken over the Alps to France as a prisoner.

When Pius died under arrest in Valence in July 1799 many presumed that the papacy had at last come to an end. But he had left secret instructions for the election of a successor. Ten months later in Venice, Luigi Barnaba Chiaramonte, a Benedictine, was elected with the style Pius VII (1800–1823). The modern age of papal history had begun. But the experience of the revolutionary decade had profound effects on the papacy. The revolutionary ideas of liberty, equality, and the overthrow of monarchy were viewed as the antithesis of Christianity by the papal government. When the clerics returned to power in 1815 they were determined that these revolutionary ideas were to have no place in the Papal States, nor in the wider Church. This was to be a disastrous policy.

Pius VII (1800–1823)

Secular assumptions of the end of the papacy were premature. Even before the death of Pius VI, the cardinals had been gathering at Venice under Austrian protection and influence.[3] Through the election of a pliant pope, the Austrians hoped to gain control of all of northern Italy. After a long, deadlocked conclave, Pius VII was elected. He quickly removed himself from Austrian influence, returned to Rome, and appointed the great papal diplomat Ercole Consalvi (1757–1824) as his secretary of state. As such, Consalvi acted as both papal prime minister and foreign minister. While on the journey to Rome, Pius VII heard about Napoleon's victory over the Austrians at Marengo (July 1800). The long struggle with Bonaparte began. At first Pius VII was happy to work with the French state. Negotiations were carried on by Consalvi and a concordat with Napoleon, who by now controlled France, was signed on 15 July 1801. The terms were weighted in favor of France and the government retained the right of nomination of bishops. The appointment of parish priests required government approval. Bishops and priests were to be paid by the state. Catholicism was recognized as the religion of the majority of Frenchmen and freedom for the Church was guaranteed. A whole new bench of bishops was nominated.

But Napoleon's *Organic Articles*, a series of measures applying the concordat, increased the power of the state over the bishops and excluded papal influence in France. Napoleon saw the Church as a department of the state. In the long term, the *Organic Articles* had the effect of forcing the French church to turn from the old-style Gallicanism to the ultramontanism of the nineteenth century. The pope attended Napoleon's coronation in December 1804, but relations between them quickly degenerated. Rome and the Papal States were occupied and integrated into the kingdom of Italy, and in July 1809 Pius VII was arrested and imprisoned, first at Savona (1809–1812) and then Fontainebleau (1812–1814). It turned the pope into a 'martyr' for all anti-Napoleonic nations and made him popular even in Protestant England.

After the abdication of Napoleon, Pius VII returned to Rome in March 1814, left the city during the '100 Days' when Napoleon escaped from Elba, and returned finally on 7 June

1815, after the French emperor's final defeat at Waterloo. Consalvi, sacked under French pressure in 1806, had been reappointed secretary of state in May 1814.

The Congress of Vienna (1815) and the restoration of the Papal States

The defeat of Napoleon at Waterloo in 1815 brought the kings back to power. The peace settlement was negotiated at the Congress of Vienna. But it was a very different Europe to which the kings were restored. The principles articulated by the Revolution and spread by French armies had brought about a new consciousness that was to change the course of European history. The Church, too, would have to come to terms with this. In the one hundred and fifty years from 1815 until Vatican II, there was a long and often bitter struggle within Catholicism between the forces of equality and liberalism on the one hand, and those of reactionary conservatism on the other. In a real sense this struggle still continues. Neither Pius VII nor Consalvi were reactionaries, but they were staunchly anti-liberal. They were faced with immediate problems, including the restoration of the Papal States, and they supported the new world order that emerged from the Congress of Vienna.

In retrospect, the settlement achieved in 1815 was moderate and successful. There was no war involving more than two great powers between 1815 and 1914. The statesmen of 1815 claimed that they wanted to return to conditions prior to 1789. At Vienna they enunciated the principle of legitimacy: the legitimate rights of rulers were to be respected. But the application was not consistent. The petty German principalities were not restored, and only persistent efforts by Consalvi secured the restoration of the Papal States. It was primarily the legitimate rights of the monarchs of Russia, Austria, Prussia, France, and Britain that were really respected. Although the papacy emerged from the revolutionary era with enhanced prestige, both the Austrians and the French had little sympathy for the restoration of the Papal States. It was Consalvi's friendship with British foreign secretary Castlereagh that finally persuaded the powers to restore the papal dominions. Consalvi had visited London in 1814 and had been received at court.

The restored Papal States straddled Italy from the Romagna in the north-west to the north-central Legations, focused on Bologna, down the Marches on the Adriatic coast, across the Apennines to Umbria and the *Patrimonium Petri*, the area immediately around Rome. These areas had little in common with each other in the nineteenth century, but Consalvi's aim was to ensure the neutrality of the papacy, while maintaining the legitimist status quo by stamping out liberalism and representative democracy. These aims proved irreconcilable. Consalvi imposed strict censorship, especially of the press. Hales correctly comments that 'Consalvi's achievement at Vienna was as remarkable as it would later prove to have been disastrous.'[4] His point is that the papacy insisted on keeping the Legations, largely because they were the only economically viable part of the state. During the Napoleonic regime they had been united with Lombardy, their natural economic, geographic, and political setting. During the French occupation laymen had shared in their government and they did not wish to return to the inefficiency of the clerical regime. But Hales's comment can be applied to all of the Papal States; they became a halter around the papal neck and linked the papacy psychologically and politically to the legitimist establishment. Consalvi's victory proved, in the end, 'only to postpone and prolong the death agonies of a temporal order that was moribund.'[5] The problem in the Papal States was the constant conflation of the spiritual and the temporal.[6] This confusion extended to the identification of the fate of the Papal States with the fate of the universal Church. The popes projected their problems with democracy and free speech in the Papal States onto the whole Church and condemned these movements everywhere. While Consalvi recognized the need for some reforms, especially in the Legations, he was opposed by the obscurantist *Zelanti* cardinals, led by Bartolomeo Pacca.

When he died in 1823, Pius VII had restored the reputation of the papacy and had turned Rome once more into an international and artistic capital. His pontificate saw the restoration of the Society of Jesus in 1814, the re-establishment of the *Propaganda Fide* in 1817, and the recognition of the Latin-

American republics in 1822. The great missionary expansion of the nineteenth and twentieth centuries had begun. Through *Propaganda Fide* (the curial department, now called the Congregation for the Evangelization of Peoples, that supervises the Church's missionary work) Rome was to play a central role in this missionary expansion, determining dioceses, appointing bishops, settling disputes, encouraging the foundation and growth of missionary orders, and bringing those orders more and more under papal control. The great missionary movement that followed European expansion in the nineteenth and early-twentieth centuries was to be an important part of the process of Roman centralization.

Romanticism and traditionalism

But other ideologies were emerging in 1815. Coterminous with the French Revolution, another movement swept across Europe—romanticism. Romanticism is difficult to define. Kenneth Clark explains it simply as 'I feel. Therefore I am.'[77] Romanticism began as a revival of interest in nature and continued as a revolt against the rationalism and symmetry of eighteenth-century classicism. Romanticism also expressed itself in a religious revival, and the classic expression of this is found in the work of Count François René de Chateaubriand (1768–1848). His 1802 book *Genié du christianisme* (*The Genius of Christianity*), attempts to negate the eighteenth-century rationalist attack on Christianity by transferring the debate about religion from the realm of reason to that of feeling. He argued that Christianity is true because it is beautiful. A similar current is present in the Protestant thinker Friedrich Schleiermacher (1768–1834).

Two other French religious writers, Louis de Bonald (1754–1840) and Joseph de Maistre (1753–1821), gave expression to the anti-democratic aspect of romanticism. Both were philosophical traditionalists. They argued that it was by adherence to the tradition which was 'handed down' that truth was maintained in a culture. Revolutions were wrong because they interfered with the transmission of truth. Family and state came from God, and there was an indissoluble union between Church and monarchy. De Maistre was a political theorist rather than a theologian. He wanted to destroy the 'satanic' evils of the Revolution and nationalism. His most important work was *Du Pape* (*Concerning the Pope*, 1819). The key to his political philosophy is the idea of sovereignty. Subjects are bound to obey the sovereign government, for it must be assumed to be right; it is, in a practical sense, 'infallible.' He held that religious truths are also social truths, and they exist for the common good. Society cannot exist without religion. For this reason the practical 'infallibility' of government becomes the absolute 'infallibility' of faith. He saw the infallible papacy as the permanent symbol of spiritual authority, and monarchy as the symbol of temporal authority. For de Maistre the Catholic Church was the one safeguard of political stability, and the pope alone had genuine access to the truth. Human reason was of no use, for it was fallible; it was only by adherence to what was 'handed down' that truth was guaranteed. Thus what the pope proclaims as true is true to the exclusion of all other truths.

These reactionary, irrational, and entirely untheological views had enormous influence on the development of nineteenth-century ultramontanism. They permeated Roman attitudes and in a real sense continue to underpin papalism. At the end of twentieth century, the pope remains the last relic of absolute monarchy, presuming that even his personal theological views are somehow true and therefore normative for Catholics. In this view, the pope alone is the source of truth, even if that truth is contradicted by historical fact. The wider world and secular scholarship has little or nothing to offer, for the papacy is the infallible vehicle of truth. Given that papalism does not take history seriously, it is useless to point out that these views are not only untheological but they are entirely without foundation in the tradition of the Church. They are, in the most precise sense of the word, 'novelties.' But their subtle, underpinning influence continues.

The influence of romanticism, de Maistre, and the ultramontane bandwagon needs to be kept in mind as we examine the disastrous history of the Papal States in the nineteenth century, and the gradual replacement of a political hegemony over central Italy by a spiritual and theological hegemony over the whole Church.

Leo XII (1823–1829), Gregory XVI (1831–1846), and Pius IX (1846–1878)

With the death of Pius VII, the tentatively moderate regime in the Papal States was quickly abolished by his successor, Leo XII. The region reverted to an economically stultified police state. Leo XII set a pattern that was to be followed by his successors. During the brief and slightly more open regime of Pius VIII (1829–1830), Catholic Emancipation was passed in the United Kingdom (13 April 1829) and the United States bishops held their first provincial synod. He in turn was succeeded by the Camaldolese monk, Bartolomeo Alberto Cappellari, who was elected as Gregory XVI.

In 1799, Cappellari had published *The Triumph of the Holy See and the Church against the Attacks of the Innovators*. In this he advocated papal infallibility and the maintenance of the Papal States. The day after he was elected there was a revolt in Bologna that was repressed by the Austrians after the failure of the corrupt papal mercenaries. Gregory refused any democratic reforms and throughout his papacy there was simmering rebellion. He even refused to allow railways in the Papal States! In 1830, liberal revolts broke out in Catholic Belgium against the Protestant Dutch monarchy, and in Catholic Poland against the Orthodox tsar. Gregory condemned both these revolts. He was utterly opposed to liberalism because he saw God, not the people, as the source of sovereignty.[8] Gregory's experience of liberalism and democratic ideas in his own state soured him against all forms of freedom, both in theory and in practice. He was convinced that liberalism was rooted in indifferentism. We have already seen his reaction to Lamennais's ideas about liberalism, and how his encyclical *Mirari vos* (1832) condemned all forms of liberalism within Catholicism (pp. 20–1).

Yet, while Gregory encouraged reactionary regimes in Europe, in the new world the Church was growing apace. In the United States, Canada, and Australia—in contrast to Europe—Catholicism began to prosper in free, liberal societies. Gregory had been Prefect of Propaganda before 1831, and as pope he encouraged the missionary movement, whose impetus really got under way during his papacy. He established new dioceses and vicariates, approved new missionary orders of both men and women, reorganized others, condemned the slave trade, and even encouraged the training of indigenous clergy and local hierarchies in mission territories. In Rome he also encouraged archaeological research. Despite these positive notes his papacy showed no comprehension of the forces at work in the nineteenth-century world. Gregory strongly reinforced the pattern of the alienation of the Church from modern culture.

When Gregory died in 1846 he was succeeded by the longest papacy in history; the conclave elected Giovanni Maria Mastai-Ferretti, who took the style Pius IX.[9] He became pope with the reputation of being a liberal. He had been critical of the papal government and he had shown some sympathy with Italian national aspirations. Citizens of the Papal States were delighted when, as soon as he was elected, he planned for railways and street lighting and declared an amnesty for prisoners. He allowed some freedom of the press and of assembly, and set up a *Consulta* (consultative assembly) in October 1847. It looked as though he would unite Italy.

However, 1848 was the year of revolutions throughout Europe. In Paris, in February, King Louis Philippe was over-thrown. In Frankfurt, the seat of the German Confederation, there were a series of revolts. In Austria, the Chancellor, Clemens von Metternich, fell, and in both Naples and Lombardy revolts broke out. Rome was affected also as revolutionary pressures increased. The pope's prime minister, Count Pellegrino Rossi, was murdered and in November 1848 Pius IX fled to Gaeta. A Roman republic was set up by Giuseppe Mazzini and the new religion of 'God and the People' was introduced. At Gaeta the Pope appointed the lay cardinal Giacomo Antonelli (1806–1886) secretary of state, and it was he who obtained French help for the recapture of Rome.[10] Pius IX re-entered the city in April 1850. The moderately progressive pope had become a reactionary.

Under the control of Antonelli, the Papal States were restored. But this arrangement was to survive for only another decade. The economic, social, and political forces of Italian unification could not be resisted: a new 'feeling of *italianita*' was spreading.[11] The prime minister of Piedmont, Count Camillo Cavour, was the ruthless pragmatist who turned *italianita* into the reality of Italy. The defeat of Austria at Solfarino and Margenta in 1859 led to Lombardy, Tuscany, Parma, Modena, the Legations, and Umbria becoming part of a united Italy under the Piedmontese monarchy. The corrupt Neapolitan kingdom collapsed in 1860. All that was left to the pope was the *Patrimonium Petri*. This was protected until 1870 by a French force, assisted by volunteers. After the downfall of Napoleon III, following the Franco-Prussian War, the French garrison was withdrawn and Italian troops occupied Rome on 20 September 1870. In 1871, the Italian government offered the pope the Law of Guarantees, which gave him possession of the Vatican and other Roman buildings and granted him important immunities. He refused this offer and retired to the Vatican. The Roman question was not settled until 1928.

Religious centralization under Pius IX

If Pius IX's papacy was a political disaster, it was enormously successful ecclesiastically. Transportation made travel easier and pilgrims flocked to Rome. The growing influence of the new ultramontanism enhanced the influence of the papacy in the Church. The Jesuits became increasingly influential. Roman centralization grew, not only bureaucratically, but also through religious orders moving their headquarters to Rome, the establishment of many new orders of pontifical right, and the building of national seminaries in Rome where elite students were trained for the priesthood and imbibed the *Romanita*. Many of them were subsequently to become bishops.

Propaganda continued its leadership in missionary work under the long-lasting Prefect, Cardinal Alessandro Barnabo. The nineteenth and early-twentieth centuries saw the greatest missionary expansion in the history of Catholicism and Christianity. Propaganda encouraged this and hundreds of new dioceses and vicariates were set up in the British, French, and German colonies, and in Asia and Africa, as well as the United States, Canada, and even Europe itself. Pius IX re-established the English hierarchy in 1850 and the Dutch hierarchy in 1853. Concordats were negotiated with Russia, Spain, Austria, and the Latin American republics.

Beatifications and canonizations were also a characteristic of this papacy. In the same vein, in December 1854, the pope defined (without any formal episcopal consultation) the doctrine of the Immaculate Conception. This encouraged the revival of Marian devotion specifically and a richer devotional life generally. Much of this was centered in France, either on specific persons, such as Saint Jean Vianney, the *Curé* of Ars, or specific pilgrimage shrines, the most important of which were La Salette (1846) and Lourdes (1858), and after 1870 this religious revival took on a new lease of life.[12]

The occupation of most of the Papal States in 1859 had an odd doctrinal consequence. The pope perceived this as a new assault on the Church and he felt it was a consequence of modern errors.[13] There had been repeated papal condemnations of modern theories and a strong emphasis on the need for a return to Thomistic philosophy. The political loss finally persuaded Pius IX to issue the *Syllabus of Errors* and the encyclical that accompanied it, *Quanta cura* (8 December 1864). The other immediate occasion was the first Catholic Congress at Malines in 1863. Inspired by French and Belgian liberal Catholics, over three thousand people gathered at the congress and unequivocally supported the call for 'a free Church in a free state.'

The *Syllabus* was drawn up by the Barnabite priest (later cardinal) Luigi Bilio. The pope's secretary of state, Antonelli, was opposed to issuing the *Syllabus* for political reasons. It was a confusing document and did not bear Pius' signature. But it represented the pope's view and was symptomatic of the alienation of Pius IX from the modern world. The essence of the *Syllabus* is expressed in the last error condemned that: 'The Roman Pontiff can and ought to reconcile himself with progress, with liberalism, and with modern civilization.'[14] The *Syllabus* was a grab-bag of propositions condemned in earlier encyclicals and speeches of the pope, and covered topics such as rationalism, pantheism, indifferentism, socialism, secret societies, Bible societies, the rights of the Church, and the pope's civil power.[15] It was an attack on liberal Catholics and liberalism, but it was also an error of judgment in view of the opposition, misunderstanding, and difficulties that it caused.

The First Vatican Council (1869–1870)

The most important event of the papacy of Pius IX was Vatican I. It was also the pivotal event in the development of modern papalism. Papal primacy and infallibility were defined at this council. It is essential to understand what happened at this gathering for it drew together and focused the ultramontane ideology of the preceding decades. It also vastly enhanced the prestige and power of the Vatican and set it apart from the rest of the Church. Certainly, Catholics have had to continue to deal with the results of Vatican I, right up until our own time. There is a sense in which the papacy of John Paul II is the natural result of all that was decided in 1870. A number of prescient bishops at Vatican I foresaw the results of the definitions of both infallibility and primacy. Further, as we shall see, questions are increasingly being asked both about the freedom of those at the Council and about the reception by the Church of its decrees. But, firstly, it is important to examine the dynamics of the Council and how and what decisions were made.

In the nineteenth century there was widespread questioning of basic Christian beliefs. As a result, there was mounting pressure in the Church for the reassertion of the fundamental dogmatic basis of Christianity. The idea of a council as a way of achieving this was first suggested in 1849. Certainly the pope began to talk to some of the cardinals about it from December 1864 onwards. Pius was also influenced by the growing influence of neo-ultramontanism—perhaps not to the extent suggested by August Bernhard Hasler, but nonetheless this movement became very important and was supported by the pope as proximate preparations for the Council got under way.[16] On 26 June 1867, Pius IX announced his intention to hold a council and he set 8 December 1869 for the opening. In a ham-fisted but well-intentioned move, all Orthodox bishops were invited to return to Roman unity so that they could attend the Council. Anglicans and Protestants were also invited to submit. Such invitations were ignored—from our contemporary ecumenical perspective they were insulting gestures.

The term 'new' or 'neo-ultramontanism' was coined by Wilfred Ward and it accurately characterizes the more extreme nineteenth-century movement, in contrast to the 'traditional ultramontanism' that had been articulated after the Reformation by Saint Robert Bellarmine (1542–1621).[17] It is Bellarmine's theory of the role of the papacy that has become the basis of the accepted teaching. In the sixteenth century, monarchical absolutism emerged with Henry VIII, Elizabeth I, Francis I, and Philip II. These monarchs were supported by increasingly efficient bureaucratic structures. In the early-seventeenth century, the theory of the 'divine right of kings' was articulated. The notion was that kings were responsible to God alone, that their will was the source of law, and that subjects owed obedience to every morally lawful command.[18] It is significant that this notion of divine right was current at the very time Bellarmine articulated his theory of the absolute papal monarchy. He argued that Christ is the supreme head of the Church. The pope is his vicar, his ministerial head on earth. The pope has absolute power to rule the Church. He succeeds to his rights and prerogatives *iure divino* (by divine right) and not merely *iure ecclesiastico* (by ecclesiastical right). Further, Bellarmine held that general councils can err and the pope must give his confirmation to a council's decrees for them to be genuine. He taught that the pope cannot be judged, deposed, or punished by a general council. If he becomes a heretic he simply ceases to be pope and then can be judged and deposed by the Church. The pope is the supreme judge in deciding controversies on faith and morals, and what he formally teaches is *ipso facto* infallible. The only limit to papal power that Bellarmine allows is in the area of direct interference in the concerns of secular authorities. 'Temporal rulers ... held their authority from God, though in his view it was mediated to them through the consent of the peoples they ruled.'[19] Nevertheless:

> No one can diminish or take away the power of the Supreme Pontiff, not the college of cardinals nor a general council, nor the Pope himself, because papal authority comes immediately from God, and is not subject to the control of any created will.[20]

This teaching of Bellarmine has, essentially, been the accepted dogmatic position on papal primacy since the early-seventeenth century.

But in the lead-up to the Council it was the neo-ultramontanes who were best organized. They focused on one aim: the most extreme possible definition of infallibility, passed without debate and by acclamation. The leaders of this movement were Henry Edward Manning, Archbishop of Westminster; Ignaz von Senestrey, Bishop of Regensberg; Victor

Deschamps, Archbishop of Malines; and Conrad Martin, Bishop of Paderborn—but there were many other supporters from France and Italy, and, to a much lesser extent, from non-Hapsburg Germany. Neo-ultramontanism developed among those who saw the French Revolution as the essence of evil, and the pope as the last stronghold of authority and stability. A strong apocalyptic note, derived from de Maistre and traditionalism, ran through this movement.

The neo-ultramontanes wanted to argue that everything the pope said was infallible. They used the popular press and their views lent themselves to the journalistic 'theology,' typified by Louis Veuillot's *L'Univers*. Veuillot had a stranglehold on the mindset of most of the French clergy.[21] Veuillot was encouraged by Pius IX, even to the extent of supporting him against the French bishops.[22] Cuthbert Butler speaks of Veuillot's 'entirely untheological extravagances.' Typical is this extraordinary *bon mot*:

> We all know certainly one thing, that is that no man knows anything except the Man with whom God is forever, the Man who carries the thought of God. We must unswervingly follow his inspired directions.[23]

Such heretical statements were never contradicted by Pius IX nor by the curia.

In England, almost all the bishops were cautious ultramontanists, but a form of extreme neo-ultramontanism was promoted by Henry Edward Manning (1808–1892), Archbishop of Westminster, and William George Ward (1812–1882) through both *The Tablet* and *The Dublin Review*.[24] Both were converts to Catholicism and Manning had a curious ability to identify his own ideas with those of God. Ward was Manning's theologian and Butler describes him as 'prone to adopt positions of extreme intransigence.'[25] Ward's position was simply that the pope's every doctrinal statement was infallibly directed by God:

> For him, all the direct doctrinal instructions of all encyclicals, of all letters to individual bishops and allocutions, published by the pope, are *ex cathedra* pronouncements, and *ipso facto* infallible. Thus he utterly rejected the idea that infallible pronouncements were few and far between.[26]

The clear influence of de Maistre's traditionalism can be seen in the positions of both Veuillot and Ward.

In Italy, the neo-ultramontanist position was held by the semi-official Jesuit magazine *La Civiltà Cattolica*, especially after the sacking of its founder, Carlo Maria Curci.[27] The position of the Roman curia was, however, more complex. There was some opposition from within it to the definition of infallibility. Antonelli, for instance, was an inopportunist on political grounds. Hasler claims that a considerable number of senior curalists and other important bishops were opposed to the definition of infallibility, and that there was understandable fear in the curia of the results of a council, including the possibility of schism.[28] His figures are probably inflated, but there certainly was quiet opposition among a minority in the curia and the papal household.

The majority of the bishops followed Bellarmine and belonged to the moderate ultramontane party, even if they had not articulated this view as their own. They saw great danger in simply defining the doctrine by acclamation without discussion, as was promoted by the neo-ultramontanes. Even the Roman universities held a moderate ultramontane view. They, like the majority of bishops, accepted infallibility, but they wanted it carefully limited. It was this view that ultimately prevailed, at least in the infallibility debate.

A sizable minority of bishops at Vatican I opposed the definition. There were two groups: those who had theological reservations about infallibility, and those who considered the timing of the definition inopportune. The first group was small. There were a few French Gallicans like Bishop Henri Maret, Dean of Theology at the Sorbonne, Augustin Verot of Savannah, Georgia, and Felix de las Casas, Bishop of Constantine and Hippo in Algeria. A number of others had their own theological objections. The most significant was the learned historian, Bishop Karl Joseph Hefele (1809–1893) of Rottenburg. In 1855 he had begun a nine-volume *Konzilien-geschichte* (*History of the Councils*).[29] Butler thinks that he was one of the few who seriously questioned the doctrine of papal infallibility.[30] It is significant that this question came from the best historian at the Council.

The layman Johann Joseph Ignaz von Döllinger, Professor of History at Munich, had great influence on the Council. He began as an ultramontane, but gradually became alienated from papalism because of his opposition to the policies of Pius IX. The call in the *Civiltà Cattolica* for infallibility by acclamation, and the extremism of people like Manning and Veuillot, worried Döllinger. He wrote a series of articles, published in book form as *The Pope and the Council* under the pseudonym Janus, attacking the whole institution of the papacy from the Middle Ages onwards, with its political pretensions, curial centralization, and ultramontanism. Döllinger constructed 'an imposing onslaught on the popes, probably the most damaging ever compiled.'[31] His book caused tremendous discussion in Germany.

Most of the rest of the minority bishops believed in a moderate infallibility, but considered it inopportune to define the doctrine at that particular time. They were supported by liberal Catholics everywhere. Many of these bishops were in touch with the broader non-Catholic world and they did not want to create further alienation between the Church and culture. They also believed that it was dangerous for the papacy to be divorced from the context of the Church and the magisterium of the bishops, as a kind of Catholic 'oracle.' These issues troubled, among many others, prelates like Cardinals Freidrich von Schwarzenberg of Prague, Josef Othmar Rauscher of Vienna, Filippo Maria Guidi of Bologna, all of the Hungarian bishops, Archbishop Peter Richard Kenrick of St. Louis (who, like many of the US bishops, was concerned about the obstacle infallibility would create for Protestants), and Bishops Felix Dupanloup of Orleans, David Moriarty of Kerry, and the famous pan-Slavic and Croatian nationalist, Bishop Josef Georg Strossmayer of Bosnia, Slavonia, and Sirmium (Djakovo in modern Eastern Slavonia).[32] In view of what has happened subsequently in the Church, the reservations of these bishops were totally justified. The pope has become a Catholic oracle and the doctrine of infallibility has become an enormous obstacle to ecumenism.

In fact, it was Strossmayer who caused the most famous 'scene' of the Council. An ecumenical man whose diocese straddled the Hapsburg and Ottoman empires, he objected to Protestants being called the source of all 'the errors of the day' in the *Proem* (introduction) to the schema *De fide Catholica*. He said: 'I believe that there exists in Protestantism ... a great crowd of men who love Our Lord Jesus Christ.' After interruptions by the presidents, Strossmayer complained about the Council's processes and freedom. This led to his being shouted down by a mob of bishops who called him 'Lucifer' and 'Luther.' Butler says about two hundred bishops took part in this ugly scene and suggests that most of them came from Catholic countries with no experience of Protestants.[33] However, the reference to Protestantism was dropped from the final schema. This 'scene' is significant insofar as it indicates that freedom of speech at the Council was limited not only by the pope-appointed presidents but, more importantly, by many of the bishops from Latin countries who were totally ignorant of Orthodoxy and Protestantism and broader European culture. These bishops were also cosseted by support from often corrupt Catholic regimes, who used the Church to support their legitimacy.

Vatican I was the largest council ever held: Butler says that by the end of December 1869 there were eight hundred present.[34] This number seems inflated; the average attendance was between six and seven hundred. Both Butler and Hales say that there were about two hundred bishops from Italy, representing about thirty million Catholics.[35] Germany and central Europe, in contrast, was under-represented, with about sixty bishops and a Catholic population of seventy million. Döllinger questioned the ecumenicity of the Council because of the preponderance of bishops from Italy and Spain, and there is no doubt that Germany and the Hapsburg territories were under-represented. Again this is a serious criticism that needs to be taken into account in judging the Council's significance. A significant minority group of bishops, numbering about one hundred and forty, opposed infallibility.[36]

The Council began on 8 December 1869. One of the most scandalous events of the Council occurred very early, at the second general congregation of 14 December 1869. Those elected to the *De fide* (on theology and dogma) deputation were virtually entirely pro-infalliblist. Not a single member of the minority was on it, except Archbishop Johannes Simor of Esztergom, Hungary, who was on the pro-infallibility list by mistake! The task of the deputation *De fide* was to revise the theological schemata according to the comments of the bishops; the final wording of texts was decided by the deputation.[37] Manning was primarily responsible for the political maneuvers that led to this. The moderate English bishop, William Ullathorne, commented that:

> All the cautious people, as opposed to the *zelantes* [sic], feel that [Archbishop Manning's] rooms are the centre of a determined intrigue, and that if they get their committee it is because they are organised, restlessly active, and have the strongest backing.[38]

Butler admits that this biased election was 'a serious blot on [the Council's] doings,' but he lamely excuses the pope, saying it was against his wishes.[39] If that is the case, why did Pius IX not do something about it, such as appointing minority bishops to the deputation? Hasler bluntly accuses the pro-infallibilists of manipulation and in this one has to agree with him.[40] It hindered the Council's freedom and destroyed the possibility of its reaching moral unanimity. Again a shadow is cast over the Council's legitimacy.

In the first months of 1870, there were widespread complaints about procedures: there was no time limit on speeches, many of which were rhetorical exercises in florid Latin, and because of conditions in the *aula* (hall) many of the speeches could not be heard. There was no clear agenda and many felt there was no real discussion; just set-piece speeches.

The Dogmatic Constitution Dei Filius

Vatican I produced only two documents: the dogmatic constitutions on the Catholic faith (*Dei Filius*) and on the Church (*Pastor Aeternus*).[41] *Dei Filius* originally came to the Council on 10 December 1869, as a schema on Catholic doctrine against the errors of the day. It was severely criticized by the bishops; Rauscher of Vienna said it was too long and elaborate, too abstract and obscure, and that it did not meet the needs of the times.[42] The pope and the curia were surprised by the vehemence of the rejection and on 10 January it was sent back to the deputation to be rewritten.

Dei Filius was returned on 18 March. One hundred and seven bishops spoke and the constitution was finally passed on 24 April 1870. It is not a particularly impressive document. Pantheism and materialism are condemned and God's creativity is asserted. It says that God can be known by the light of natural reason but faith, inspired by the Holy Spirit, leads to a knowledge of God's revelation. Faith is a free act that finds its fullest expression in membership of the Catholic Church, which itself is a witness to faith. Lest ecumenical ideas creep in here, *Dei Filius* says bluntly: 'The situation of those, who by the heavenly gift of faith have embraced the Catholic truth, is by no means the same as that of those who, led by human opinions, follow a false religion.'[43]

The third chapter contains a statement that has had vast repercussions for the contemporary Church. It introduces *for the first time* the term 'ordinary and universal magisterium.' As we have already seen, both Pope John Paul II and Cardinal Ratzinger use this term frequently and, at times, seem to interweave it with the notion of an infallible magisterium. The statement in *Dei Filius* is almost hidden away:

> Wherefore, by divine and catholic faith all those things are to be believed which are contained in the word of God as found in scripture and tradition, and which are proposed by the Church as matters to be believed as divinely revealed, whether by her solemn judgement or in her ordinary and universal magisterium.[44]

The history of the term is interesting.[45] It first appeared in a papal document in the letter *Tuas libenter* to Archbishop Gregor von Scherr of Munich in December 1863.[46] Von Scherr had allowed Döllinger to organize a conference of Catholic scholars in Munich and he was rebuked by Pius IX for this. The term 'ordinary magisterium' was first coined by the Jesuit theologian Josef Kleutgen, and he was one of the redactors of *Dei Filius*. Through him the term passed into the conciliar decree. 'Ordinary magisterium' has been used as a catchall phrase for virtually all papal teaching. The ordinary magisterium is now being conflated by the Vatican with the infallible magisterium.

The final chapter of *Dei Filius* asserts that there can be no disagreement between faith and reason. It says that any appearance of contradiction is 'specious,' for it is the result of the fact that the human reason is mistaken or has embraced unsound views.[47] The Church alone determines:

> the truth of enlightened faith ... Hence all faithful Christians are forbidden to defend as the legitimate conclusions of science those opinions that are known to be contrary to the doctrine of faith, particularly if they have been condemned by the Church.[48]

Hence the source of all truth is faith as defined by the magisterium. In this way *Dei Filius* establishes an ideology of faith that sets, in advance, the parameters of 'the legitimate conclusions of science.' Thus the papal magisterium attempted to protect its teaching, not only from historical and critical examination, but even from examination by theology itself. This was to become a major issue in the twentieth century.

The Council also considered reforms of ecclesiastical discipline, which were debated between 10 January and 18 March. These 'disciplinary schemata were subjected to the same fire of criticism as the dogmatic schema.'[49] In the light of Vatican II, and what has happened subsequently in the Church, some of these discussions were prescient. The first reform schema was *De episcopis*. It was attacked by Cardinals Schwarzenberg of Prague and Melchers of Cologne, along with Archbishop Darboy of Paris, as being far too theoretical and lacking any real sense of the bishops' status, power, and position in the Church. Both Melchers and Schwarzenberg spoke of over-centralization in Rome and of the need to reform the curia. Eastern patriarchs and bishops were also concerned, especially with the strong centralizing tendencies of Propaganda and its prefect Barnabo. The Patriarch of the Chaldeans, Joseph Audu, was 'scolded' by the pope for defending Eastern Catholics against the Latin regime and Western canon law. A revised version of *De episcopis* was never returned to the floor of the Council.

The primacy and infallibility of the pope

Debate on the schema that eventually became *Pastor Aeternus* began on 13 May 1870. Two versions of the schema had already been circulated and written comments submitted. On 27 April the deputation *De fide* began recasting the schema in the light of these written comments. The theologians of the deputation produced a report 'of a pronounced ultramontane hue.'[50] They argued that infallibility was part of original revelation and that therefore historical problems were apparent rather than real.[51] Here is the difficulty I highlighted previously: ideology determined what was accepted as historical fact. It was claimed that historical problems had already been sufficiently answered, but the reality is that the historical objections to both infallibility and primacy were not dealt with at Vatican I and remain unanswered to this day.

The debate on this schema on papal primacy and infallibility was the decisive debate of the Council. It lasted until foreclosure on 6 June; sixty-five bishops spoke, thirty-nine in favor, twenty-six against—a significant percentage. The major objections were that infallibility was not part of the apostolic tradition but, as Vérot said, 'was an opinion introduced by piety and zeal.'[52] Cardinal Schwarzenberg and Bishop William Clifford of Clifton argued that both primacy and infallibility could not be considered apart from a theology of the Church. The Eastern-rite bishops stressed that the doctrine would place an insurmountable obstacle in the path to reunion with the Orthodox. A number of bishops pointed out that the doctrine would alienate Protestants and prevent conversions, because it would be intolerable to non-Catholics of good will. In a clear reference to Veuillot, Archbishop Darboy of Paris said that the bishops were being forced against their better judgment to define infallibility by demagogues outside the Council. He stressed that he opposed a definition that emphasized a personal and separate papal infallibility, cut off from the context of the Church.

Two of the most telling speeches were delivered by Bishops Hefele and Maret. Hefele argued that the orthodoxy of Leo the Great's *Tome*, which was an *ex cathedra* statement, was judged (and approved) by the bishops at the Council of Chalcedon in 451. True to his historical training, he also argued that the pro-infallibilists could not posit the doctrine as revealed and then argue that historical facts to the contrary could be dismissed. Here is the clash between ideology and history again. He forcefully referred to the condemnation of Pope Honorius I (625–638) by the Third Council of Constantinople in 680.

Bishop Maret was reproved by the president, Cardinal Bilio, when he argued that if the Council declared the pope to be infallible, the Council was, *ipso facto*, superior to the pope.[53] This, said Bilio, was intolerable. The Council was merely confirming rights the pope already had! But Maret had pointed to the essential problem: the irreconcilable approaches taken by the two groups of protagonists. Bilio was *assuming* that the pope was infallible and that all arguments to the contrary were invalid because facts could not be facts in the face of 'doctrinal truth.' The Council could not give something to the pope because he already had it. But what about historical evidence to the contrary? Such evidence had to be wrong because it was already established that the pope was infallible. Papalist apologists still use these circular arguments today.

The best arguments for the definition were put by Archbishop Deschamps of Malines. He stressed that infallibility was not personal and absolute, but that it belonged to the papal office and could be exercised only under the most strict conditions. This was to be borne out in the actual definition. When Archbishop Manning spoke, he said that as the only convert in the Council he was sure that infallibility, far from being an obstacle to conversion, was:

> a powerful attraction for those outside the Church. The religious Protestant mind in England desired an escape from the confusion and chaos of the innumerable sects, and the lack of any tribunal able to teach with authority ... the definition will more than anything else promote conversions and the return of [England] to the faith.[54]

Manning said that infallibility was *already* a Catholic doctrine and 'all are already obliged to hold it.'[55]

Following this general debate on *Pastor Aeternus*, the Council turned to the specific question of the primacy; the debate lasted from 6 June to 13 July. Butler correctly recognizes that papal primacy is more of an ecumenical problem than infallibility.[56] In fact, primacy, as defined at Vatican I, has now become a major difficulty for the Catholic Church itself. The basic reason for this was pointed out by many bishops at the Council: the ecclesiology of the Council was defective and incomplete. 'Here ... is a summary of Catholic doctrine on the Church in which there is no account taken of the hierarchy, episcopate, ministry, ecumenical councils: simply Church and pope.'[57] '*Stupefacti sumus'* (We are astonished), said one bishop. A recast schema on the Church, including an emphasis on the role of bishops, was prepared, but the Council was prorogued before it saw the light of day. This was to have tragic consequences. The pope emerged from the Council in solitary splendor; and with more and more petty centralization of all authority in Rome, the bishops were increasingly seen as mere representatives of head office. The first two chapters of *Pastor Aeternus*, on Peter and the continuation of the Petrine primacy in the popes, aroused little discussion. It was the third chapter on the definition and extent of the primacy that caused most controversy. The fact of the primacy was accepted by the vast majority. But the problem was that there was no context for it. This highlights the lack of an ecclesiology at Vatican I. The definition of primacy has created the situation of an isolated, all-powerful pope with no corresponding balancing and countervailing forces in the Church.

There is a sense in which primacy was not carefully considered at the Council. The bishops were under enormous pressure, not just from the pope, the curia, and demagogues like Veuillot, but also from the need to deal with the agenda quickly. This came from internal forces in the Council, but also from the outside. These debates about papal power were ironically occurring just as the strategic pressure of the Italian *risorgimento* was growing on the remnants of the Papal States. The Franco-Prussian War broke out on 18 July 1870, the day the Council ended. The great irony is that within two months of being declared infallible, Pius IX finally lost Rome to a united Italy.

The primacy question quickly focused around two issues: the meaning of the 'ordinary and immediate' jurisdiction of the pope, and the role of the episcopate in the Church. The word 'ordinary' here is used in the canonical sense meaning 'not delegated.' In other words it means that the power of the office comes with the office itself; one has the power if one has the office. The word 'immediate' means that the pope can act directly in any part of the Church; he does not have to go through another person or body. But where does this leave bishops? Are they simply representatives of the Vatican? Can the pope go over their heads? Bishops also have ordinary jurisdiction in their dioceses, but the pope's immediate power means that he can simply overrule or ignore them.

This sense of absolute power was reinforced when, in what Butler describes as 'a grave error of judgement on the part of the deputation,' a clause strengthening papal power even more was suddenly introduced without debate into the canon at the end of the chapter on primacy.[58] The purpose of the canon was to sum up the chapter. The clause inserted is here given in italics:

> If anyone says that the Roman pontiff has merely an office of supervision and guidance, and not the full and supreme power of jurisdiction over the whole church, and this is not only in matters of faith and morals, but also those which concern the discipline and government of the church dispersed throughout the whole world; *or that he only has the principal part, but not the absolute fullness, of this supreme power*; or that this power of his is not ordinary and immediate both over all and each of the churches and over all and each of the pastors and faithful: let him be anathema.[59]

In this purely legal definition the Church is totally handed over to the pope. He exercises the 'absolute fullness' of power without any check other than the law of God and the defined teaching of the Church—and, of course, the pope is the final interpreter of both! This definition leads straight to the view that the pope owns the Church without any countervailing centers of authority to restore the balance of power. In this legalistic ecclesiology the pope equals the Church, and the Church equals the pope.

The debate on the schema on infallibility began on 15 June and ended on 4 July. Key minority speeches came from Cardinals Rauscher and Filippo Maria Guidi of Bologna. Rauscher emphasized the formula of Saint Antoninus (1389–1459), a Dominican theologian at the Council of Florence and later archbishop of that city. 'The successor of St Peter using the counsel and seeking the help of the universal Church, cannot err.'[60] Rauscher emphasized that infallibility cannot be divorced from the indefectibility of the Church. Guidi, who Hasler maintains was a natural son of Pius IX, was also a Dominican.[61] He argued that the pope was not personally and in and of himself infallible, but only within the context of the Church's belief and only to the extent that the pope's teaching reflected that of bishops and theologians. This was another attempt to keep infallibility within the context of the Church and to avoid creating a papal oracle. Both Butler and Hasler report that Guidi was upbraided by Pius IX for his speech, Hasler adding extra spice by saying it was an Oedipal, father–son conflict![62]

Against this emphasis on episcopal consultation, Cardinal Paul Cullen of Dublin put forward the formula that was eventually used. He said:

> When the pope acts as vicar of Christ he acts by his own authority given him by Christ, not the authority of the bishops or the consent of the churches. Christ did not say to Peter, 'Thou art the rock' provided you consult bishops or theologians.[63]

But the minority still argued for a papal authority placed firmly within the context of the Church. Archbishop Thomas Connolly of Halifax, Canada, put the question bluntly: Is the pope infallible by himself, or does he require the counsel and assistance of the Church? Hasler asserts that Pius IX used Barnabo of Propaganda to threaten missionary bishops, such as Connolly, to get them to switch to the pro-infallibilist side.[64] After eleven midsummer days of exhausting speeches without time limits, the problem had focused around whether papal infallibility was personal, separate, and absolute. The presidents decided to foreclose the debate.

The schema and amendments went back to the deputation *De fide*. As Butler stresses, the request of the minority was utterly reasonable. They feared that the separate, personal, and absolute notion would divorce the pope from the Church—which is exactly what did happen.[65] But the *De fide* deputation simply would not listen to them. They were determined to exclude the Gallican position, which had been articulated by Maret, that the pope was infallible only when the Church accepted his teaching. A week later, on 11 July the deputation *De fide* reported back through Bishop Vincent Gasser of Brixen in the Austrian Tyrol. His exposition on the schema is important for an understanding of the eventual definition. He made it clear that infallibility was personal and that it was independent of the consent of the Church. Two days later there was a trial vote. Out of 601 bishops voting, 451 voted *placet*,

88 voted *non placet*, and 62 voted *placet iuxta modum*. It was now clear that infallibility would be passed and minority bishops began leaving Rome rather than vote against *Pastor Aeternus*. Only two stayed on to vote *non placet* on 18 July: Edward Fitzgerald of Little Rock, Arkansas, and Luigi Riccio of Cajazzo, in the kingdom of Naples.

What had been approved? The key text of *Pastor Aeternus* is the actual definition:

> We teach and define as divinely revealed dogma that when the Roman pontiff speaks *ex cathedra*, that is, when, in the exercise of his office as shepherd and teacher of all Christians, in virtue of his supreme apostolic authority, he defines a doctrine concerning faith or morals to be held by the whole church, he possesses, by the divine assistance promised him in blessed Peter, that infallibility which the divine Redeemer willed his church to enjoy in defining doctrine concerning faith or morals. Therefore such definitions of the Roman pontiff are of themselves, and not by the consent of the church, irreformable.[66]

Because there had been so much debate, the actual definition is reasonably moderate and infallibility has truly only been exercised once since, in the definition of the Assumption of Mary by Pius XII in 1950. In the process the pope consulted all of the world's bishops before the definition. The real problem for the Church after Vatican I has not been infallibility, but primacy and the ordinary magisterium. They have had much more effect on subsequent Church history.

The definition of papal infallibility led directly to the Old Catholic schism. Small groups in Germany, Austria, and the Netherlands rejected the doctrine. No bishop joined them. They united with the Church of Utrecht and eventually formed a loose confederation with the Anglicans. Vatican I also led to a strengthening of anti-clericalism that found its most potent expression in the German *Kulturkampf*.

The most serious failure of the Council was its lack of response to the real needs of the modern period and, despite enormous efforts from scholars, this marginalized the Church from the major intellectual currents for the next ninety years. The paradox is that Vatican I set out to face up to the 'errors of the day' in the most inappropriate way imaginable: by defining papal infallibility and primacy. The Council was blind to the real issues that shaped the modern era: materialism, the myth of progress, the vast increase in world population, environmental destruction in both the Old and New Worlds, migration from Europe on a vast scale, and exploitative colo nialism. And the only response of the Council: the proclamation of a unique form of authoritarianism.

1 J. N. D. Kelly, *The Oxford Dictionary of Popes*, Oxford: Oxford University Press, 1986, p. 301.

2 Hales, *Revolution*, pp. 67–79, and John McManners, *The French Revolution and the Church*, New York: Harper and Row, 1969, pp. 38–79.

3 Hales, *Revolution*, pp. 130–8.

4 Ibid., p. 234.

5 Ibid., p. 236.

6 Ibid., p. 258.

7 Kenneth Clark, *Civilisation*, London: BBC/John Murray, 1969, p. 274.

8 Hales, *Revolution*, p. 280.

9 E. E. Y. Hales, *Pio Nono: A study in European Politics and Religion in the Nineteenth Century*, London: Eyre and Spottiswoode, 1954.

10 Frank J. Coppa, *Cardinal Giacomo Antonelli and Papal Politics in European Affairs*, Albany: State University of New York Press, 1990, pp. 57–72.

11 Denis Mack Smith, *Italy: A Modern History*, Ann Arbor: University of Michigan Press, 1969, p. 9.

12 Thomas A. Kselman, *Miracles and Prophecies in Nineteenth Century France*, New Brunswick: Rutgers University Press, 1993, pp. 113–40.

13 Coppa, p. 139.

14 Barry, vol. 3, p. 74.

15 Ibid., pp. 70–4.

16 August Bernhard Hasler, *How the Pope Became Infallible: Pius IX and the Politics of Persuasion*, New York: Doubleday, 1981, pp. 57–103. There are problems with this translation, which is really a summary of the two-volume German original.

17 Wilfred Ward, *William George Ward and the Catholic Revival*, London: Macmillan, 1893, pp. 84, 116–17. For Bellarmine see James Brodrick, *Robert Bellarmine: Saint and Scholar*, London: Burns & Oates, 1961.

18 Brodrick, p. 265.

19 Ibid., p. 105.

20 Bellarmine quoted in ibid., p. 257.

21 Adrien Dansette, *Religious History of Modern France*, Edinburgh-London: Nelson, 1961, vol. 1, p. 282.

22 Hales, *Pio Nono*, pp. 282–3.

23 Cuthbert Butler, *The Vatican Council, 1869–1870*, London: Collins/Fontana, 1962 (first published 1930), p. 44. See also Butler's *The Life and Times of Bishop Ullathorne: 1806–1889*, London: Burns, Oates & Washbourne, 1926, vol. 2, pp. 40–79.

24 Frederick J. Cwiekowski, *The English Bishops and the First Vatican Council*, Louvain: Publications Universitaires de Louvain, 1971.

25 Butler, *Council*, p. 57. See also Butler, *Ullathorne*, vol. 2, pp. 305–8.

26 Butler, *Ullathorne*, vol. 2, p. 41.

27 Hales, *Pio Nono*, pp. 283–6.

28 Hasler, pp. 53–5.

29 Butler, *Council*, p. 110. The nine volumes were published between 1855 and 1890.

30 Ibid.

31 Ibid., p. 89.

32 Remigium Ritzer and Pirminum Serfin, *Hierarchia Catholica Medii et Recentioris Aevi*, Pavia: It Messaggero di S. Antonio, 1978, vol. 8, p. 153.

33 Butler, *Council*, pp. 236–9.

34 Ibid., p. 149.

35 Ibid., p. 139. Hales, *Pio Nono*, p. 305.

36 Hales, *Pio Nono*, p. 307. Butler, *Council*, pp. 400–3.

37 Cwiekowski, p. 120.

38 Ullathorne (14 December 1869), in Butler, *Council*, p. 141. Butler dates this letter 16 December, but is incorrect.

39 Ibid., pp. 145, 146.

40 Hasler, pp. 70–2.

41 Norman P. Tanner, *Decrees of the Ecumenical Councils*, London: Sheed and Ward, 1990, vol. 2, pp. 804–16.

42 Butler, *Council*, p. 158.

43 Tanner, vol. 2, p. 808.

44 Ibid., p. 807.

45 John P. Boyle, 'The Ordinary Magisterium,' *Heythrop Journal*, 20 (1979), pp. 380–98, and 21 (1980), pp. 14–29.

46 Ibid., p. 381.

47 Tanner, vol. 2, p. 809.

48 Ibid.

49 Butler, *Council*, p. 188.

50 Ibid., p. 304.

51 Ibid.

52 Quoted in ibid., p. 312.

53 Hasler, p. 173.

54 Quoted in Butler, *Council*, p. 309.

55 Quoted in ibid., p. 308.

56 Ibid., p. 330.

57 Ibid., p. 332.

58 Ibid., p. 345.

59 Tanner, vol. 2, pp. 814–15. Emphasis added.

60 Quoted in Butler, *Council*, p. 352.

61 Hasler, pp. 89–92.

62 Ibid., p. 91.

63 Quoted in Butler, *Council*, p. 355.

64 Hasler, pp. 96–9.

65 Butler, *Council*, pp. 396–9.

66 Tanner, vol. 2, p. 816.

CHAPTER 3

The infallible and absolute monarch of the Church

The effects of Vatican I

Almost unnoticed, Vatican I embodied a radical break with a long Church tradition. For centuries it was held that there were three *munera*, or functions, operative in the running of the Church. The first of these was the doctrinal or teaching function. It was through this that matters of faith, belief, and morals were decided. Traditionally, the process was that theologians debated these issues, and bishops and synods made decisions about them. Finally, if the *congregatio fidelium* (the Catholic people) received the teaching it was accepted as the doctrine of the Church. The papacy was involved only at the end of the process, or when Church unity or order was threatened. The second function was that of *ordo*, the celebration of the worship and sacraments of the Church. The third was the jurisdiction or the government of the community. Clearly, the papacy played an important role in both of these functions, especially the latter. What Vatican I and its doctrines of ordinary magisterium and primacy did was to subsume the teaching and doctrinal function to that of order and jurisdiction, and concentrate all three in the pope and the Roman curia. Alberigo argues that this created a magisterial monopoly in the church with the abolition of a sense of theological pluralism. In other words, what was lost was the sense of doctrinal Catholicity. The history of the Church following Vatican I demonstrates the ongoing constriction of theological diversity in the Church. We have now reached the point where the idiosyncratic agenda of a particular pope is increasingly identified with the established teaching of the Church.

We can see this progressive constriction of Catholicity in the decades between 1870 and 1960. Pius IX died in 1878 and he was succeeded by Cardinal Gioacchino Pecci, who became Leo XIII (1878–1903). He was sixty-eight at the time and was seen as a 'caretaker' pope. He had traveled widely and was conscious of contemporary culture. He inaugurated a more intellectually open and challenging papacy. He used the encyclical letter as his major means of communication with the Church and bishops. He was convinced that the theology of Saint Thomas Aquinas would help Catholicism deal with cultural currents in the modern world. Thomism was to remain normative in Catholic universities and seminaries until Vatican II. Leo also insisted, in his letter on historical studies in 1883, that scholars ought to return to the original sources and not depend on subsequent interpretations of the Christian classics. He also allowed certain scholars access to the Vatican's secret archives.

Leo XIII was aware of the development of critical methods in biblical research, especially among Protestants, and he encouraged biblical studies and even literary criticism. In 1902 he set up the Pontifical Biblical Commission. He had what we would call an ecumenical sense and was concerned about both the Orthodox and Protestants. The social question was a major focus of Leo's papacy. The contexts in which he wrote were industrialization, an increasing population, and the capitalist exploitation of workers. The socialists and communists had proposed radical, revolutionary solutions to social problems, but moderate reformers, many of them Catholics, encouraged the development of a social conscience, workers' rights, education, and basic economic justice.

Leo XIII attempted to respond to all of this. He rejected the socialist and communist solution, and in defining the nature of the relationship between Church and state he maintained that civil authority came from God and not from the people. He argued that the ideal state was arranged according to gospel principles. However, he did admit that the Church is indifferent to the *form* that the government takes and that Catholics ought to take part in the public affairs of all forms of government. In his famous encyclical *Rerum novarum* (1891), he provided the foundation of the development of Catholic social doctrine in the twentieth century.[2] It is a carefully balanced document that is essentially very conservative. The pope blames capitalism for the condition of the working class, but he warns against a socialist and revolutionary solution. The right to own property is a natural right. But this natural right must be balanced by the fact that God has given the earth to all. Leo says that inequalities are inevitable and that the class war is wrong.

While all of this might seem to contradict my comments about the constriction of Catholicity after Vatican I, the fact is that Roman centralization continued apace under Pope Leo. The very fact that he felt that he could speak so authoritatively on all of these issues meant that the papal or Roman view immediately became the dominant, normative view to be held by all Catholics. The fact that the pope felt that it was his task to take the initiative meant that his view immediately dominated the field, and theologians were seen as mere apologists for the papal teaching. This doctrinal centralization was reinforced by the increasing control of the world Church by Rome. The enormous expansion of Catholicism outside Europe continued during this papacy, with the establishment of two hundred and forty-eight dioceses worldwide.[3] Emigration from Europe to the United States, Canada, and Australia led to the growth of the Church in these areas. In the new world the Church prospered within the context of democratic and liberal regimes, and to an extent Leo XIII recognized this. However, the unfortunate condemnation of 'Americanism' in 1899 showed that Rome still had little real understanding of the Church's relationship with the democratic regimes that characterized the English-speaking world.

Pius X (1903–1914) and the rejection of modern culture

If Leo XIII's papacy had been a cautious attempt to come to grips with the modern world, Pius X's was a repudiation of it. Giuseppe Sarto, Patriarch of Venice, was elected after a difficult conclave in which controversy centered on the possible election of Cardinal Mariano Rampolla, who was expected to continue the political policies of Leo XIII. Eventually Sarto was elected because he would be a 'religious' rather than a 'political' pope. Roger Aubert calls Pius X 'a conservative reform pope' who 'instinctively mistrusted' anything progressive.[4] Sarto certainly tried to renew the inner life of the Church. He reorganized the curia, codified canon law, reformed seminaries and catechetical instruction, changed the emphasis in Church music, and encouraged frequent communion. Nevertheless, Pius X's anti-intellectualism was to result in the Catholic Church turning inward for the next six decades, largely divorcing itself from the cultural currents of modernity and setting up a false sense of separation between Church and world.

This primarily resulted from the condemnation of modern-ism. On 3 July 1907, the decree *Lamentabili* condemned sixty-five propositions from the works of several authors, and on 8 September 1907 Pius X issued the encyclical *Pascendi dominici gregis*, which attacked supposed covert enemies of the Church as 'modernists.' In the first chapter (pp. 24–7) I have already described the appalling results of the witch-hunt against Modernism. Here we simply need to remind ourselves of its tragic results for the Church in the decades that followed. Fundamentally, Modernism was symptomatic of a split between those who wanted the Church to deal with and express itself in terms of the emerging modern cultural forms of the twentieth century, and those who rejected this reconciliation completely. Aubert speaks of 'the disastrous consequences of the anti-modernist suppression upon Catholic scholarship.'[5] An extraordinary constriction of Catholicity occurred through the anti-Modernist oath imposed by Pius X on all ordinands, bishops, and priests appointed to teaching or administrative offices in the Church. The oath demanded acceptance of papal teaching *in eodem sensu* (in the same sense) and *eadem semper sententia* (always with the same meaning) as that proposed by Rome. In other words, there was no possibility of any form of dissent, even interior. The conscience of the person taking the oath was forced to accept not only what Rome proposed, but even the sense in which Rome interpreted it! Not only was this contrary to the traditional Catholic understanding of the role of conscience, but it was a form of thought control that was unrivaled even under fascist and communist regimes. It was

Orwell's *1984* in 1910! The imposition of this oath was not removed until 1966.

Two other actions of Pius X had long-term, centralizing effects on the Church. In rejigging the Roman curia in 1907 (one could scarcely call it a 'reform'), the pope enhanced the power of the Congregation of the Holy Inquisition, renaming it the Sacred Congregation of the Holy Office and making it the 'supreme' congregation of the curia. Its power over theology was absolute. But the reordering of the curia did not lead to a change of attitude on the part of the Vatican bureaucrats; in fact, their power was enhanced. In the 1917 *Code of Canon Law* (can. 246), all determination of theological truth was entrusted to the Holy Office. As a result it controlled the Church during the period 1910 to 1960.[6] It delayed Catholicism's participation in ecumenism for decades, it excluded millions of Catholics from the sacraments (in Spain, Mexico, and later Italy) for voting for communists, and it created a difficult obstacle course of condemnation and prohibition for those theologians who were to be the foundational thinkers of Vatican II. It went far beyond the traditional task of discerning orthodoxy from heresy, and its procedures were above control or appeal. It completely suppressed licit and discussable areas of thought and conduct, and imposed on the Church an extraordinarily narrow orthodoxy.

The other aspect of Pius's reordering of the Vatican was the codification of canon law. This work began in secrecy in 1904 under the guidance of Pietro Gasparri, who became a cardinal and secretary of state in 1914. Parts of the Code were issued at various times, such as the decree *Ne temere* (2 August 1907), which required Catholics to marry before an authorized Catholic priest and two witnesses, and declared invalid any marriage contracted outside the Catholic Church by a Catholic. Again, this was an arbitrary restriction of the freedom of Catholics; in its reform the sixteenth-century Council of Trent had never imposed the necessity of marrying before a priest for the *validity* of a marriage. The *Code of Canon Law* was finally published in 1917 and it considerably inflated centralization and the juridical and legalistic aspects of the Latin Church. In the Code the solemn and the ordinary teaching authority were equated (can. 1323), and heresy and error were conflated (can.

1324). Thus basic and traditional distinctions were abandoned in a purely canonical context, without reference to theology.

In this way a defensive pattern of rejection of contemporary culture was established in the Sarto papacy. It was to characterize Catholicism until Vatican II.

Benedict XV (1914–1922)

Benedict XV, along with John XXIII, is one of the great popes of the twentieth century. His papacy, overshadowed by the First World War, has been consistently underestimated by historians.[7] An experienced diplomat and a protege of Rampolla, he put an end to the worst excesses of anti-Modernist integralism, and he worked for peace and justice in war-torn Europe. One of his greatest achievements was the maintenance of papal neutrality throughout the First World War. He laid the foundations for the settlement between the state of Italy and the Holy See, he restored relations with France, and he encouraged the study of Orthodox theology and practice and established the Pontifical Oriental Institute in Rome. He was interested in missionary work and insisted that missionaries focus on the task of evangelization and not just be agents of their own national brands of European cultural imperialism. He also called for the training and ordination of indigenous clergy in missionary countries, which laid the long-term foundations for the enculturation of the Church in the third world.

Benedict died tragically early at the age of sixty-seven, and was succeeded by the Archbishop of Milan, Achille Ratti. He took the style Pius XI. A scholar himself, he continued the reversal of anti-Modernist integralism, but only within the cautious limits set by the Holy Office. In fact, throughout this whole period the dominance of the Holy Office continued. The Lateran Treaties of 1929, negotiated with Benito Mussolini, were the great diplomatic achievement of the Ratti papacy. The Holy See recognized the kingdom of Italy, with Rome as its capital. The Vatican City was established as an independent state, Catholicism was recognized as the official religion of Italy, and Catholic canonical legislation on marriage became the norm for Italian civil law. A large compensation was paid to the Vatican by Italy for the loss of the Papal States.

Pius XI was confronted with the problems of both left- and right-wing totalitarianism, and he attacked communism in the encyclical *Divini Redemptoris* (1937). Despite the Lateran Treaties, the pope's relationship with Mussolini became increasingly strained. In retrospect, one of the disasters of this papacy was the concordat with Nazi Germany, signed in July 1933. While motivated by fear of Soviet Communism, it gave Hitler the respectability he needed. By 1937, Pius XI was denouncing Nazi racism in the encyclical *Mit brennender Sorge*. He also had to deal with the persecution of the Church in Mexico and the problems of the Spanish Civil War.

On the theological front, Pius promoted Catholic action and the lay apostolate, but always in terms of the laity assisting the Church because of a shortage of clergy and because priests could not enter some areas because of their clerical dignity. Lay Catholic action was always to be under the control of priests, who in turn obeyed their bishops, who themselves reported to Rome. While it gave many laity a sense of their Christian dignity and encouraged their participation in the apostolate, it was always subsumed into the hierarchical and priestly ministry and was always ultimately under the control of Rome. Pius XI was concerned with the influence of secularization on Christian institutions. The encyclical *Casti connubii* (1930) attacked the modern vision of marriage and reproduction. It was significant that its strong condemnation of contraception came just after the Lambeth Conference of the Anglican Church had given cautious approval to the limited use of contraception.

When Pius XI died in March 1939, right on the eve of the Second World War, he was succeeded immediately by his secretary of state, Eugenio Pacelli. Pius XII (1939–1958) had had wide experience and had traveled further than any other pope. The first six years of his papacy were dominated by the war, and subsequent debate has centered on his attitude toward Germany and his failure to condemn the Jewish Holocaust. In theology, he at first permitted a cautious opening to broader influences. Even during the war he published the encyclicals *Mystici corporis* (1943), which shifted the focus away from the hierarchical Church toward the Christian community as the body of Christ, and *Divino afflante Spiritu* (1943), which permitted the use of modern historical and critical methods in biblical study. It was the beginning of the contemporary Catholic interest in scripture. This openness was continued in *Mediator Dei* (1947), which provided the basis for the work of Vatican II in liturgy. He reformed the Holy Week liturgy in 1953, and set a pattern for the renewal of worship.

However, it was still the pope making all the running. The only licit doctrinal or moral position for a Catholic was what Rome approved. It was seen as the task of theology to explain and justify papal teaching. Pius XII literally pontificated on a myriad of topics and all of this became normative for belief and practice. Those theologians who were pushing the edges of Catholic thought were bluntly brought to heel in the encyclical *Humani generis* (12 August 1950). It was basically directed, as we have seen, against the theologians of the French *Nouvelle théologie*. This encyclical was the apex of the influence of the Holy Office's repressive approach to theology. The new theology was accused of attacking the foundation of Christian culture, and theologians were told that the papal magisterium was the proximate and universal norm of truth, that a decision by the pope in controversial questions was final and binding, and that the task of theology was to show how the doctrine of the magisterium was found in the sources. The Church was paralyzed by this encyclical for another decade, and it negated much of the good that had been achieved earlier in Pius XII's papacy.

The high point of Pius's papacy was probably 1950. It was a Holy Year and millions came to Rome on pilgrimage. Papal audiences became very important and it was in these audiences that the tall, ascetic-looking pope lectured those present on a vast range of topics. He was the first pope to realize the importance of the media and used it widely. He expanded the college of cardinals both numerically and nationally, although his authoritarian and solitary style increasingly diminished the role of cardinals. He was popularly seen by many ordinary people as almost 'quasi-divine.'

However, during the illnesses of Pius's declining years, power slipped into the hands of the curialists who surrounded him. His death in October 1958 marked a turning point. He was succeeded by the greatest pope of the twentieth century, John XXIII. A decisive break with myopic Roman centralism and the extraordinary renewal that would take place at the Second Vatican Council were at hand.

John XXIII (1958–1963)[8]

Angelo Giuseppe Roncalli, who was born near Bergamo in 1881, came to the papacy with long experience in the diplomatic service in Bulgaria and Greece, where he established good relations with the Orthodox. During the Second World War he served in Turkey and from 1944 to 1953 was Papal Nuncio in Paris.[9] He left Paris in January 1953 and was appointed a cardinal and Patriarch of Venice. Here he found his true metier in full-time pastoral work. Roncalli was a mixture of the pietistic attitudes of his generation of Italian clerics and an openness that allowed him to live and let live. His spirituality was traditional and simple, but it always remained humane and gentle. Despite his long years in the diplomatic service he was never a curialist. He never saw himself as an 'intellectual,' but he was a competent historian and antiquarian.

The long illness that led up to the death of Pius XII had left the curia in disarray, but still under the control of the career curalists. Roncalli emerged as one of the possible candidates before the conclave, but it took eleven ballots to elect him. He took the style John and the numeration XXIII indicated that Baldassare Cossa, elected by the Council of Pisa in 1410 as John XXIII, was considered an antipope by Rome. As pope, Roncalli was clearly perceived as transitional. However, his humanity, affability, and humor were in sharp contrast to his austere and remote predecessor and he quickly became popular. People sensed in him warmth, gentleness, and a genuine spirituality. Right from the start the themes that were to typify his papacy quickly emerged: unity in the Church, ecumenism and unity with other Christians, and justice in the world.

Anyone wishing to understand the problems of contemporary papalism must understand the pivotal, watershed role the Second Vatican Council played in the recent history of Catholicism. It was the moment of liberation, the break with the narrow and uncatholic orthodoxy of the previous two centuries. In many ways the history of the papacy since the close of the Council in 1965 has been a long, painful retreat from Vatican II. But the forces for change unleashed at the Council have never been quite defeated. While Catholics are now in the post-post-Vatican II era, the vision of Vatican II has never actually been realized in Church structures. The papacy itself is the major obstacle to this. So it is worth reviewing what happened at the Council if only to reinvigorate the sense of freedom that was realized between 1962 and 1965.

The initiative to hold a council seems to have come primarily from Pope John himself. In the new *History of Vatican II*, Giuseppe Alberigo comments:

> The calling of a new Council was ... the fruit of a personal conviction of the pope, one that slowly took form in his mind, was strengthened by others, and finally became an authoritative and irrevocable decision during the three-month period after his election to the pontificate. It was a free and independent decision such as perhaps was never made before in the history of ecumenical or general Councils.[10]

The pope announced his intention on 25 January 1959, to an unenthusiastic group of cardinals in the chapter house of Saint Pauls Outside the Walls. John intended that the Council be open and ecumenical in the broadest sense, and in October 1959 invitations were sent to the 'separated Christian churches.' Control of the conciliar preparations was in the hands of the secretary of state, Cardinal Domenico Tardini, and the curia. Their aim was an in-house council approving, but not debating, documents previously prepared by the curia. Rome simply presupposed that its views were the only possible ones.[11] Most of the curalists were very similar to each other: Italian career bureaucrats usually of limited theological knowledge and ability. Some were good canon lawyers and most were educated within the narrow confines of the Roman seminaries.[12] The prevailing view in the Vatican was that John had made a bad mistake in calling the Council, which, from the viewpoint of Roman centralism, was correct.

But there were other powerful forces at work in the Church. In order to facilitate ecumenism, John set up the Secretariat for Christian Unity in March 1960, directed by the German Jesuit biblical scholar, Cardinal Augustin Bea, who had been the main author of *Divino afflante Spiritu*. Some of the bishops began to demand that preparation for the Council turn outward to the world and its needs. The French, for instance, asked that the Council confront the problems of the developing world, an idea echoed by Cardinals Josef Frings of Cologne and Bernard Alfrink of Utrecht, who also spoke of the need for decentralization in the Church. Archbishop Lorenz Jaeger of Paderborn wanted a broad, ecumenical approach, and Cardinal Giovanni Battista Montini of Milan said that the Church must adapt to the needs of the age.

In the period prior to the Council there was also a parallel preparation carried on by theologians. Archbishop Jaeger, for instance, called for a Council that would be democratic, collegial, and open. He urged lay participation. But it was Hans Küng, then a young, outspoken Swiss theologian, who succeeded in spelling out the alternative agenda. In *The Council and Reunion* he outlined a conciliar program that was extraordinarily prophetic.[13] He wanted:

- reform of the Catholic Church leading to reunion with other Christians
- emphasis on the use of the Bible in theology and worship
- development of a vernacular liturgy
- an emphasis on the universal priesthood of all believers
- dialogue with other cultures and religions
- reform of the Roman curia and abolition of the *Index of Forbidden Books*
- a de-politicization of the papacy

The book—and Küng's lectures all over the world—enjoyed enormous publicity and offered a real alternative program. In the three years leading up to the Council it was theologians like Küng who broke the stranglehold of the Holy Office and the curia; the curialists were simply caught unprepared, especially for the intense media interest in preparations for the Council. The theological foundations of the Council had been laid—at times at great personal cost—by scholars during the previous thirty years. The groundwork was already in place for a new view of the Church.

The Council opened on 11 October 1962.[14] The pope's opening address sketched a vision of vast optimism. He insisted that the Church must look outward into contemporary existence. He disagreed with the 'prophets of doom who announce ever more unhappy events.'[15] The Council was not about condemnation: 'Today ... the Bride of Christ prefers using the medicine of mercy rather than severity.' The agenda of Gregory XVI was bluntly turned around and it was clear to perceptive observers that the theological schemata prepared by the curia did not correspond to the attitude that the pope had emphasized in his opening address.[16] The way was left open for the reformist majority. They were not slow in seizing the initiative.

It was the largest council in Church history: there were 2640 voting participants, the vast majority of whom were bishops. Superiors general of clerical religious orders also had a vote. Participants included 1041 Europeans, 956 North and South Americans, 300 from Asia and Oceania, and 279 from Africa. The numerical superiority of the Italians, who had dominated Trent and Vatican I, was gone. Present throughout the sessions were about fifty Orthodox and Protestant observers. They were there despite the attempts of the curialists who opposed their presence. These 'separated brethren' and the psychological influence they exercised were to be profoundly important. Their attendance constantly reminded the Council that Catholicism did not exhaust Christianity, and that the imperative of Christian unity must be kept before the Council.

The first session (13 October to 8 December, 1962)[17]

Each morning the bishops gathered in Saint Peter's Basilica— there were tiered stands erected on both sides along the length of the nave—for Mass and then debate in Latin. Afternoons and evenings were increasingly taken up with meetings, conferences, and lectures as participants and theologians attempted to sort out the issues for themselves. On the first day, the curia tried to stampede the Council into accepting its list of members of conciliar commissions. Led by Cardinals Achille Liénart (Lille) and Josef Frings (Cologne), the Council put off these elections for three days and the commissions were given a much broader spread of representation. This is not to say that it was only the group of curialists aligned with Cardinal Alfredo Ottaviani who opposed what was quickly to become the progressive majority. There were always different constellations of bishops who opposed various reforms, and there was a small but consistent group who really opposed everything for which Vatican II stood.

The first session debated schemata on the liturgy, revelation, communications media, Church unity, and the nature of the Church. The schemata prepared by the curial theologians under the guidance of Ottaviani—revelation, Church unity, and ecclesiology—were summarily rejected by the large majority. Among the bishops there was strong emphasis on an ecumenical approach. Bishop Emile De Smedt of Bruges (Belgium), the finest speaker of the Council and one of its best theologians, summed up the majority view of the three schemata prepared by the Holy Office when he said that they (he was referring to the schema on the Church) smacked of 'Romanism' and were characterized by triumphalism, clericalism, and juridicism. De Smedt also emphasized the importance of ecumenism.

This was summed up in the debate about the schema on revelation, which, having been prepared by the Ottaviani commission, was a restatement of the old 'two separate sources' notion: the Bible was one source of God's revelation and the Church tradition another. But in the years prior to the Council the view of Josef Geiselmann gained ground: there was no distinction between scripture and tradition, and that tradition was actually the Church's ongoing interpretation of scripture in the demands of everyday life, which meant that scripture was not a second and independent source of revelation; it was simply the flip side of tradition. Such a view was much more biblical and more acceptable to Protestants. This open attitude was constantly repeated by the other leaders of the majority, Cardinals Paul Léger (Montreal), Franz König (Vienna), Bernard Alfrink (Utrecht), Léon-Joseph Suenens (Brussels), and the Melkite Patriarch, Maximos IV Saigh.

Because the pre-conciliar liturgy commission was fairly widely representative, debate on the schema on worship reversed the roles of progressives and conservatives. The progressives supported much that was in the schema and the conservatives wanted it radically changed. The debate centered on the issues of the use of vernacular languages in the Mass and sacraments, communion under both kinds, the concelebration of Mass, and, perhaps most importantly, whether local conferences of bishops could decide on liturgical changes for their own cultures with only general reference to Rome. While there was strong opposition to liturgical reform from some Italians, interestingly it was some of the English-speaking bishops who provided the stoutest opposition to the use of the vernacular, concelebration, and to communion under both kinds. No decisions were taken at the first session and, like all other topics, the schema went back to the commission for rewriting. Little was achieved in what was a superficial discussion of the media. The discussion was shelved for the next session.

The first session concluded on 8 December with very little in terms of concrete results. But the bishops had begun to think for themselves and to make their own decisions. It was now clear that this would not be a Council that merely approved prepared texts. It had gained its own momentum. A coordinating commission was set up with wider representation, and the schemata had gone back to much broader commissions for rewriting. The curia had been put firmly in its place.

Pope John XXIII died on 3 June 1963, the most important pope of the twentieth century. He had succeeded in initiating a revolution and things would never be the same again. But the future of the Council lay in the hands of his successor.

Paul VI (1963–1978)[18]

Giovanni Battista Montini was elected on the sixth ballot of a two-day conclave that was the largest in history.[19] He took the style Paul VI. In the conclave the anti-conciliar cardinals had at first tried to exclude both Giacomo Lercaro of Bologna (who was considered very liberal) and Montini.[20] He had been born near Brescia in 1897. His father was a newspaper editor who was later a member of the Italian parliament and who was strongly opposed to Fascism. From 1922 to 1954, with the exception of a brief stint in the Warsaw nunciature, Montini worked in the Secretariat of State, eventually becoming assistant to Pacelli. When Pacelli became Pius XII, he worked closely with the pope. Always a moderate, he was anti-Fascist and widely read in French Catholic thought. He was also deeply involved in the Catholic student movement and, after the war, in support of moderate elements in the Italian

Christian Democratic party. His nine years in Milan gave him considerable pastoral experience and in 1958 he was made a cardinal. Pope John involved him in preparations for the Council and he was an active member of the Central Preparatory Commission. In 1960 he visited Brazil and the United States (where he met President Eisenhower), and in 1962 he took an extended trip to Zimbabwe (then known as Southern Rhodesia), Upper Volta, Nigeria, and Ghana.[21]

Paul VI felt he faced a daunting task: how to continue the Council and, at the same time, win over the persistent curial opposition. Hebblethwaite outlines the problem clearly:

> The fact that some twenty-two to twenty-five cardinals declined to vote for Montini, even when his election was assured, remained a worrying handicap. They were mostly Italian, and mostly in the Curia. Their refusal to vote for him meant they were not prepared to yield an inch. ... He would have to find some way of winning the Curia over to the Council while at the same time reassuring it that orthodoxy would not thereby collapse.[22]

In some ways this is the key to this papacy, and to subsequent papal history: it was a constant compromise between keeping the reactionaries in the curia and the wider Church onside, while attempting to grapple with modernity and the realities of contemporary ministry. This same compromise infected the Council, and much that has happened to the Church since 1965 has resulted from it. The tragic fact is that it is because the Church failed to make an unequivocal commitment to the contemporary world at the Council and in the years following it that Catholicism is now facing profound theological and ministerial problems that make it seem irrelevant to more and more of its own people.

The second session (29 September to 4 December, 1963)

Pope Paul VI immediately announced that the Council would continue. When the second session began, he set out four major tasks for the succeeding sessions.[23] Firstly, he called for a doctrinal presentation on the nature of the Church; secondly, he wanted an inner renewal of the Church; thirdly, he pledged the Church to work for Christian unity and asked forgiveness for the papacy's part in causing disunity; and fourthly, he broadened ecumenism to include a dialogue with the wider world.

The Council followed the papal suggestions and the debate opened with a consideration on the revised schema on the Church. It contained chapters on the people of God (laity), the hierarchy, and the role of Mary in the Church. A fierce debate broke out over the chapter on the hierarchy and specifically on the question of collegiality. A minority saw this as an encroachment on papal primacy and denied that it was based in either scripture or tradition. At this time the restoration of the permanent deaconate was also debated. Many speakers saw this as a threat to celibacy: who would choose to be celibate if they could be full-time deacons and marry? Most support for the deaconate came from missionary countries that were already short-staffed.

Discussion on this schema dragged on, and it became clear that the Council was floundering and in crisis. The only ones to profit from this were those who wanted the Council to fail. To break the deadlock a straw vote was taken and it became clear that both collegiality and the permanent deaconate would gain the necessary two-thirds vote. The schema on the pastoral office of bishops was introduced. It reflected a pre-conciliar, legalistic approach, and was rejected and sent back to the commission for a complete rewriting.

In November, the schema on ecumenism was introduced. It was more widely accepted, but debate immediately focused on the relationship of the Catholic Church to the Jewish people and the issue of religious liberty. Introducing the schema, Cardinal Bea spoke of the terrible consequences of anti-Semitism and of the difficult question of the status of the state of Israel. This became a crisis issue for Arabic Christians. It was De Smedt who focused the religious liberty question: every person who follows their own conscience in religious matters, he argued, has a right to authentic religious freedom. Nothing can take the place of a free judgment of an individual conscience. It had been the American Jesuit John Courtney Murray who had developed the theory of the compatibility of Catholicism and a free society, and the strongest push for religious liberty came from the bishops of the United States. For those bishops from countries with a democratic tradition there was no problem with this. But there was strong opposition from many Latin bishops where Catholicism was the majority religion. The two problem chapters on the Jews and religious freedom were eventually pushed into a temporary limbo in the second session.

Meanwhile some work had been brought to a conclusion. The *Constitution on the Sacred Liturgy* and the *Decree on Social Communications* were adopted on 4 December 1963. The liturgy constitution laid the foundation for the most radical overhaul of Church worship in history, and had great impact on ordinary Catholics in the parishes. But the ill-considered *Decree on Social Communications* has been subsequently consigned to the oblivion it deserves. However, there was a sense in which something had at last been achieved. To many, Paul VI's role in the second session seemed ambivalent. Throughout his papacy he often seemed to vacillate. At Vatican II he seemed unwilling to support the majority, to make a stand. But he had to guarantee the freedom of all, and humiliation and confrontation is not the way of the Vatican in dealing with its own. And the main opponents of the Council were the curalists themselves.

The pope concluded the session by announcing a pilgrimage to Jerusalem and a meeting with the Ecumenical Patriarch of Orthodoxy, Athenagoras, which took place in January 1964. This action strengthened the ecumenical thrust of the Council and, as one of the first major papal journeys, it had a worldwide impact. Much work went on between the sessions. A liturgy committee was set up with Cardinal Lercaro as president and Annibale Bugnini as secretary.[24] But there were enormous problems in combining the work of this committee with existing bodies, the Congregation of Rites and the conciliar commission. Another problem was the escalating cost of the Council. Many felt that the third session would have to be the last.

The third session (14 September to 21 November, 1964)[25]

This session saw both the climax and the major crisis of the Council. The session began with the presentation of nine schemata: on the ministry and life of priests, the missions, the lay apostolate, religious life, Christian education, the Church in the modern world, the sacrament of marriage, the Eastern churches, and the Church. Eventually several of these were combined, eliminated, or integrated. The text on the laity was inadequate and dated: it still said that the ministry of laity was delegated by the clergy. There was no appreciation that ministry flowed directly from baptism and that all Christians shared in the priesthood of Christ. Likewise the text on the priesthood emphasized piety, avoided the question of celibacy, and gave the impression that priests were second-class and unimportant compared to bishops. This schema also was sent back for rewriting.

The important schema on *The Church in the Modern World* was introduced on 20 October. Pope Paul was one of the prime movers of this schema and he was determined to see it through the Council. It eventually evolved into the greatest document of the Council, with far-reaching implications: its aim was to shift the focus of the Church outward to the world, which was the context of the Church's ministry. The discussion on this schema ranged across a whole range of modern issues including contraception, social justice, sexuality, population, and a total ban on nuclear weapons.

However, dissatisfaction with the administration of the Council had been simmering throughout the third session. It focused on the secretary-general, Archbishop Pericle Felici, who, it was felt, was manipulating the Council on behalf of the conservative minority.[26] Feelings reached a crisis point on 14 November when the revised schema *On the Church* was given to the bishops. The third chapter on collegiality was the storm center. Felici informed the Council that a 'superior authority' (whom everyone presumed to be Paul VI) had imposed a *nota explicativia praevia* (an explicative note) to the chapter to preclude any encroachment on the papal primacy by the notion of collegiality. Confusion reigned: was the *nota* part of the text? 'No,' said Felici. What was its purpose, then? Felici said the bishops had to understand the text and to vote in terms of the *nota*. Why had the pope imposed the *nota* on the Council as a precondition for voting? As Hebblethwaite shows, the pressure on the pope from the minority conservatives from the beginning of the session was considerable.[27] The pope wanted moral unanimity when the text was voted on and he knew that the minority conservatives would never agree unless the *nota* was imposed. However, many bishops were furious over this action, which was considered arbitrary and unnecessary. The *nota* probably did not alter the sense of the text but the question remained: Did the pope have the right to determine the interpretation of the text in advance? A somewhat gloomy Council eventually adopted the texts *On the Church*, *Christian Unity*, and the *Eastern Churches* on 21 November 1964. The schema *On the Church* has been viewed by most as the theological highlight of the Council, but the unresolved problems in the text still cause trouble for Catholics today. The now separate declarations on religious liberty and the Jews were put off until the next session.

When the third session of the Council closed it was clear that there would have to be a fourth session and that enormous work would have to be done before it. Most of the majority bishops were depressed, as were the observers from the other churches. But the reactionaries were happy. There was a core group of two to three hundred who formed the *Coetus Patrum Internationalis* (the international group of fathers) who opposed religious liberty, collegiality, ecumenism, and the deaconate.[28] Many were also anti-Semitic. Between the sessions work continued on all the outstanding documents.

The fourth session (14 September to 8 December, 1965)[29]

Prior to the opening of the session, Paul VI announced that he would reform the Roman curia and that canon law would be revised. The questions of mixed marriages and birth control continued to be openly discussed. This session was largely fought out in the committees framing the schemata, rather than in Saint Peter's. It also saw the beginning of the debate about the role of women in the Church. The pope opened the session with the announcement that he would set up:

> in accordance with the wishes of the Council, an episcopal synod of bishops to be chosen for the greater part by the episcopal conferences and approved by us, which will be convened ... by the Roman Pontiff, for consultation and collaboration when ... this will seem most opportune to us.[30]

It was a concession, but it was a toothless tiger. The pope called it at his discretion, presided over it, determined its agenda, and decided how its results would be communicated. While Paul VI made desultory efforts to make it work, it was nothing more than a parody of a synod.

The Council was under pressure; this had to be the last session, if only because of financial concerns. The *Declaration on Religious Liberty* was the first item on the agenda. The debate was protracted and the reactionary *Coetus* opposed it in every possible way. The core of the declaration was that no human power could command conscience. Modern society was recognized as essentially pluralistic. The declaration did not pass until the second last day of the Council. The decrees on *The Pastoral Office of Bishops* and *The Renewal of the Religious Life* passed without a great deal of trouble. Few people took post-conciliar renewal more seriously than did religious orders, but the decree itself was not an impressive document. Debates continued on schema on the *Church in the Modern World*, priestly life, and the missions. Simmering under the surface of the discussion of priestly life was the celibacy issue. Paul VI became quite emotional over this and discussion of it was forbidden as 'inopportune.' This was the first issue to be withdrawn from the Council by the pope.

The revised *Declaration on Relations with Non-Christian Religions* (an expansion of the *Declaration on the Jews*) came before the Council again in mid-October. The issue was as divisive as ever. Bishops from Arab countries were still convinced that a declaration on the Jews would imply recognition of the State of Israel. Despite the fact that the declaration was directed to Hindus, Buddhists, Moslems, and the other religions, it was the section on the Jews that received the most attention. Two hundred and fifty bishops opposed the *Declaration* to the end. The rewritten *Constitution on Divine Revelation* was also opposed to the end by a small minority. The decrees on the *Apostolate of the Laity*, the *Missionary Activity of the Church*, and the *Ministry and Life of Priests* were passed by mid-November. These were unimpressive documents. As we shall see later (pp. 102–7), the decree on the priesthood has been particularly problematic.

The last big issue for the Council to surmount was the schema on the *Church in the Modern World*. Despite enormous work on the document by ten subcommittees, there were still many problems to be resolved when it was submitted to the Council. There was a long discussion on marriage and sexuality, but the question of birth control was unhappily skirted on the pope's request. This was the second issue withdrawn from the Council by the pope, significantly both of them being related to sexuality. Over four hundred and fifty bishops said the schema was too soft on atheism and communism. The question of nuclear war and deterrence was fully debated. This was the time of the escalation of the Vietnam War, and the question of conscientious objection also arose. World population was also mentioned and there was a group that attempted to use the pope's name to introduce a condemnation of contraception into the schema. The schema was finally approved on 7 December 1965.

That same day the pope and the Orthodox Patriarch Athenagoras agreed to 'consign to oblivion' the mutual excommunications that had poisoned the relationship between Catholics and Orthodox since 1054. On 8 December 1965, the Council ended. In itself it had been the most extraordinary event in the history of Catholicism since the Reformation, and perhaps in the whole of the second millennium of Christianity. But in order to bring it to fruition major compromises had been made. Catholics are now living with the consequences of those compromises and of all that happened after 1965.

The conciliar implementation under Paul VI

The work of Vatican II did not finish on 8 December 1965. It continued through the application of the practical reforms right across the life of the Church—worship, ecumenical relations, the establishment of episcopal conferences, the rejigging of the curia, the updating of religious orders and the priesthood, the rewriting of canon law—and through a whole new spirit of openness that spread throughout the Church. But the compromises that had been made, and the failure to reform the Vatican thoroughly, meant that there was always a window of opportunity for those who wished to maintain the old values and structures.

Enormous expectations had been built up by Vatican II. Much of the bitterness and disappointment of the present, the alienation of so many Catholics from the Church, and the loss of so many able clergy from the ministry, results from the hopes that were built up in the immediate post-conciliar period. Enormous energy was expended in the renewal of the Church and its institutions, but to many that all seems to have been betrayed by the Church's current leadership. The novelist Morris West has spoken of 'the deep hurt and division ... within the post-Vatican II generation, who see the fading of the hopes they had invested in the updating and renewal of the church.'[31] This sense of alienation has only become apparent fifteen to twenty years after the Council, although the condemnation of contraception in *Humanae vitae* (1968) led many to abandon the practice of Catholicism.

The immediate period after 1965 saw a whole series of post-conciliar documents applying and expanding the reforms of Vatican II.[32] Between 1963 and 1981, forty separate documents were issued on the reform of the liturgy and set out practical applications of the *Constitution on the Sacred Liturgy*. There were sixteen documents on ecumenism and ecumenical activities, fifteen on the reform of religious life, six on priesthood, and six from the Synod of Bishops. Of these the most important were clearly those on worship, ecumenism, and the religious life.

Ecumenism was a priority for Paul VI and his meetings with Archbishop Michael Ramsey of Canterbury (23 March 1966) and the Ecumenical Patriarch Athenagoras I at Istanbul (25 July 1967) and Rome (26 October 1967) were highlights of his papacy. One most significant yet least noticed of the ecumenical documents was the Apostolic Letter of Paul VI *Matrimonia mixta* (7 January 1970).[33] It dealt with the complex problem of 'mixed marriages' between non-Catholics and Catholics, especially in countries where there was a significant number of both Catholics and Anglican and Protestant Christians. The pope tried to engage the bishops of the world in the preparation of the letter but received little response. Collegiality is a two-way street. Probably because of the lack of input, it is not as radical as it could have been. There has still been very little work done to support mixed marriages ecumenically.

In the Apostolic Constitution *Regimini Ecclesiae Universae* (1967), Paul VI reformed the Roman curia. This reform broke the tenure of cardinals prefect of Roman congregations. Their position was to be reviewed every five years, they had to retire at seventy-five, and their tenure lapsed altogether on the death of the pope. Secondly, the Secretariat of State (or Papal Secretariat) emerged as the core of the Vatican. All business now flows through this body; it has become a curia within the curia. The Council for the Public Affairs of the Church administers Church relationships with civil governments and the papal diplomatic service. In a further streamlining under John Paul II, the secretariat of state has been divided into two sections: the first deals with general Church affairs and the second with relations with states. In this sense, the secretary of state has now truly become a kind of papal prime minister. But, like the rejigging of Pius X, this was ultimately a superficial exercise. It did nothing to confront the notion that the curia 'owns' and 'runs' the Church. The structures and even some of the personnel changed, but the underlying attitudes remained the same.

In 1969, the French Cardinal Jean Villot was appointed secretary of state, succeeding the aged Cardinal Amleto Cicognani. But under Paul VI the key men were the *Substitutes*, Archbishops (later Cardinals) Giovanni Benelli and Agostino Casaroli. The industrious and dynamic Benelli dealt with ordinary affairs and Casaroli with the controversial *Ostpolitik*, the Vatican's attempt to negotiate with the communist regimes of Eastern Europe.

Giancarlo Zizola has pointed out that the Papal Secretariat, which was meant to be a coordinating body of the curia, has, in fact, become a duplicate curia that surrounds and protects the pope.[34] The 'old' curia remained pretty much as it was, with a certain amount of tinkering and renaming. The Holy Office, for instance, became the Congregation for the Doctrine of the Faith (CDF), and its first prefect was the friendly Yugoslav, Cardinal Franjo Seper. The Louvain scholar, Monsignor Charles Moeller, was brought in as CDF Secretary, but he soon returned to Belgium. The International Theological Commission was set up in 1967 to work 'alongside' the CDF. The CDF's processes had been 'reformed' by the decree *Integrae servandae* in 1965. But the fact that this institution had changed its name but not its methods was quickly illustrated by the attempt to muzzle the maverick American monsignor, Ivan Illich. Despite the fact that the absurd 'case' against him was quickly abandoned, his two inquisitors continued their careers: Giuseppe Casoria became a cardinal and Sergio de Magistris is still the Regent of the Apostolic Penitentiary.

But a whole series of new secretariats and other bodies were set up between 1960 and 1967, such as the Secretariat for Christian Unity (1960), the Secretariat for Non-Believers (1965), and the Pontifical Council for Justice and Peace (1967). Further bodies, such as the Pontifical Council for the Family and the Pontifical Council for Culture, have been set up by John Paul II. The increase in the number of curial officials is significant—although by modern bureaucratic standards the numbers are small. At the turn of the century there were fewer than two hundred curial staff; at the time of the election of John Paul II that number had grown to around three thousand. It is this increase in staff that has largely contributed to the Vatican's financial deficits right up to the present time.

Guiseppe Alberigo comments that it was in the decade 1967 to 1977 that the restructuring of the curia was really abandoned and that, in fact, the new curial offices brought even more aspects of the Church under Vatican control.[35] The reforms of 1967 actually enhanced papal power. This is not to say that the curia did not change; it did. The sense of curial officials as baroque noblemen disappeared and there was a certain streamlining of administration. Particularly in the 'new' curia some able and broad-minded people were appointed, although there are not many of these left now. But at heart, things did not change: the same self-enclosed, ministerially inexperienced, and narrow attitudes characterize those who work in the contemporary curia.

The encyclical Humanae vitae (1968)

Paul VI's encyclical *Populorum progressio* of 1967 is one of the most radical of all papal documents and it is truly international in its approach. It deals fundamentally with the north–south divide, the gap between the rich and the poor. This, the pope says, will be resolved only by the full human development of all people. The problem with the encyclical is the ambivalence of the meaning of the word 'development,' which so often occurs at the expense of the environment. However, the pope does seriously question theories of rationalist economics and the dominance of market forces. The inspiration of the encyclical was the papal visit to India, French Catholic social thought, and the influence of Barbara Ward, who had spoken to the Council.

However, it is not Paul VI's social radicalism that is remembered, but his moral conservatism. So often his papacy is defined by the encyclical *Humanae vitae*. The history of the encyclical is now well known.[36] The contraceptive pill, which made artificial contraception readily available, only came into widespread use in the 1960s. Prior to that, in *Casti connubii* (1930) Pius XI had condemned all forms of artificial contraception. The introduction of oral contraceptives seemed to shift the focus of the discussion, and some Catholic moralists said that the use of the pill was morally permissible. They argued that the pill was not a direct physical intervention against conception—also *Lex dubium non obligat* (a doubtful law does not oblige). Many Catholic couples, for whom the issue was more than theoretical, began to use the pill. Pope Paul used the Birth Control Commission set up by John XXIII to advise him. The only nonprofessional 'experts' on the commission were Pat and Patty Crowley, a married couple and the founders of Christian Family Movement, who provided the most telling evidence against the so-called rhythm method. If rhythm is the only way to space births, one woman asked, 'How can we imitate God's love by rationing ours?'[37] In 1966, a final majority report recommended change in papal teaching. However, a minority on the Commission wanted the maintenance of the traditional teaching. The report remained secret until it was leaked to the US *National Catholic Reporter*, which handed it on to *The Tablet* in London.[38]

The curia and conservative moralists, of whom one of the most influential was the American Jesuit John C. Ford, put Paul VI under intense pressure to maintain the old line. They argued that any change would gravely weaken papal teaching authority, for it would contradict the condemnation of contraception by Pius XI. In other words, the real issue was papal power and not the question of the moral status of contraception. The pope appointed another, secret, commission headed by Ottaviani.[39] The arguments put to the pope by this commission can be deduced from a letter of Ottaviani to Josef Reuss, Auxiliary Bishop of Mainz. The arguments were:

1) it is not possible to contradict *Casti connubii*, for that would undermine the doctrinal authority of the magisterium and seriously endanger the confidence of the faithful. 2) In the existing atmosphere of general eroticism, in taking an open position, one risks opening the door to hedonism. 3) If one permits the use of contraceptives for individuals, governments will be able to claim recognition of their right to state-organized family planning.[40]

These are the real reasons for *Humanae vitae*. But the actual argument in the encyclical is based on natural law. It said that conception was a natural result of intercourse and the processes of nature could not be artificially vitiated. Every conjugal act must be open to the transmission of life.

All bishops, priests, Catholic faithful, and—since the letter was addressed to them—'all men of good will,' must give internal assent and commit their consciences to the papal teaching. The pope admitted that many would not agree with him in his interpretation of natural law, but he wanted them to obey nevertheless. This was interpreted by many as hypocrisy and it did enormous damage to the papacy.

The results of this encyclical have been incalculable, most of them bad. An untold number of Catholics left the Church, never to practice again. Others, bereft of sensible advice, limped along for years denying themselves communion. Most priests were as confused as laypeople, but their pastoral sense guided them toward a tolerant and helpful attitude. Tragically, it led to many good priests and even to one bishop leaving the ministry. There has been a precipitous drop in Mass attendance, especially in the fertile age group. Many Catholics have come to see the Church as *in*credible in the area of sexuality. Young people today simply ignore the Church, and especially the papacy, which they see as irrelevant to their needs and aspirations. Perhaps the encyclical had one good result: it brought many Catholics to moral maturity in one step. They assumed personal responsibility for their own moral behavior. No longer would they ask the Church to decide their morals. They learned to use and develop their own consciences.

In 1968 *The Economist* commented bluntly: 'This encyclical is not the fruit of papal infallibility but of papal isolation.'[41] This is the core of the tragedy: today we can see clearly that everything was sacrificed to preserve papal power. This encyclical was not a collegial action. The pope had called a synod in 1969 to discuss collegiality, but as Cardinal Suenens pointed out, Paul VI had ignored collegiality in the extremely important contraception decision.[42] Suenens was quickly supported by Karl Rahner, Hans Küng, Bishop Christopher Butler, and other theologians. Nothing was resolved at the synod on collegiality, and for the rest of his papacy Paul VI remained stuck between primacy and collegiality, with a very strong emphasis on primacy.

Financial scandals

I previously mentioned (pp. 91–4) the financial problems of the Vatican in the context of the cost of the expansion of curia after Vatican II. But the problems went deeper: in a series of spectacularly foolish moves, Paul VI and his financial advisers allowed themselves to become involved with some of the most notorious thieves and con men of the century. Highly centralized and secretive administrations like the Vatican are pecularily vulnerable to scams, for there are insufficient checks and balances. While the general lines of these scandals are clear, the exact interconnections between the Vatican and the shadow side of international finance are hard to clarify. Certainly by the late 1960s it was clear that the Vatican had financial problems. The Chicago-born Archbishop Paul Marcinkus was the rising star at the *Istituto per le Opere di Religione* (IOR)—the Institute of Religious Works—set up by Pius XII in 1942 as an investment arm of the Vatican. It acted as a merchant bank and was thus involved in the morally ambivalent world of international finance. As an ordinary bank most of its deposits came from religious orders, private individuals, and other church-related agencies. It is popularly known as the 'Vatican Bank.'

In the context of this book it is fascinating that a whole series of Church councils from Arles (314) to Vienne (1311) condemned usury: that is, the taking of interest on a loan. As late as 1745, Benedict XIV issued the encyclical *Lex pervenit*, which repeated the long-standing tradition that usury was sinful. It was only in the nineteenth century that the view began to change, when moderate rates of interest were approved. So what was the status of this teaching of councils and popes for fifteen hundred years? Was it infallible? Why could it have been dropped so quickly that within a century the Vatican itself was running a bank that speculated in the short-term money market? Again, we are confronted with the issue of teaching that is held to be binding and definitive, only later to be jettisoned.

Appointed head of the IOR in 1969, Marcinkus thought that Vatican investments should be moved out of the Italian stocks favored by his predecessor, Cardinal Alberto Di Jorio, and placed in various international companies that were felt to be safe. However, there were also justifiable accusations that the Vatican was trying to sidestep Italian taxes on its portfolio.[43] The IOR was also used by some Italians as a channel to the tax havens of Switzerland and the Caribbean to avoid Italy's financial regulators. Operating within the Vatican, which is an independent country, the IOR can sidestep Italy's currency laws.

In a secret meeting in 1969, Marcinkus introduced Paul VI to the Sicilian banker Michele Sindona. This was an extraordinarily foolish move, for Sindona's Mafia and criminal connections were well known. He was a member of the notorious right-wing, pseudo-Masonic lodge, *Propaganda Due* (P-2), founded by the Fascist, Licio Gelli.[44] Sindona was asked to dispose of Vatican shares in the giant holding company, *Società Generale Immobiliare*. Sindona did this by taking over the company and it is clear that he used his Vatican connections to facilitate criminal financial deals, and it is also clear that Marcinkus did nothing to stop him. By 1974 two banks run by Sindona had crashed and he was wanted in both Italy and the United States. The Vatican tried to distance itself from him, but it had lost a massive amount of money through the Sindona connection. Estimates range between US$30 million (the official figure) and US$200 million. Sindona died of poisoning in suspicious circumstances in an Italian prison in 1986.

Through a connection with Paul VI's private secretary, Don Pasquale Macchi, the Vatican then brought in the Milanese banker Roberto Calvi, president of the prestigious Catholic Banco Ambrosiano. The IOR quickly became a large stockholder in the Ambrosiano. It was another unmitigated disaster. Calvi was probably the most talented con man and thief of the century. Like Sindona, he used his Vatican connections to facilitate a whole range of illegal dealings. In July 1981, Calvi was convicted of the illegal export of Italian currency. Further investigations by Italian banking authorities uncovered massive fraud by Calvi. He was found hanged under Blackfriars Bridge in London in June 1982. Through Calvi the Vatican had become involved in the theft of US$1.6 billion from the Banco Ambrosiano. In late 1982, John Paul II appointed a committee of cardinals to investigate the fiasco. Marcinkus was eventually charged by Italian authorities, but he was protected by Vatican diplomatic immunity and eventually retired to the United States.

While denying all responsibility in the Ambrosiano affair, the Vatican made 'reparation' by paying US$250 million to the bank's creditors. The source of this money has not been explained although various suggestions have been made.[45] It has now been almost certainly established by the British authorities that Calvi was murdered, probably by the Mafia whom he had deceived and cheated.

Many have subsequently charged the Vatican with criminal misbehavior in the whole sorry affair. The best that can be said is that its administration was utterly irresponsible. It vividly demonstrated the stupidity of allowing priests to play in the world of international finance. On Marcinkus' part there seemed to be a complete lack of moral and ethical sensitivity. While the affair has led to the Church being accused of criminal misbehavior, in fact, the IOR was probably more likely to have simply been remarkably stupid. Vatican finances are now under the control of Cardinal Edmund Szoka, formerly the Archbishop of Detroit, who has balanced the books. This is quite an achievement!

The last years of Paul VI's papacy were overshadowed not only by financial scandals, but also by the growing right-wing Lefebvrist schism, the departure of many priests and religious from the active ministry, and a spreading disillusionment among Catholics across the world as they perceived that the renewal of the Church was grinding to a halt. Many hoped that Paul would retire at seventy-five and that a synod of world bishops would elect his successor. The pope seems to have toyed with the idea for a while, but eventually only tried to broaden the internationalization of the college of cardinals even more, and to decree that cardinals over eighty years of age would be excluded from future conclaves. Again, a chance was lost. He suffered from ill-health for the last couple of years of his life and was deeply depressed by the murder of his lifelong friend, Aldo Moro, by the Red Brigades in 1978. The power and influence of Benelli in the curia throughout this last period of Paul's life was considerable.

Paul VI died on 6 August 1978. He left a profoundly ambivalent legacy. He had saved the Church from open schism and he had honestly tried to implement Vatican II. However, for the vast majority of Catholics he had never gone far enough, and he had never been strong and decisive in dealing with the curial and reactionary attempts to subvert the Council. Try as he might, he could not escape from the thought categories with which he had grown up. And with most people his reputation never recovered from the disaster of *Humanae vitae*. While there was never a significant right-wing schism (that of Lefebvre is numerically totally insignificant), the inactivity of Paul VI has contributed to a kind of schism of indifference. Many Catholics feel that the Church has come to a grinding halt. This feeling began under Paul VI, as he failed to deal decisively with the reactionaries in the curia, hierarchy, and elsewhere, was exacerbated by *Humanae vitae*, and is now deeply entrenched after eighteen years of John Paul II.

Even in 1978, time had not run out and there still was a chance to realize the radical vision that was inherent in Vatican II. In a month of optimism between 26 August and 28 September 1978, it seemed as though that radical vision might be realized.

The year of three popes [46]

The conclave that met on 25 August had a record one hundred and eleven cardinals, and was the first to meet under Paul VI's reforms. Cardinals over eighty were excluded, although their influence on the pre-conclave discussions was considerable. There were only twenty-seven Italians eligible as electors. The cardinals met daily to prepare for the conclave. In the public discussions before the conclave it became clear that what people wanted was, in the words of a group of theologians that included Hans Küng, Yves Congar, and Edward Schillebeeckx, a man of holiness, a man of hope, a man of joy … .who can smile. A pope not for all Catholics but for all peoples. A man totally free from the slightest taint of financial organizational wheeling and dealing.[47]

The Latin-American cardinals were looking for similar qualities. On 26 August 1978, twenty days after the death of Paul VI, the Patriarch of Venice, Albino Luciani, was elected on the third ballot. It was an extraordinarily quick conclave. He promised to be a new style of pope. He was from a working-class background and all of his priestly and episcopal experience had been in pastoral work and seminary teaching. He had never had anything to do with the curia, although he had been active in the Italian Bishops' Conference. He chose the unusual—some might say odd—title of John Paul. It is impossible to say where he would have stood on theological matters, despite the assertions that he was assassinated because he was going to 'disown' *Humanae vitae* and clean up the Vatican Bank and the curia.

He died late in the evening of September 28, 1978, while reading in bed. There was no autopsy and rumors of murder by poisoning found concrete form in the book *In God's Name* by David Yallop.[48] Yallop maintained that John Paul was murdered by a coalition that included Cardinals Jean Villot (secretary of state) and Cody of Chicago, as well as Archbishop Marcinkus, Sindona, and Calvi.[49] These fabrications were completely repudiated by John Cornwell's excellent book *A Thief in the Night*. Cornwell maintained that the pope died because no one took care of his health or made sure that he took medication for his heart condition.[50] The short reign of John Paul I seemed like another lost opportunity.

And so Rome prepared for another conclave. This time it was clear that the pastoral candidate would also have to have good health and probably be younger. The conclave was much longer and clearly more divided. At first the candidates were Benelli, by then Archbishop of Florence, and the reactionary Siri of Genoa. It is extraordinary that a person such as Siri could still be a serious candidate. It was only when it became clear that neither could get the necessary two-thirds-plus-one that the cardinals began to look beyond the Italian candidates. Cardinal Franz König of Vienna put forward the name of Karol

Wojtyla of Krakow. He had travelled widely, spoke fluent Italian, and came from a communist country. Aged only fifty-eight, he seemed to have much to recommend him. After eight ballots he had obtained a large majority. He took the style John Paul II. This brings us to the papacy of the present day.

1 Alberigo in Swidler and Fransen, pp. 124–5.

2 John Molony, *The Worker Question: A New Historical Perspective on Rerum Novarum*, Melbourne: Collins Dove, 1991. Bruce Duncan, *The Church's Social Teaching: From Rerum Novarum to 1931*, Melbourne: Collins Dove, 1991, pp. 20–91.

3 Kelly, p. 312.

4 Aubert in Jedin and Dolan, vol. 9, p. 386.

5 Ibid., p. 464.

6 For an outline of the work of Holy Office before its incarnation as the CDF see Peter Canisius van Lierde, *The Holy See at Work: How the Catholic Church is Governed*, London: Robert Hale, 1964, pp. 55–61.

7 See W. H. Peters, *The Life of Benedict XV*, Milwaukee: Bruce, 1959.

8 For detailed studies of aspects of John's papacy see Giancarlo Zizola, *The Utopia of John XXIII*, English trans., Maryknoll: Orbis, 1978. For biography see Peter Hebblethwaite, *John XXIII: Pope of the Council*, London: Geoffrey Chapman, 1984.

9 Zizola, pp. 81–99.

10 Giuseppe Alberigo, 'The Announcement of the Council,' in Giuseppe Alberigo and Joseph A. Komonchak (eds), *The History of Vatican II: Volume 1*, Maryknoll: Orbis and Leuven: Peeters, 1995, p. 13. This is the first of a projected five-volume definitive history of the Council. See also Zizola, pp. 233–42, and Hebblethwaite, *John XXIII*, pp. 283, 306–9.

11 Alberigo in Alberigo and Komonchak, pp. 44–9, and Hebblethwaite, *John XXIII*, p. 337.

12 Zizola, pp. 165–80.

13 Hans Küng, *The Council and Reunion*, English trans., London: Sheed and Ward, 1961.

14 I have described the workings of Vatican II in some detail in *Mixed Blessings*, pp. 20–49.

15 Quoted in Zizola, pp. 258–9.

16 Ibid., p. 260.

17 Xavier Rynne, *Letters from Vatican City: Vatican Council II (First Session): Background and Debates*, London: Faber and Faber, 1963.

18 Peter Hebblethwaite, *Paul VI: The First Modern Pope*, London: HarperCollins, 1993.

19 Kelly (p. 323) says it was the fifth ballot. Hebblethwaite's *Paul VI* (p. 329) says the sixth.

20 Hebblethwaite, *Paul VI*, pp. 318–32.

21 Ibid., pp. 292–4; 301–2.

22 Ibid., p. 331.

23 Ibid., pp. 348–69, and Rynne, *Second Session*.

24 Annibale Bugnini, *The Reform of the Liturgy 1948–1974*, English trans., Collegeville: Liturgical Press, 1990.

25 Xavier Rynne, *The Third Session*, London: Faber and Faber, 1965.

26 Ibid., pp. 238–45.

27 Hebblethwaite, *Paul VI*, pp. 384–401.

28 Ibid., p. 401.

29 Xavier Rynne, *The Fourth Session*, London: Faber and Faber, 1966.

30 Paul VI, opening address, quoted in Hebblethwaite, *Paul VI*, p. 432.

31 Morris West, 'One Man's Voice,' *Eureka Street*, August 1994, p. 31.

32 These documents can be found in Austin Flannery (ed.), *Vatican Council II: The Conciliar and Post Conciliar Documents*, Dublin: Dominican Publications, 1975, and *Vatican II: More Post Conciliar Documents*, Grand Rapids: Eerdmans, 1982.

33 Text in Flannery, *Vatican Council II*, pp. 508–14.

34 Giancarlo Zizola, 'Secretariats and Councils of the Roman Curia,' in the *Concilium* entitled *The Roman Curia and the Communion of Churches*, New York: Seabury Press, 1979, p. 43.

35 Giuseppe Alberigo, 'Serving the Communion of Churches,' in *Concilium* 1979, pp. 24–5.

36 Robert Blair Kaiser, *The Politics of Sex and Religion: A Case History in the Development of Doctrine 1962–1985*, Kansas City: Leaven Press, 1985. (A revised UK edition of Kaiser's book was published as *The Encyclical that Never Was: The Story of the Commission on Population, Family and Birth, 1964–66*, London: Sheed & Ward, 1987.) Kaiser's account has been confirmed and amplified by Robert McClory, *Turning Point: The Inside Story of the Papal Birth Control Commission*, New York: Crossroad, 1995.

37 Quoted in McClory, p. 92.

38 Kaiser, pp. 183–7.

39 Ibid., p. 183.

40 Ibid., p. 193.

41 Quoted in ibid., p. 198.

42 Hebblethwaite, *Paul VI*, pp. 532–5.

43 Luigi DeFonzo, *St. Peter's Banker: Michele Sindona*, New York: Franklin Watts, 1983, pp. 8–10. This book is determined to attribute the worst possible motives to Paul VI.

44 Ibid., pp. 67–74.

45 Michael Walsh, *The Secret World of Opus Dei*, London: Grafton, 1989, p. 157.

46 Peter Hebblethwaite, *The Year of Three Popes*, London: Collins, 1979.

47 Complete in *The Tablet*, August 1978, p. 811.

48 David A. Yallop, *In God's Name: An Investigation into the Murder of Pope John Paul I*, London: Corgi, 1985.

49 For Cody in Chicago see Charles Dahm, *Power and Authority in the Catholic Church. Cardinal Cody in Chicago*, Notre Dame: University of Notre Dame Press, 1981.

50 John Cornwell, *A Thief in the Night: The Mysterious Death of John Paul I*, London: Viking, 1989.

CHAPTER 4

Papalism triumphant: John Paul II

High papalism

The papacy of John Paul II has brought the Catholic Church to a crossroad. Never before has the papacy been so powerful. Its theological claims are now supported by the global reach of modern communications. Pope John Paul's ability to use his office and his personality to project his vision of the Church has brought him superstar status. This gives him a peculiar ability to impose his agenda on the Church. By his constant travel he has *de facto* turned himself into a kind of 'world bishop.' Television and the speed and facility of air travel have created an entirely new situation in Church history: the seemingly omnipresent papacy. Previous popes, such as Innocent III and Boniface VIII, had claimed a universal jurisdiction and pastorate, but they did not have the facilities to realize it. The peripatetic John Paul II has made this a reality. He has taken the notion of primacy as defined at Vatican I to its logical conclusion. In its entire history, the Catholic Church has never, in fact, been more centralized. In the popular mind and in television images, the Church and the papacy have become identified. The pope has given a new lease of life to the papal monarchy.

There is no doubt that John Paul II has met the needs of some people. He has made the papacy *seem* present. People see him, especially on television, where he is a consummate performer, as an accessible and humane figure who stands for justice and for a return to traditional values. Despite his often unpopular message, he is still admired by many. He is no longer remote, like the 'quasi-divine' Pius XII, but a man of the masses. This certainly meets the religious needs of some people in a world of disintegrating values and changing meaning structures. For some Catholics the Wojtyla papacy has become the point of stability in a world of rapidly changing values. De Maistre's theory of traditionalism maintained that God's revelation is handed down through the unbroken line maintained by the papacy. John Paul sees it as his task to maintain that tradition into the postmodern world. That deeply *non*-historical view of reality is the antithesis of the view put forward in this book.

In this exaltation of the papacy, the notions of collegiality and subsidiarity are pushed into the background. The notion of subsidiarity is derived from Catholic social teaching and refers to the fact that large institutions should not usurp the prerogative of lower, more intimate ones. The role of larger institutions is to support decision-making processes at the lower level. It was first enunciated by Pius XI in the 1931 encyclical *Quadragesimo Anno*.

Local leadership, and local bishops and communities, fade into insignificance beside the papal star. It is the captain, not the team, that is highlighted. If, for instance, John Paul came on his visits to learn from the local church and bishops, and, after genuine dialogue, to reinforce the priorities of Catholics to confront local realities, the visits might have some real pastoral value. But there is no discussion, and local participation is vetted well in advance. While there is a certain limited consultation on the content of the papal speeches, no views are allowed to be expressed except those approved by Rome. The local church is simply silenced. The identification of pope and Church is reinforced.

This triumphalism is in sharp contrast to the real sense of despair that is palpable among those middle-aged and older Catholics who committed themselves with energy and generosity to the renewal of the Church after Vatican II. They now feel there is nowhere to go and that their good will has been betrayed. Much of the passion and enthusiasm has gone out of the best people in the Church. Bishops and priests have turned inward, and only a small minority are now willing to stand up and offer leadership. Younger, idealistic people are forced to look outside the Church for the commitments that direct and develop their generosity. Part of the reason for this is that, unlike the more synodal structures of the other Christian churches, the Roman Church seems impervious to the wishes and priorities of its members. Decisions are made far from the grassroots and simply imposed from on high. There are few structures of consultation, and Catholics do not even have a say in the appointment of their parish priest (if they have one), let alone in the appointment of their bishop. Some of those who are still committed to the Church look inward to the development of personal spirituality, or they commit themselves to issues at the local level and simply block out wider issues. Among Catholics there is a deep, unspoken sense of alienation and a feeling that the Church that once challenged them has now failed them.

The reason for this is clear: it is the failure to resolve the disjunction inherent in many documents of Vatican II, but especially in *Lumen Gentium*. In the first two chapters the Church is described as a sacramental community along New Testament lines, but in chapter three it is portrayed primarily as a hierarchical structure. I referred to this disjunction a decade ago in *Mixed Blessings* and nothing has changed.[1] The usual line is that the two models are complementary, and that the hierarchy exercises a genuine leadership in a community church.

> [But] Catholics are discovering that the two models are not only not complementary, but that their side-by-side existence has created an enormous tension. Many Catholics (including some in the hierarchy) view the Church *fundamentally* as a community. Many others (including a lot of laity) view the Church *fundamentally* as a hierarchy. It cannot be *fundamentally* both. Father J. Rémy has said that these two models are 'mutually exclusive' and 'mutually corrosive.'[2]

Remy is right: the corrosive results of the disjunction are clear to anyone with perception. An absolute monarchy cannot be superimposed on a more democratic-synodal structure. A community model based on New Testament images of the Church, and a hierarchical model based on an imperial notion of *sacra potestas*, are simply incompatible, and the time has come to acknowledge this.

John Paul's use of the power of both his office and his superstar influence, his treatment of the synod of bishops as a mere rubber stamp for his own views, and his increasing identification of his personal agenda with the established teaching of the Church have heightened the destructive tensions inherent in the disjunction. The community-oriented, consultative vision of the Church that emerged at Vatican II has simply never been embodied in Church structures. This is the most important issue on which the Catholic Church has failed over the last thirty years. The reason why acknowledgment of this problem has been put off for so long lies in the Vatican's persistent refusal to surrender any of its power. Nothing will change during John Paul's pontificate and the schism of indifference will continue.

The crisis in the priesthood[3]

Another example of the corrosive disjunction inherent in the documents of Vatican II, and another clear symptom of the pervasive malaise in the Church, is the crisis in the role of the priest. Significantly, this is also an issue that John Paul emphasizes. The fact is that the contemporary clerical priesthood is in crisis. The leadership cadre of the Church has lost confidence in itself, as well as losing the confidence of many of the Church's members. Catholics are alienated not because they have lost faith, but because they do not perceive that the Church is showing leadership in addressing the issues that are important to them. The priestly leadership of the Church has become increasingly self-engrossed with problems of identity, lifestyle, and role. Also, the criminal sexual misbehavior of some priests has understandably led to a very negative perception of the Catholic priesthood in popular opinion and in the media.

The French Dominican Christian Duquoc claims that there is an essential conflict between the post-Tridentine theology of a cultic priesthood outlined in the Vatican II *Decree on the Ministry and Life of Priests* and the same decree's stress that priestly ministry consists in an 'openness to non-believers ... profound involvement in everyday life ... [and] service of the poor.'[4] Duquoc says that this places the priest in an irreconcilable bind between the demands of a modern ministry and an

outdated theology of priesthood.[5] He argues that this underlying tension manifests itself in all of the other contemporary
problems related to the Catholic priesthood. Pope John Paul
has actually heightened this tension by his constant emphasis
on this inadequate and outdated theology and spirituality.

One of the most serious problems facing the Church is a
complex set of questions relating to the priesthood and
sexuality. The question of the actual observance of celibacy has
been raised in the two recent books of A. W. Richard Sipe.[6] He
claims that at most only about forty percent of clergy in
the United States actually practice celibacy at any one time.
The same is probably true of other countries in the West. It is
the secrecy that Sipe especially emphasizes.[7] Because of the
nexus between secrecy and power, Sipe argues that once secrecy
is broken clerical power will then be challenged. This public
discussion has understandably made most priests wary of
public leadership, and especially public controversy. Personally, I am ambivalent about Sipe's books. Much that he says is
true, especially the connection between celibacy, clericalism,
and power, and the way in which this is all maintained by
secrecy and compromise. Perhaps my ambivalence is because I
am a priest and cannot face the hard truth about myself and
the clerical system. But my problem with Sipe's view is that my
life is not defined exclusively in terms of my sexuality and, like
everyone else, I would not want to be judged in terms of my
worst behavior.

Sipe's exclusive focus on sexuality actually distorts an even
more complex issue. Nowhere does he mention the disjunction
indicated by Duquoc, nor the massive process of adjustment
and change that priests have had to face during the thirty years
since Vatican II. They have had to face more fast-moving,
ambivalent, and complex situations, both institutionally and
ministerially, than any other generation of clergy before them.
Not the least of the issues that they have had to confront is
voluntary disempowerment, as they hand over aspects of their
former role to the laity. They have also had to face the problem
of the departure of so many of their friends and colleagues from
the active priestly ministry. None of this context is to be found
in Sipe. And he is not the only one to write about this. Recently
there has been a spate of books, some serious, some merely 'kiss

and tell' stories, about relationships between priests and women. It is not surprising that many priests are increasingly on the defensive.

However, there is also a sense in which Sipe is right. There is a connection between secret sexuality and power, even though most priests do not experience themselves as powerful. In fact, many of them feel powerless and frustrated, caught as they often are between the expectations of the laity and the immobility of the established Church. But it is clear that some priests have seriously abused their position of influence and trust. It is becoming almost commonplace now to open the newspaper to read of another priest found guilty in the courts of criminal sexual misbehavior. The accusations reach to the top of the hierarchy and include an Austrian cardinal and an Irish bishop, but it is largely in common law countries, such as the United States, the United Kingdom, Ireland, Canada, and Australia, that culprits are being brought to book.

The widespread nature of this scandal indicates that its causes are pervasive and deeply embedded in the institutional Church. Its repercussions affect not just bishops and religious superiors, but the whole Catholic community. The blame for this cannot be shifted to the media, or to anyone outside the Church. It is a problem embedded at the core of its institutional and clerical structure. It is also true that many priests justifiably feel that they are the 'fall guys' who have to bear the understandable but often undifferentiated anger of the laity, not only over sexual issues, but also over the way in which renewal of the Church has completely stalled. As the most accessible Catholic authority figures, priests feel that their good names, personal relationships, and ministries are unfairly—but constantly—on the line.

The fact is that the underlying problem does not lie with local bishops and church leaders who are struggling to deal with these issues. The core issue is the attitude of Rome. For example, in Ireland throughout 1995, the *Alice in Wonderland* attitude to celibacy has been publicly manifested for all to see. Ireland has been shocked by a series of clerical scandals of which the Bishop Eamon Casey case was only the first. Recently the prime minister of Ireland was forced to resign over the attempted delay of the extradition to Northern Ireland of

Brendan Smythe, a priest later found guilty of abusing children. Public discussion in the Irish media has been dominated by clerical scandals. As a result, several bishops modestly suggested that obligatory celibacy is an issue that needs to be openly discussed for the good of the Church. For their pains these bishops were quickly assured by Rome that this issue was 'beyond discussion.' They were also publicly chastized by the Irish Primate, Cardinal Cahal Daly, and the Prefect of the Congregation for Bishops, Cardinal Bernardin Gantin. But all of this is a symptom of something deeper. The crisis of obligatory celibacy and clericalism points beyond itself, for both are key elements in the institutional structure of the Church. It indicates that at the heart of the hierarchical and clerical lifestyle there is a pervasive dysfunction that is slowly becoming more obvious. The issue is not one of individual priests, but of an increasingly dysfunctional institution that serves neither the needs of those within it nor the needs of the ministry. Abusive priests are actually a symptom of the disease at the center of clericalism. One is reminded of Marcellus' comment in *Hamlet*, where the imagery of disease and rottenness points beyond itself to the secret corruption at the core of the state: 'Something is rotten in the state of Denmark' (act 1, scene 4).

Research into dysfunctional, addictive families can help us understand this rottenness. As Neil and Thea Ormerod suggest, the present-day clerical structure of the Catholic Church can be compared to a problematic and dysfunctional family.[8] In these families the addictive father sets up a pattern of control and abuse. In order to survive, everyone colludes and tries to appease and placate him by turning inward to protect the family's reputation. The dominant abuser determines everything that the family will do and think; loyalty to him becomes the test of membership. In this process everyone becomes co-dependent in the addiction, and thus the system continues. The only way to break this pattern is for someone in the family to have the courage to recognize what is happening, to name the reality, and break out. This can give courage to others to follow the same path to freedom. But this can release terrible anger, accusations, expulsion from the family, and attempts at revenge. It is not an easy path to take.

There is, of course, no exact comparison between clericalism and the dysfunctional family, but there are suggestive parallels and connections. In order to tease these out I want to begin with something apparently unconnected—the ecclesiastical priorities that have emerged during the Wojtyla papacy. Over the last few years the pope has increasingly identified his personal theological agenda with the established teaching of the Church. In this context it is significant that he has consistently highlighted the importance of the sexual issues linked to *Humanae vitae*—contraception, and celibacy. He sees *Humanae vitae* as infallible. But in the process of emphasizing this, he has seemingly distorted the traditional theological priority given by the Church to questions about God, the divinity and humanity of Christ, the role of the Holy Spirit, and the living of a faith commitment. Also, his apparent conflation of the ordinary and infallible magisterium is very worrying. As a result of this, he has made issues such as loyalty to *Humanae vitae* and the support of obligatory celibacy for priests the litmus tests of genuine Catholicism.

What is the connection between the papal agenda, the increasing dysfunctionality of institutional Catholicism, and problematic families? Firstly, it is clear that the pope is willing to force his personal agenda on the Church, to make it normative for all 'loyal' Catholics. Any dissenters, especially those who are perceived as having an important role in the Church, are expelled. A recent example of this is the scandalous treatment of the French Dominican, Jacques Pohier, but there are many better known theologians, such as the American Charles Curran, who have been driven out of the Catholic system and forced to teach in secular or Protestant universities. This threat of expulsion and punishment goes right through the system. Local hierarchies and superiors of religious orders are expected to toe the line and 'deal' with critics and dissenters. They might resist for some time, but they normally give in 'for the greater good' of the family. What is really encouraged is *external* conformity. It does not matter what you think personally, or say in private. As long as you never confront problems publicly. But there is a highly critical underground. Anyone who knows priests well, knows what they say to each other about the pope, their superiors, and the system in which they work. Most of them feel powerless to change anything. But no matter what they say in private, they are rarely willing to speak out when given the opportunity. The malaise has pervaded the whole clerical system. Because it is pervasive, it is hardly ever noticed.

Sipe argues that control of sexuality has historically been used by the Church as a form of power over people, especially women. This is not to say that most priests are motivated by a lust for power. In fact, the contrary is probably true. Even the most healthy priests feel powerless in the face of the hierarchical institution that employs them. They feel they cannot change the system and are forced to make constant compromises to remain within it and to continue the ministry to which they have given their lives. A considerable number feel trapped in the only lifestyle that they know. Some think themselves unqualified for anything else.

All of this adds up to a major crisis of leadership at both the local level and the broader level. The fundamental problem facing the Church is a crisis of credibility of leadership. Given the widespread nature of the problem, the only solution can come from a general council. But before I turn to solutions I want to look at what theologians have been saying about the papacy since Vatican II.

Contemporary theologies of the papacy

Between Vatican II and the 1990s, several theologians have examined the role and function of the papacy. The background to this examination was the encyclical, *Humanae vitae*. Despite the fact that the topic was contraception, the encyclical actually focused discussion on the role of the pope. Vatican insiders persuaded Paul VI to ignore the report of the Birth Control Commission that approved contraception. Their argument was clear: any change in the teaching on contraception would gravely weaken papal teaching authority. But the irony is that the widespread dissent from the teaching of the encyclical has highlighted the question of papal authority even more. It has raised questions: What is the status of a teaching that was ignored on such a widespread scale? Is this a case of non-reception? Emphasis on the encyclical and its status has had the result of focusing theological attention on the question of infallibility. Most theologians argue that *Humanae vitae* is an exercise of the ordinary magisterium. But the problem is that John Paul clearly thinks that it is infallible. This leads to the further problem of the confusion and even the conflation of the ordinary and infallible magisterium.

John Paul II told the United States bishops in 1988 that 'the charism of infallibility' is not *only* found in 'the solemn definitions of the Roman Pontiff and of ecumenical councils,' but also in the 'universal ordinary magisterium which can be regarded as the usual expression of the Church's infallibility.'[9] This is an extraordinary statement that goes well beyond the careful distinctions made at Vatican I. That Council made it clear that the 'charism of infallibility' only operated under the most restricted and solemn circumstances. Infallibility cannot be somehow injected into the 'universal ordinary magisterium.' A definition is either infallible or it is not. Something cannot be quasi- or semi-infallible. It is reasonable to argue that if the pope, or the pope and the bishops, make a statement it has an authoritative status. But that does not make it infallible. And if it is not infallible, it can be changed.

But this modern focus on infallibility and the status of the papal magisterium has meant that the theology of the primacy has been neglected. Combined with the issue of the ordinary magisterium, this is where the real problem of modern papalism lies. Despite the confused conflation of the ordinary magisterium with *infallibility*, the doctrine is hedged in with considerable restrictions. But there were far fewer restraints built into the definition of *primacy* at Vatican I. Primacy also has the worst ecumenical consequences. Unlimited papal power is simply not acceptable to the Orthodox, Anglicans, or Protestants, although in one form or another they may be willing to accept some form of papal leadership of the Church. In a more ecumenical Church of the future, there would have to be considerable limits placed on papal power.

Hans Küng's Infallible? An Inquiry

At the beginning of Vatican II, two youthful German-speaking theologians emerged as important influences on the Council: Josef Ratzinger and Hans Küng. Of the two, Küng's books quickly became accessible in English, the most important of which was *Structures of the Church*.[10] Küng described an ecclesiology that drew on the broad tradition of the Church and thus offered an alternative to the more recent monarchical-papalist model. His vision of the Church stressed its synodal structure and the role of the laity. Ratzinger, at that time, shared a similar vision of the Church.

Küng has always believed theology is done within the context of the living Church. Thus Küng's *Infallible?* was a response to *Humanae vitae*.[11] Most bishops and theologians had seen *Humanae vitae* as an exercise of the ordinary magisterium and, for that reason, despite a lot of anguish, felt that Catholics of fertile age could, in good conscience, ignore the encyclical's teaching. Few, however, were prepared to say openly that Paul VI was wrong. Many contorted arguments were advanced to explain the encyclical away. Küng was more honest. He argued that in the Roman view the encyclical was infallible, and this raised the stakes if the teaching was widely rejected within the Church. Taking this as his starting point, Küng went on to argue in *Infallible?* that the whole doctrine was seriously flawed, that the processes of Vatican I had limited the freedom of the conciliar fathers, and that the validity of its acts could be questioned. He further maintained that the traditional arguments for infallibility were completely unconvincing.

He asked directly if the doctrine should be abandoned.[12] He questioned whether it was possible to make 'infallible statements.' He argued that it is only since Descartes that theology had assumed that knowledge reflects reality.[13] Küng traces the connection between Cartesian rationalism and theology's attempt to attain definitive clarity.[14] From this, he says, it is an easy step to claim that clear, infallible statements can be made. But Küng argues that Cartesian rationalism (and the Neo-Scholasticism that apes it) has been shown to be fatally flawed.[15] It was specifically against the attempted closure of ongoing discussion that Küng protested. Basically, he said that all that scripture guaranteed was the indefectibility of the Church. It did not guarantee that the pope could speak infallibly, even on behalf of the Church, for infallibility was a philosophical impossibility.

There was an avalanche of response to *Infallible?*, both for and against.[16] Most agreed with Küng's attack on the Church's *de facto* extension of infallibility to any and every kind of papal statement. Many sympathized with the need to re-examine the scriptural and historical foundations of the doctrine, and for the need to revise customary teaching. But he was criticized as anti-authority and for the narrowness of his perspective. Küng returned to the fray in his introduction to August Bernhard Hasler's book on Vatican I, *How the Pope Became Infallible*,[17] In this Küng called for a re-examination and reformulation of the Vatican I dogmas and for an investigation of infallibility by an *ecumenical* commission.[18] Peter Hebblethwaite says that it was this introduction that persuaded the Doctrinal Congregation to take action to cancel Küng's 'canonical mission' to teach Catholic theology.[19] Significantly, it was in the second year of John Paul II's papacy that Küng was deprived of his canonical mission.

If Paul VI never spoke about *Humanae vitae* again, John Paul II has regularly discussed the encyclical and the issue of its binding status.[20] He has not hesitated to declare it 'infallible' and to demand submission to it. In fact, his emphasis on the encyclical has threatened to distort the hierarchy of the truths of faith. This is the principle that arranges beliefs according to their relative importance. Clearly, the teaching on contraception is hardly as important as beliefs about the Trinity, Incarnation, or eucharist, yet one could be forgiven for thinking that the teaching on contraception is part of the core of faith!

Tierney and the origins of the doctrine of infallibility

Just after the publication of Küng's *Infallible?*, the medieval canonist at Cornell University, Brian Tierney, published his *Origins of Papal Infallibility*.[21] Tierney was aware of the debate over Küng's book, but he says his purpose is to provide a historical description of the origin of the doctrine.[22] As Tierney points out, the doctrine was used in the nineteenth century to enhance papal power. However, it actually limits such power, for the pope is bound by the definitions of all his predecessors, as Paul VI learned in the lead-up to *Humanae vitae*. Tierney says: 'The earliest defenders of the doctrine [of infallibility] were much more interested in limiting the power of the pope than in enhancing it.'[23] Modern protagonists of infallibility have maintained that the doctrine reaches back to the origins of the Church, even though it was never actually mentioned. The reason for this was that everyone accepted it. However, Tierney says that the first evidence of the doctrine emerged in the years around 1300. In the eleventh and twelfth centuries, Gratian and the canonists distinguished papal jurisdiction from Church indefectibility. They held that the pope had the right to pronounce on disputed questions of faith, but that he could and did err. For them the key question was Christ's promise to Peter that the Church would always survive. In the twelfth century, it was the Church, the *congregatio fidelium*, not the papacy, that could not err. The theory of a specific papal infallibility was first raised by the Franciscan Spiritual, Pietro Olivi (*c.* 1248–1298). He argued that Saint Francis' teaching on poverty exemplified the lifestyle that Christ taught the apostles.[24] The Spirituals persuaded the pro-mendicant Pope Nicholas III (1277–1280) to issue the bull *Exiit qui seminat* (1279), which stated that it was an official teaching of the Roman Church that the Franciscan way was the way of Christ.[25] Olivi maintained that no subsequent pope could change the teaching of Nicholas III on the superiority of Franciscan poverty. Thus infallibility was meant to restrict the power of future popes to change doctrine. Certainly the Avignon pope, John XXII (1316–1334), did not want his power restricted and he denounced Olivi's position on poverty as heretical.

It was only later—against Protestantism and Gallicanism— that the popes slowly came to accept the notion of infallibility. Tierney says that:

> There is no convincing evidence that papal infallibility formed any part of the theological or canonical tradition of the church before the thirteenth century; the doctrine was invented in the first place by a few dissident Franciscans because it suited their convenience to invent it; eventually, but only after much reluctance, it was accepted by the papacy because it suited the convenience of the popes to accept it.[26]

If this is the case, then the Vatican I presupposition that the doctrine reached back to the origins of the Church is exposed as nonsense. This gives substance to Küng and Hasler's objections to the Council.

A theological response—Peter Chirico

A decade after *Infallible?* and the historical work of Tierney, the American theologian Peter Chirico tackled the theology of infallibility.[27] Küng had questioned the epistemological possibility of infallibility. It has become even more problematic in a postmodern world where all 'meta-narratives' are summarily dismissed Chirico's epistemological argument roots infallibility in the possibility of what the medievals called 'universals,' and what he calls 'universal meanings'—which is very problematic for the contemporary mind. Chirico argues that there are perennial meanings that can be comprehended in every age and culture.[28] These meanings can be compared to the appeal of the work of great artists, such as Dante, Mozart, Shakespeare, or Beethoven, although one could argue that these artists really make sense only within the context of Western culture broadly defined. Chirico says that without these 'universal meanings' human communication would be impossible. Equivalent to these universal meanings there are, in the religious sphere, 'universal Christian meanings,' or 'dogmatic meanings.'

He then proceeds to apply this to infallibility. He argues that human beings are able to attain infallibility in the sense of being able to embrace and articulate universal meanings. Within the specific context of the Church he concludes that the pope or the bishops in council can articulate universal meanings for the belief of Christians.[29]

However, he cautions that this does not mean that the pope and the bishops can know, let alone define, the fullness of Christian mystery. Infallibility, then, is the gift of being able to articulate the central issues of the Church's faith. Chirico's argument is that within the Christian context the pope and bishops can articulate beliefs through their perception of the significance of these beliefs for the Christian community. In this context infallibility is a process of discernment and then of articulating that discernment. The rest of his book is taken up with reconciling this with the teaching of Vatican I.

This is argued at length with considerable originality, but it is unconvincing. The basic reason for this is that Chirico seemingly ignores the warning that postmodernism highlights:

that the relevance and meaning of any belief or institution is profoundly embedded in a particular cultural and historical context, and it is dangerous to forget that context. The Christian belief we have inherited was largely expressed within a European cultural framework, but it will survive today as meaningful belief only if it is reinterpreted in different cultural contexts. Certainly there is a continuing reality that is the mystery at the core of the belief. This is inexpressible and no definition will exhaust it. The problem with Vatican I is that it believed that the pope could give exhaustive, 'irreformable' definitions of Christian mysteries that were to be binding and valid for all time. But the very nature of mystery is that it cannot be expressed in any definition; it essentially defies such categorization and verbal expression. It can be talked about, but it has to be said that all such talk is essentially analogical and limited. Ultimately one has to say with Küng that the scriptural and traditional position of the Church is better represented by the notion of ecclesial indefectibility than by papal infallibility. Indefectibility means that the Church will ultimately be true to its founder, its tradition, and itself.

The question of primacy—J.-M. R. Tillard

Jean-Marie Roger Tillard is a Dominican teaching in Ottawa who is deeply interested in ecumenism. The title of his book *The Bishop of Rome* (1983) gives a clue to Tillard's approach.[30] This is the pope's original and primary title. Today he is usually called the 'Vicar of Christ.' This title only came into common use with Innocent III (1198–1216) and his successors. The more traditional term is 'Vicar of Peter' (or of Peter and Paul), but the pope's fundamental role is as Bishop of Rome.[31] Ecumenically the papacy has become an urgent problem and Tillard hints, without saying so directly, that it has also become a difficulty for the Roman Catholic Church itself. He points out that even those Orthodox well disposed toward Rome consider the definitions of Vatican I's *Pastor Aeternus* to be heresy. Tillard has sympathy with this view, for he thinks that the Council's definitions make the pope 'more than a pope' in ordinary Catholic attitudes.[32] He says bluntly that the attitudes of ultramontane Catholics 'obscure the essential characteristics of the Bishop of Rome's function.'[33] He cites numerous examples of popular theology from the period between Vatican I and Vatican II in which the pope is endowed with almost divine, and certainly heretical, qualities.[34]

Vatican II placed the teaching of Vatican I in a much broader context: that of the theology of the episcopate and the ecclesiology of communion.[35] However, Tillard stresses that while Vatican II emphasized the sacramental nature of the episcopate and stressed the power inherent in episcopal ordination to govern a diocese, it did not clarify the practical relationship between pope and bishops.[36] Tillard discreetly suggests that the theology of Vatican II is now being ignored and pope-centric notions have returned. He was writing, of course, in the early 1980s before the worst excesses of the Wojtyla papacy became clear.

Tillard sketches out an ecumenical model of papacy for the future. In this the pope is the center and heart of the Church. He helps the local churches take responsibility for their ministries, while drawing them together in a communion of churches united in the oneness of faith. Tillard takes Leo the Great (440–461) as a model for this.[37] But the practical problem remains: How is this to be realized when the papacy still has complete control over the entire Church, and still thinks of itself in terms of complete dominance over local communities? An immediate practical problem is the relationship of the local bishop and the Roman bishop. To which of the two do we owe primary allegiance? Tillard says that:

> You share in ecclesial communion in so far as you are in communion with the bishop of your local church, who is himself in communion with all his brother bishops because he and they are in communion with the Bishop of Rome ... To speak only of communion with the Bishop of Rome while considering communion with the local bishop as 'incidental and secondary' is, to use an expression from the debates during Vatican I, to go *ad destructionem Ecclesiae.*[38]

It is a pity that those reactionaries who constantly go over the heads of their own bishops to Rome do not take this to heart. According to Tillard they are involved in the destruction of the Church.

The limits of papal power—Patrick Granfield

Patrick Granfield is a Benedictine who teaches at the Catholic University in Washington. He has written two books on the papacy: *The Papacy in Transition* and *The Limits of the Papacy*.[39] Granfield shows considerable concern about the Wojtyla papacy. He cites a series of cases from the 1980s in which theologians, bishops, and activists have been either silenced, dismissed, or investigated. Thus the program of John Paul II raises the question of the limits of papal power.[40] This is an important question, for there are many in the Church who believe that there are *no* limits to papal primacy. They think that the pope owns the Church and can do what he likes. To the theologian, of course, it is obvious that there are limits, for the pope is bound by God's law, the decisions of ecumenical councils, and the Church's established dogmatic teaching. But beyond these circumscriptions there are divided opinions about the limits to primacy. Granfield says that these limits are in the moral and religious sphere rather than the canonical. He cites the passage from 2 Corinthians (10:8) where Paul says that authority is given by God 'for building you up and not tearing you down,' and he says that the behavior of popes must be seen within the light of this. Papal actions must support the purpose and unity of the Church.[41] Granfield admits that this notion of 'building' is vague. It certainly is. How does one tell what 'builds up' the Church and what destroys it? The pope may well think that 'disciplining' a theologian is constructive, whereas many Catholics might disagree with him. Who is right? Without stated and defined legal limits, these pious statements about 'building up' the Church remain vague. A strongly self-opinionated pope, like John Paul II, simply interprets 'edification' his own way.

Granfield then moves on to examine the actual legal limits to primacy. We have already seen that the pope is bound by the divine and natural law. But is he bound by ecclesiastical law? Yes and no, says Granfield. Yes, he is bound by the spirit of the law, but no, he can change ecclesiastical law when and if it is his will. Granfield argues that the pope is further circumscribed by practical circumstances, such as his own limitations, lack of acceptance of his authority, hostile secular governments, and concordats with sovereign states. But despite all this, one is tempted to say: So what? The theory of unlimited papal sovereignty remains.

Granfield then discusses the theology of collegiality. He says that primacy and collegiality cannot be separated, for the pope is part of the episcopal college, not separate from it. All of his primatial acts have to be collegial.[42] But the fact remains that the pope does not have a legal obligation to act collegially by, for instance, holding a synod of bishops or consulting the bishops about major issues. Ultimately Granfield has to admit that, despite the fitful attempts of Paul VI to make it a reality, collegiality remains, in the words of Gabriel Daly, the 'sleeping princess' of Vatican II.[43] Collegiality will work only if the pope makes it work.[44]

Granfield then examines the relationship of the local churches and national episcopal conferences with Rome. Again, despite his discreet discussion, the picture is not good. He cites the notion of granting faculties to bishops as though they did not have governance in their own dioceses. He quotes the bishops of Scandinavia and Finland, who claim that most people have the impression that bishops are mere representatives of the pope and the Vatican.[45] This was seemingly confirmed by the treatment meted out to Archbishop Raymond Hunthausen of Seattle, and more recently to Bishop Jacques Gaillot.

In working through both Tillard's and Granfield's books one has the sense of encountering a reasonable and orthodox ecclesiology that is being largely ignored in practice by Rome. Reading these books one constantly thinks, 'Yes, but ... '— the 'but' here referring to the reality of the situation in the Wojtyla papacy. The simple fact is that the modern Vatican has long abandoned Vatican II and, in practice, acts out of a thoroughgoing papalist ideology.

Luis M. Bermejo's Infallibility on Trial[46]

Bermejo is a Spanish Jesuit who, until recently, taught at the Pontifical Athenaeum at Pune in India. He is a theologian who takes history seriously.[47] His work is remarkably brave; he does not resile from tackling some very hard issues. This is the result of his historical perspective. His context is ecumenical. It is now recognized that the doctrines of primacy and infallibility have created ecumenical gridlock. Bermejo says that attempts by theologians such as Avery Dulles to set Vatican I's *Pastor Aeternus* in the new context of Vatican II, and to promote a 'moderate infallibilism,' have failed. The reason is simple: the universal magisterium and the authority claimed by *Pastor Aeternus* will always be rejected by other Christians. Bermejo takes this ecumenical rejection seriously.

Bermejo begins with a fundamental question: Where can we find today the Church founded by Christ? Can it be identified fully with any existing church?[48] In the process of answering this question he sets out four fundamental ecclesiological principles:

1. He says that the Church of Christ subsists and is present in the non-Catholic churches in varying degrees, as well as in the Roman Catholic Church.
2. It is an accepted Catholic theological principle that the body of the faithful as a whole cannot err. This, Bermejo claims, should be extended to all Christian people, not just to Roman Catholics.
3. He then turns specifically to the councils of the Church and says that those held during the second millennium should be considered to be 'general' councils rather than 'ecumenical' councils. In other words, the second millennium councils represented most of the Western Church, but not the whole, worldwide Church, because the Orthodox (and later Protestants) did not attend.
4. He claims that conciliar unanimity must be reached for decisions concerning the faith of the entire Church; that is, almost all of the bishops must give assent to the teaching.

In the light of these principles Bermejo conducts a radical reappraisal of Vatican I. He focuses on two fundamental issues concerning Vatican I: firstly, the freedom of the Council, and secondly, the reception of the Council by bishops and the faithful. He also asks if this reception has now been withdrawn by faithful Catholics.

Firstly, was the Council free? In other words, were the minority bishops bullied into voting *placet* to *Pastor Aeternus?* Hasler had already argued that Vatican I was not free; Bermejo re-examines his evidence, plus several other documentary sources that have now become available.[49] His conclusion: there are serious doubts about Vatican I's freedom, but he emphasizes this is still an open question.[50] Secondly, Bermejo examines whether there was the required moral unanimity on *Pastor Aeternus* among the minority bishops. It is significant that we now know that between one-fifth and one-quarter of the bishops either opposed, or considered to be inopportune, the teachings of *Pastor Aeternus*, especially infallibility.[51] After detailed examination, he concludes that many of the minority bishops did not accept *Pastor Aeternus*. But how many is 'many'? And how do you establish 'moral unanimity'?

> Would 100–120 negative votes be necessary to question the new dogma, or would only eighty suffice, or fifty? To my knowledge nobody raised that figure above 100–120 ... We saw ... that the final strength of the minority votes was *at least 115, probably around 130*. The required moral unanimity was not reached [at Vatican I].[52]

This is an important claim, for the lack of moral unanimity renders the Council's deliberations invalid.

Bermejo then examines the question of reception. Traditionally, this is a key issue for the ultimate truth of any Church teaching. Theology had neglected the notion of reception, but it has undergone a revival since Vatican II. Reception is the confirmation and acceptance by the people of the teaching of a council, a pope, or the Church's magisterium. If a teaching is not received then those responsible (bishops or pope) need to re-examine the teaching and the reasons for the lack of reception. (This is yet to be done in the case of *Humanae vitae*.) Vatican II's *Lumen Gentium* simply assumes reception for infallible teaching: 'The assent of the Church can never be lacking to such definitions on account of the same Holy Spirit's influence' (n. 25). But what happens when this assent is, in fact, lacking? Or what happens if reception is withdrawn?

Bermejo argues that a significant portion of the minority bishops at Vatican I only submitted under obedience, or out of fear of schism. Others simply never mentioned the definitions again. Bermejo thinks that reception is never valid unless it is free.[53] While he argues that Vatican I eventually was received, he admits that Hasler has created 'nagging doubts' about this. He points out that in the German-speaking universities as many as twenty theologians were excommunicated and two-thirds of Church history professors left the Church rather than accept the doctrine of infallibility.[54] His conclusion is that 'one is forced to acknowledge that the papal dogmas met with considerable resistance, during and after the Council, from a qualified minority of bishops and theologians.'[55] There is no doubt that the doctrine was accepted by the vast majority of ordinary Catholics. But by extending reception to non-Catholic Christians, Vatican I was definitely not received by either Orthodox or Protestants. This non-reception continues today, which means that Vatican I is not received by about forty-seven percent of all the Christian faithful.

Bermejo argues that reception is an ongoing process.[56] He says that while Vatican II may have accepted Vatican I, there is considerable ambivalence among many Catholics today about infallibility. A growing number of Roman Catholic theologians challenge the doctrine by arguing the non-ecumenicity of the Council. Bermejo points out that the Second Council of Nicaea (787) laid down three characteristics of ecumenicity: universal participation by all five patriarchates, universal post-conciliar reception, and a vertical consensus with the apostolic tradition.[57] Vatican I lacks all three. Turning to the laity, the best that Bermejo can come up with, even among Roman Catholics, is that 'the overall impression is that whatever the reason, we can no longer speak of a peaceful, universal, and unquestionable reception of Vatican I.'[58]

Overall, Bermejo shows that the Vatican I doctrines are based on problematic theological foundations and that serious questions can be raised about them. This may well become important in the future if and when Rome begins to take ecumenism seriously. Then the Vatican I doctrines might well have to be rethought entirely.

The unfinished achievement of Vatican II

There is a sense in which we are now in the post-post-Vatican II era. A whole generation has grown up for whom Vatican II and what happened before it are history. They know nothing except the contemporary Church. But the tensions and ambiguities created by both the past and the Council are still with us. This is because a combination of forces—the peculiar agenda of John Paul II, the attitude of many in the curia, the aging and loss of energy for reform in the post-conciliar generation, the collapse of priestly leadership, and the activities of a tiny but determined minority of disgruntled reactionaries—have succeeded in halting the renewal set in train by Vatican II. This combination of forces has stopped the Church in its tracks, and created a high level of alienation and cynicism among many contemporary Catholics of good will.

The French writer Pierre Dentin expresses this in more positive terms. He describes Vatican II as *La symphonie inachevée* (the unfinished symphony).[59] He lists the great achievements of the Council—openness to the world, ecumenism, and the development of a climate of joy and hope. He contrasts these achievements to the clerical elitism, hierarchicalism, and closed attitudes of the councils of Trent and Vatican I, and the Church in general, before what he calls the 'Copernican revolution' of Catholicism: Vatican II. 'Never before had the world known so remarkable a deliberative assembly.'[60] Dentin is right: it was an extraordinarily open and consultative achievement. It was a tremendous effort of the ecclesiological imagination. But he argues that it remains incomplete. It is true that all councils remain unfinished, for they mark a new phase in the evolution of the tradition, the moment when a new approach first emerges. The work of a council simply points in a new direction. Vatican II remains incomplete because its ecclesiological revolution has never been encapsulated in structures. The direction in which it points has not been taken up because there has never been a commitment to turning the Council's insights into structural forms in the Church. The new *Code of Canon Law* was an opportunity to do this but, while it points in the direction of Vatican II, it never encapsulated the Council's insights in Church structure. Of course, in Church history several other councils have suffered the same fate. But none have been followed by the diametric opposite of what the conciliar decrees had proposed. There is a sense in which the high papalism of John Paul II is the very antithesis of the more balanced model of Church proposed at Vatican II.

This is illustrated by four significant ambiguities that Dentin says Vatican II failed to resolve. The first is what he calls *La solitude du pape*.[61] By this phrase Dentin means that *Pastor Aeternus* left the pope in isolated splendor at the peak of the hierarchical triangle. 'Papal aloneness' leads straight to modern papalism, in which pope and Church become interchangeable. This 'solitude of the pope' has been reinforced by the superstar status of John Paul II. Ecumenically this is totally unacceptable to the other Christian churches, for, as the Orthodox Patriarch Athenagoras told Paul VI in 1969, the pope needs his brothers in the episcopate.[62] Traditionally the Bishop of Rome is not *primus solus* (first alone), but *primus inter pares* (first among equals). Ironically, one good thing that the Wojtyla papacy has achieved is that it vividly illustrates the papalist notion of *La solitude du pape*.

The second ambiguity that Dentin highlights is the doctrine of the episcopate.[63] Vatican II's *Lumen Gentium* says that bishops exercise their supreme authority in general councils, and the Council of Constance (1414–1418), in the decree *Frequens*, decreed that there ought to be a council every decade. Yet between Trent and Vatican I there was a break of over three hundred years and between Vatican I and Vatican II there were ninety-seven years. These are extraordinary breaks without the exercise of general episcopal authority. Moreover, the papacy has not had the same scruples as Peter when Matthias was *elected* by 'the believers' after the suicide of Judas (Acts 1: 15–16). The modern popes have broken that long tradition of episcopal election by priests and people, and in the appointment of bishops they act more like dictators. They have also taken to themselves the full panoply of episcopal titles, and claim the primacy of both honor and jurisdiction. So Dentin asks: 'If the pope is a universal bishop, where does that leave the episcopate?'[64] Vatican II tried to right the balance. It stressed the importance of the local church and the collegiality of bishops. Yet, as Dentin says, Rome is still 'allergic' to episcopal conferences, whether they be national, regional, or international.[65] Collegiality has been ignored in the Wojtyla papacy.

Dentin also points to a closely related ambiguity: what he calls 'the hegemony of the curia.'[66] While the curia has certainly been internationalized under Paul VI and John Paul II, the intellectual quality and attitudes of those who work in it have been widely questioned in the Church. For instance, while Josef Ratzinger is a serious theologian, there have been constant allegations that the doctrinal and other congregations are served by second- and third-rate theologians who live in cosseted worlds far away from the real frontier of ministry. The quality of other curial bodies varies widely. Some, such as the rather small Pontifical Councils for Justice and Peace, for Promoting Christian Unity, and for Inter-Religious Dialogue, are staffed by experienced and intelligent clergy with wide international contacts and experience. But much of the rest of the curia is run by unimaginative bureaucrats with limited theological and pastoral backgrounds. And finally there are reactionary pockets whose attitudes are antithetical to any change or development in the contemporary Church.

The last and most important ambiguity resulting from Vatican II that Dentin highlights is the division between the two priesthoods.[67] This corrosive disjunction is the separation between the common priesthood of all believers and the ordained priesthood. In the New Testament, baptism marks a new birth in Jesus Christ, an entry into the bodily structure of Jesus' existence. The First Letter of Peter says that *all* Christians form 'a holy priesthood' (2:5), and later refers to them as 'a chosen race, a royal priesthood, a holy nation' (2:9). So the New Testament is quite clear that baptism is the fundamental condition of entry into the priesthood of all believers. But in practice in Church history the word 'priest' has been largely confined to the ordained ministers of the Church. There is a sense in which the New Testament's doctrine had been 'forgotten.' The New Testament doctrine was revived by Luther during the Reformation, and he emphasized the priesthood of the laity at the expense of the clerical priesthood. The Council of Trent (1545–1563) reacted to Protestant theology and defined the ontological superiority of the clerical priesthood over that of the laity. Trent's teaching was reinforced at Vatican II, and, in a sense, *Lumen Gentium* (n.10) went further than Trent. The problem embedded in this issue has not been referred to very often in post-Vatican II theology, but it is an important ambiguity in the Council's teaching. Vatican II argues that the ministerial priesthood is essentially different from the priesthood of all believers, and that it is not merely a difference in degree. The Council, in fact, created a double difference: (1) of nature—the priest undergoes a 'metamorphosis' from an ordinary Christian, to become (2) a superior 'superchristian' whose priesthood is essentially different from that of the baptized.[68]

Vatican II says that the priesthood of all believers 'is ordered' to the ministerial priesthood. Whatever that means, the question has still not been resolved as to what ordination adds to baptism. Dentin tries to explain it by saying that:

> ordination is a public ecclesial sign of commitment to the Kingdom of God, the giving of one's existence to the pastoral ministry and, in the case of priests of the Roman rite, the personal consecration of one's most intimate being in celibacy through love for Christ.[69]

Celibacy aside, surely anyone can give one's existence to the pastoral ministry? Also, why talk about priestly ordination in terms of ontological or 'essential' change? The question concerning the relationship between the two priesthoods remains to be resolved.

The ambiguity between the two priesthoods has been exacerbated by the contemporary shortage of clergy, their widespread collapse of confidence, and criticism of their performance and behavior. More and more laity are moving into various forms of ministry and priests are perforce surrendering many areas previously under their control. The ministerial priesthood is retreating to the purely sacramental area and is even confined to specific aspects of that: the laity have always been able to baptize and to minister the sacrament of marriage. They are now involved increasingly in preparation for many of the sacraments. But as laity they still have no *potestas*—power— in the Church. They are clearly called to ministry, but they are granted no corresponding authority to carry out that ministry. In the New Testament, gift and authority are always linked; if you have the call to a specific ministry you are granted the authority to carry out that ministry. Yet authority is still confined to priests, and more particularly to bishops, but it is increasingly the laity who are doing the work. This disjunctive ambiguity is crying out for resolution.

The Church needs a broad consultative process whereby these ambiguities can be resolved. The only solution that would involve a broad enough cross-section of Catholics is a general council. Here, once again, we are back at the need for a new council. But before we turn to that subject, we need to sort out a way into the future.

1 Collins, *Mixed Blessings*, pp. 53–8.

2 Ibid., p. 56. Emphasis in original.

3 See my article 'Coming Clean,' *Eureka Street*, March 1996, pp. 32–5.

4 Christian Duquoc, 'Clerical Reform,' in Giuseppe Alberigo (ed.), *The Reception of Vatican II*, Washington: Catholic University of America Press, 1987, p. 298.

5 Ibid., p. 299.

6 A. W. Richard Sipe, *A Secret World: Sexuality and the Search for Celibacy*, New York: Brunner/Mazel, 1990 and *Sex, Priests, and Power: Anatomy of a Crisis*, London: Cassell, 1995.

7 Sipe, *Sex, Priests and Power*, p. 111.

8 Neil and Thea Ormerod, *When Ministers Sin: Sexual Abuse in the Churches*, Sydney: Millennium, 1995, p. 80.

9 *Osservatore Romano*, 16 October 1988.

10 London: Burns & Oates, 1964.

11 *Infallible? An Inquiry* was published in English in 1971 by Collins (London). In 1994, an edition with a new introduction was published by SCM (London) and Continuum (New York) as *Infallible? An Unresolved Inquiry*.

12 Küng, *Infallible? An Unresolved Inquiry*, p. 103.

13 Ibid., p. 135.

14 Ibid., p. 138.

15 Ibid., p. 140.

16 For a useful summary of the response see John T. Ford, 'Infallibility: A Review of Recent Studies,' *Theological Studies*, 40 (1979), pp. 273–305.

17 Hasler, pp. 1–26.

18 Ibid., p. 25.

19 Peter Hebblethwaite, *The New Inquisition? Schillebeeckx and Küng*, London: Collins/Fount, 1980, pp. 81–5.

20 Tad Szulc, *Pope John Paul II: The Biography*, New York: Scribner, 1995, pp. 253–5, makes the unlikely claim that John Paul, as Cardinal Wojtyla, was a drafter of *Humanae vitae*.

21 Brian Tierney, *Origins of Papal Infallibility 1150–1350: A Study on the Concepts of Infallibility, Sovereignty and Tradition in the Middle Ages*, Leiden: E. J. Brill, 1972.

22 Ibid., p. vii.

23 Ibid., p. 6.

24 Ibid., p. 97.

25 Ibid., pp. 97–8.

26 Ibid., p. 281.

27 Peter Chirico, *Infallibility: The Crossroads of Doctrine*, Wilmington: Michael Glazier, 1983.

28 Ibid., pp. 53–4.

29 Ibid., p. 163.

30 J. M. R. Tillard, *The Bishop of Rome*, Wilmington: Michael Glazier, 1983.

31 Ibid., pp. 58–60.

32 Ibid., p. 18.

33 Ibid.

34 Ibid., pp. 20–34.

35 Ibid., p. 35.

36 Ibid., pp. 42–3.

37 Ibid., pp. 123–4.
38 Ibid., p. 129.
39 *The Papacy in Transition*, Dublin: Gill and Macmillan, 1981 and *The Limits of the Papacy: Authority and Autonomy in the Church*, New York: Crossroad, 1990.
40 Granfield, *Limits*, p. 7.
41 Ibid., p. 61.
42 Ibid., p. 83.
43 Quoted in ibid., p. 81.
44 Ibid., p. 86.
45 Quoted in ibid., p. 118.
46 Luis M. Bermejo, *Infallibility on Trial: Church, Conciliarity, and Communion*, Westminster: Christian Classics, 1992.
47 Ibid., p. 310.
48 Ibid., p. 43.
49 Ibid., pp. 118–43.
50 Ibid., p. 143.
51 Ibid., pp. 143–67.
52 Ibid., p. 167. His emphasis.
53 Ibid., p. 196.
54 Ibid., pp. 196–7.
55 Ibid., p. 197.
56 Ibid., p. 199.
57 Ibid., pp. 70–4.
58 Ibid., p. 219.
59 Pierre Dentin, *Les Privilèges des Papes devant l'écriture et l'histoire*, Paris: Les Editions du Cerf, 1995, p. 191.
60 Ibid., p. 201. Translations from this work are my own.
61 Ibid., p. 209.
62 Ibid.
63 Ibid., pp. 211–17.
64 Ibid., p. 214.
65 Ibid.
66 Ibid., pp. 220–5.
67 Ibid., pp. 217–19.
68 Ibid., p. 218.
69 Ibid., p. 219.

CHAPTER 5

Where do we go from here?

What is tradition and can it help us?

There is a sense in which the modern papacy could not become more powerful without swamping and absorbing Catholicism. We are now at the end of the development of the hierarchical model of the Church. For the continued health of Catholicism new ways of dealing with power and authority have to be discovered. To achieve this we need to move in two directions: back into the tradition to rediscover ways in which people dealt with these issues in the past, and forward as we create models that make sense in our context. Two things stand out in this process. Firstly, notions of the pope as lord and absolute monarch of the Church have to be jettisoned, as Catholics rediscover the New Testament concept of Church leader as servant and the one who facilitates the gifts of the community. Secondly, we have to move from a notion of the Church as a strict hierarchy to a more synodal, collegial model, whereby there are structures for the participation of Church member-ship in ecclesiastical processes, particularly decision-making processes.

To move in these directions will be construed by some as a revolution. In fact, what I am advocating is very conservative—in the true sense of the word. For I am suggesting that we should reanimate and adapt structures that have been long dormant in the Church. What I want to do is to draw on tradition in the strict theological meaning of that word. So in the rest of this book I want to start to sketch out what the papacy of the future might be like and something of the role it will play in the governance of the Church. One of the essential elements of Christian faith is a sense of hope for the future, and the imagination to be able to conceive of what that future might be like.

Tradition and how it helps creativity now

There are two key elements in the process of religious creativity: tradition and imagination. In English, 'tradition' is a problematic word. It is usually taken to refer to a harking back to the past, with its beliefs and attitudes. But that is not the original meaning of the word, nor is it the meaning that I am giving it here. Tradition is a process. It helps us to see ourselves as part of a long historical progression that is moving toward the future. The Catholic tradition was not invented yesterday. Its deep historical roots give it a strength and durability that can provide a firm foundation to work toward something new. It is precisely at this moment of despair for many in the Church that the greatest opportunity exists to move toward the creation of the future. So let us tease out how tradition can assist Catholicism to look to the future.

One unexpected result of Vatican II within Catholicism has been the development of a somewhat myopic focus on the Bible. This has led to the neglect of the other source of revelation—tradition. The problem has been the narrow, literalist interpretation assigned by theology to tradition since the sixteenth century. The English word 'tradition' is derived from the Latin *trado*, which means 'give up,' 'hand over,' or 'consign to.' It has a strongly active sense of passing something on to another. It is essentially a creative process. Creativity— fuelled by imagination—and a broad sense of fidelity to the past are essential components of tradition. Catholics take tradition as a source and norm of faith. God, Catholic theology says, reveals God's self to us through the Bible *and* through the tradition of the Church. But tradition has never been definitively defined. Probably it cannot be: it is one of those dynamic concepts that defies precision.

One notion of it, popular during and after the Council of Trent, saw it as the spoken but unwritten words and teachings of Jesus handed down in oral form from the apostles through the Church community. The idea was that over the centuries the Church gradually articulated these unwritten teachings of Jesus. Thus the conception gained ground that revelation was contained partly in scripture and partly in tradition. Another explanation, popular around the time of Vatican II, linked the Bible and tradition together in an intimate bond by pointing out that the New Testament itself was the product of the early oral tradition of the Church. The Church had been in existence for perhaps thirty years before any of the Gospels were written, so the community's oral teaching was the source of the New Testament itself. This approach also held that the Church's ongoing interpretation of scripture was actually the essence of its tradition. That view strongly influenced the formulation of the teaching of Vatican II, was deeply ecumenical, and geared to strengthen the theological bonds between Protestants and Catholics.

But in contrast to the modern focus on the *content* of tradition, the early Church was as much concerned with the *process* of tradition, the way in which it worked in practice. At the first Church councils, bishops and theologians saw themselves and their deliberations as the tradition working itself out in the life of the Christian community. They realized that it was their duty to maintain and develop the faith that had been handed down to them. More recently the papacy has taken to itself the sense that its magisterium is *the* tradition. During Vatican I, Cardinal Filippo Guidi spoke of the bishops as witnesses of tradition. Pius IX angrily responded: 'Witnesses of tradition? There's only one; that's me.'[1] This notion that the pope personifies tradition has been a key part of the process whereby Rome has come to presume that it monopolizes the teaching of the Church.

But Pius IX was wrong and Guidi was right: the whole Church has a role in developing and authenticating tradition. The Roman view is that it owns and controls tradition. But in fact it is only consensus by the whole community over a long period, and eventual universal acceptance, that authenticates Church teaching. Theologically, this is called *reception*. It is what John Henry Newman meant by the phrase 'consulting the faithful in matters of doctrine.'[2] For authentication of teaching, the question has to be asked: What do ordinary, faithful Christians accept or reject? For instance, it could be reasonably argued that the teaching of the encyclical *Humanae vitae* has not been authenticated. For, despite the attempts of John Paul II, the teaching on contraception has consistently not been received by many in the Church most affected by it. If the teaching has not been received then there are good grounds to argue that it is simply wrong. No one who has worked through the history of the papacy could possibly imagine that the papacy was always right, or pretend that papal teaching was never abandoned or changed. Otherwise what would we do with the bull *Unam sanctam* of Boniface VIII, *Mirari vos* of Gregory XVI, or the *Syllabus* of Pius IX?

Until now I have emphasized the historical aspect of tradition. But there is also a sense in which the word points to a profoundly creative urge in the Church. The life of the Church is never static and there is no way in which we can ever return to the 'simplicity' of the Gospels, or to the early Church, or any other period of Church history. The Christian challenge is not to retreat to a paradise in the past, but to hand on creatively what has been received. Tradition is as much about the imagination as it is about the deposit of faith. This implies a process of dynamic and creative change. Tradition is not something merely 'handed down' in an antiquarian sense, but something 'handed over' in a transformative sense. It is the *process* that is important. There are, of course, within Christianity a number of traditions, different ways of comprehending and living the Christian faith. There is the Orthodox tradition, the Roman Catholic tradition, the Anglican tradition, the Lutheran, Baptist, Calvinist, and other Protestant traditions: all emphasize specific aspects of the totality of Christian faith, while retaining much in common with the other traditions. But I am not focusing on those specific traditions here. I want to examine the process of tradition, rather than its content. The process operates when something is handed to me from the past and I transform it as I hand it on to the succeeding person. Living, dynamic, historical realities never remain exactly the same; the very act of passing them on transforms them.

The papacy itself is a very good example of tradition in operation. It has not remained static. It is the product of the development of doctrine, which is the tradition evolving as it is passed on from one generation of Catholics to the next. When I say the papacy 'develops,' I mean that the institution unfolds and changes, often in historical fits and starts. In this sense tradition frees us to act in a transformative, creative way. Development means that what we have now is not the normative, final model that can never change. It actually means that it will survive only if it changes. In that sense those who demand change are often more concerned about the future welfare of the institution than the institution is itself!

Of course, not every change is for the good. Often enough a wrong course is taken, there are incorrect emphases, things go off the rails. The Reformers were absolutely correct: there is a sense in which the Church remains *semper reformanda*, always needing to be reformed. Examples of wrong development were the nonsensical developments of papal power and pretensions in the medieval period, culminating in the excesses of Boniface VIII. This is where the papal triumphalism is so dangerous. It is as though there was nothing new to learn, no wrong turns to correct. In many ways the present pain and despair in the Church results from the sheer arrogance of the past, the assumption that there was only 'one true church,' that Roman Catholicism was it, and that everyone else was wrong. In a way, the rest of this book is about the creative element of tradition, as we discuss the struggle of Catholicism to tease out a structure and model of governance that will more effectively meet the needs of people and ministry today.

What can we learn from tradition about papal leadership? There is a sense in which the New Testament and the early Church are normative for all later theological and functional developments in the history of the papacy. The earliest period is also useful in that the essential lineaments of the office can be discerned before too much baggage is overlaid by history. While the high papacy that we have today is the immediate result of all that has happened over the last two centuries, the office has evolved over a long historical period since the early days of the Christian Church. The earliest period of the evolution of all historical structures often gives clues, shorn of the accretions of time, to the essential elements of that reality. Just as the overture often introduces the best melodic tunes of an opera, so the early period of the papacy reveals the essential elements of the office.

This period is also profoundly important ecumenically. For Protestant Christians the Bible is the fundamental norm for all later Church life, and the New Testament concept of leadership is decisive for all later developments of ecclesiastical government. For the Orthodox the normative development occurred in the period of the first seven ecumenical councils—up to the Second Council of Nicaea in 787. Because of both these ecumenical emphases, it is important to try to highlight the basic elements of the papal office in the early history of the Church, especially those that make sense to other Christians. So it is to the role of Peter and the popes in the early Church that I will now turn.

'Get behind me, Satan!' (Matthew 16:23)

Usually Catholic apologists for the papacy go straight to the famous text in Matthew's Gospel where Peter is called the 'rock' upon which the Church is built. But this needs to be placed in a broader context: that of the New Testament notion of Church leadership and the significant emphasis on Peter's failure and his betrayal of Jesus. Peter does not emerge from the Gospel as an ideal leadership figure, but as a scarred, sinful man whose authority in the Church is accepted only in a limited sense.

There is an extraordinary text in Matthew's Gospel: it begins with Peter's well-meaning, but ham-fisted remonstration with Jesus about the dangers of his forthcoming confrontation with the religious authorities in Jerusalem. It leads to Jesus' sudden, vicious rebuke: 'Get behind me, Satan! You are a stumbling block to me; for you are setting your mind not on divine things but on human things' (16:23). In the Gospel, 'Satan' refers to the adversary who attempts to divert Jesus from the work assigned to him by God, and here Peter is identified with this same Satan. The fact that this incident is found in Matthew has an additional irony because it is this Gospel that records the classical text that the papacy has used since the fourth century to authenticate its claims to primacy: Matthew 16:13–19. In this passage Peter is appointed leader of the apostolic group, is called the 'rock' upon which the Church is founded, and is given 'the keys of the kingdom' and the power of 'binding and loosing.' Papal apologists rarely refer to the incident just four verses later where Peter is called a 'stumbling stone' (the Greek word is *skandalon*) by Jesus and this rebuke is accentuated by the reference to 'Satan.'

Peter later betrayed Christ publicly. Again Jesus had warned him at the last supper: 'Truly I tell you, this very night, before the cock crows, you will deny me three times.' Peter replies adamantly: 'Even though I must die with you, I will not deny you' (Matthew 26:34–35). Yet Peter denies Jesus in the very same chapter: 'He denied it with an oath, "I do not know the man" ' (26:69–75). And it is not as though Peter were under *real* pressure: he is only challenged by two 'servant girls,' who in contemporary estimation were nobodies, without influence. John P. Meier holds that this story of failure is a warning directed at Church leaders.[3]

Catholic preachers tend to stress Peter's repentance rather than his failure: 'And he went out and wept bitterly' (Matthew 26:75). But given that the Gospels were written within the context of the early Church communities, these references to Peter's betrayal and the rebukes of Jesus have a broader context, for the Gospel does seem to harp on Peter's failures. The provenance of Matthew's Gospel is a Jewish–Christian community, probably in Syrian Antioch in the years after AD 70.[4] This group clearly recognized Peter's leadership in the early Church. Meier speaks of Matthew's concern about forms of 'nascent clericalism' that threaten the early Church.[5] However, ecclesiastical leaders could not take themselves too seriously if they were public sinners! Peter is an appropriate leader precisely *because* he had failed so seriously. He had committed the worst sin: apostasy. He had buckled under pressure and denied his Lord. Thus Peter could never take himself too seriously, or 'lord it over' the community (1 Peter 5:3). He could not be self-righteous, nor indulge in messianic pretensions. He was the humbled man who could be trusted precisely because his leadership emerged from his own failure. Thus he is normative for all Church leadership, which should be judged in the light of Peter's humility.

The New Testament model of leadership

This is further reinforced by the New Testament description of the leader as one who serves:

But Jesus called [the disciples] to him and said, 'You know that the rulers of the Gentiles lord it over them, and their great ones are tyrants over them. It will not be so among you; but whoever wishes to be great among you must be your servant, and whoever wishes to be first among you must be your slave; just as the Son of Man came not to be served but to serve . . .' (Matthew 20:25–28)

The contrast here is between secular models of power and the Christian emphasis on leadership as service, the type of service modeled by Jesus at the last supper when he washed his disciples' feet. Peter protests: 'You will never wash my feet.' Again Jesus responds bluntly to the man the Church calls the 'first pope': 'Unless I wash you, you have no share with me' (John 13:3–11). It is a far cry from the model of ecclesiastical leader as owner of the Church and papal oracle.

Matthew emphasizes that leadership is not about the perks and symbols of office (this is where we find Meier's 'nascent clericalism'). Jesus accused the religious leaders of his own day of making:

their phylacteries broad and their fringes long. They love to have the place of honor at banquets and the best seats in the synagogues, and to be greeted with respect in the marketplaces, and to have people call them rabbi. But you are not to be called rabbi, for you have one teacher and you are all students ... The greatest among you will be your servant. (Matthew 23:5–8, 11)

In this context the Church leader is both disciple and servant. The contrast is between worldly power and leadership as service. Because the New Testament sees the Church as a unique community, it demands that the leaders of the community act in a way that is different from political leadership.

Of course, it is impossible to maintain such a generous attitude. Throughout history the ecclesiastical establishment has more or less abandoned the gospel ideal of leadership. Human beings are the creatures of their own time and culture, and we naturally import secular political models into the Church. I am not suggesting that we regress to the fundamentalist reductionism espoused by radical reformers from various stages of Church history. It is impossible to return to the 'primitive gospel.' Even in New Testament times it is clear that Christians did not achieve their own ideals and that power, politics, and manipulation were part of the fabric of Church life. *A fortiori*, it is even more difficult to achieve the evangelical ideal after two thousand years of Church history. But, as Martin Luther said, the contemporary Church stands judged by the cross of Christ— *Crux probat omnia*. By any New Testament norm of leadership the modern papacy is seriously deficient. The New Testament description of the Church leader as a vulnerable, even sinful, servant has no place in the ideology of papalism. This is almost exclusively focused on the 'Petrine text' in Matthew.

The Petrine text (Matthew 16:17–19)

The dogmatic teaching of the Roman Catholic Church is clear: Christ appointed Peter the leader of the apostles, and the popes are the direct successors of Peter. They share in his power of ruling and teaching. However, it was not until the time of Pope Damasus I (366–384) that papal apologists appealed to the Gospel of Matthew as the *locus classicus* for papal primacy and leadership. Certainly the text seemingly gives great authority to the leader of the apostles. Jesus says:

> Blessed are you, Simon son of Jonah! ... And I tell you, you are Peter, and on this rock I will build my church, and the gates of Hades will not prevail against it. I will give you the keys of the kingdom of heaven, and whatever you bind on earth will be bound in heaven, and whatever you loose on earth will be loosed in heaven. (16:17–19)

Nineteenth-century Protestant scholars, such as Adolf von Harnack, contended that this text was an interpolation added later to support the fact of papal primacy. These doubts have now been generally dismissed; everything in the text indicates that it is clearly an authentic part of the Gospel.

What is the text actually saying? It comes after Peter's confession that Jesus is 'the Christ, the Son of the living God' (16:16). Peter has replied in what Meier says was probably a 'confessional formula' of Matthew's community.[6] His act of faith elicits a corresponding response from Jesus. He is now the *Petros* (in Aramaic *Kepha*), the 'bedrock' on which Jesus will found his Church. The passage contains an elaborate play on words that is only really clear in Aramaic, the language Jesus spoke.[7]

There are strong Old Testament overtones here: Abraham was the 'rock' from which the Jewish race 'was hewn, and the quarry from which [the Jews] were dug' (Isaiah 51:1). God also is a 'rock': 'Trust in the Lord forever, for in the Lord God you have an everlasting rock' (Isaiah 26:4). The Church is the new people of God who will be built upon the bedrock of Peter. The 'gates of Hades [hell]' refers to the powers of evil that oppose the new people of God.

The reference to the keys draws on an incident described in Isaiah (22:15–25), where God tells the prophet to confront and remove Shebna, the steward (prime minister) of King Hezekiah. The keys (to the palace), the symbols of office, are taken from Shebna. As steward with authority, Peter is given the keys of the kingdom of heaven. As possessor of the keys he can 'bind and loose.' These terms come from the rabbinical tradition and refer to the rabbinical decisions to allow opinions to be held, or to outlaw them. The term also refers to the rabbis' ability to bind (that is, to impose excommunication) and to loose (that is, to absolve from excommunication).

It is generally recognized today by all scholars that this interpretation of the text is authentic. For instance, the Protestant Reformed scholar Oscar Cullmann, in his book *Peter*, accepts that the leadership of the apostolic Church is conferred on Peter.[8] Cullmann argues that the role of the apostle is to witness to the resurrection and to lay the foundation of Church. Peter has a primary role in each of these functions. But Cullmann maintains that this unique apostolic work cannot survive beyond the time of the apostles. In fact, he tends to limit this even further to the period of the earliest Church in Jerusalem, when Peter's primacy was clear.[9] Cullmann denies that there can be successors to Peter. He is the rock upon which the foundations of the Church are laid.

While in many ways the discussion has moved on since Cullmann's *Peter*, there is still a clear recognition that there is a sense in which he is profoundly right. As a witness to the resurrection, and in his function as the rock on which the Church is built, Peter cannot have a successor. Tillard clearly states, 'It is … impossible to speak of a "Petrine succession" … without qualification.'[10] But, at the same time, it has to be asked whether Cullmann has not pushed the idea of the uniqueness of the apostolic age too far. Even in the New Testament, the work of Paul is continued by Timothy, Titus, and others referred to in the pastoral epistles. The unique role of the founder does not exclude succession. The mission of Christ is obviously unique, yet he tells the apostles, 'As the Father has sent me, so I send you' (John 20:21). The fact is that successors did continue the work of the founding generation.

At first there was little worry about succession, for the immanent end of the world was expected. But as that apocalyptic vision faded, the Church had to sort out what was of permanent value in the New Testament pattern. There was a realization that the community needed structural forms, and slowly the notion dawned that the work of the apostles continued in the ministry of bishops. The episcopate emerged only in the sub-apostolic age (probably first in Syrian Antioch), and it is clear that the Church only gradually sorted out various roles and functions. Christ did not found the Church as a fully developed entity.

Peter and Paul in Rome

As mentioned above, Matthew's Gospel was most probably written in Antioch, which was the first city of the Roman Empire to become a Christian center. The strong emphasis in Matthew on the role of Peter indicates that he must have spent time in the city and that he probably was somehow pivotal in the life of that community. It is clear that there was a deep split in the early Church between Paul, with his mission to the pagan Gentiles, and the conservative Jewish–Christians led by James in Jerusalem. The problem was the imposition of Jewish practices on Gentile converts. The council in Jerusalem, glowingly described in the Acts of the Apostles (15:1–22), only resolved that the Gentile mission could go ahead and that the two sides would avoid competition for converts. In fact, the unresolved issues in the dispute between Jewish and Gentile Christians came to a head some time later in Antioch.[11]

Writing very soon after this dispute in his letter to the Galatians, Paul says:

> But when Cephas [Peter] came to Antioch I opposed him to his face, because he stood self-condemned; for until certain people

came from James, he used to eat with the Gentiles. But after they came he drew back and kept himself separate for fear of the circumcision faction. And the other Jews joined him in this hypocrisy ... I said to Cephas before them all, 'If you, though a Jew, live like a Gentile and not like a Jew, how can you compel the Gentiles to live like Jews?' (2:11–14)

It is clear from the conflict described in Galatians that Peter and Paul were both closely associated with the life of the Antioch church, as they were later to be associated with the Roman church through their martyrdoms. Obviously Paul saw Peter as weak and reneging on the logical consequences of the agreements hammered out in Jerusalem. However, Peter saw his role as preventing schism and moderating the divisions between the two groups of Christians.

The other point worth noting in the quotation from Galatians above is the fact the Paul confronted Peter 'to his face.' In other words, in the early Church Paul did not hesitate to disagree with the 'rock' upon which the Church was built. He not only disagreed but, unable to accept the Petrine compromise, he set off on an independent mission. (Peter and Paul were presumably not to meet again until they both came to Rome and were martyred in the capital in the 60s.) The disputes of the New Testament Church indicate that Christians will always hold passionate convictions and that they have every right to act on them. The fact that Peter was the Church's 'bedrock' did not faze Paul. He felt that he had the right to go his own way. He is a potential model for those who do not accept the papal 'line.'

So Paul set out on his missionary journeys to Asia Minor and Greece. We can more or less work out the detailed progression of Paul's missionary journeys and roughly assign dates to the key events in his life. No such chronology can be reconstructed for Peter. There is good evidence that he was martyred, like Paul, during the persecution by the emperor Nero in Rome

Raymond Brown thinks that Peter probably did not come to the capital before 58, and even possibly not until just before his martyrdom. He was not the original missionary to Rome and 'there is no serious proof that he was the bishop (or local ecclesiastical officer) of the Roman church—a claim not made till the third century.'[12] The evidence is strong that the Christian community in Rome dates back to the early or mid-40s. There was a thriving Jewish community of up to 50 000 in the capital during the first century. So it would be natural for a Christian group to form within this larger context.

Peter and the Christian community in Rome

Many attempts have been made to clarify Peter's relationship to the Roman Christian community. Over the last forty years the most interesting has been the discussion about the archaeological evidence of Peter's martyrdom in Rome. One of the fascinating places to visit in the present-day Vatican is the *scavi*—the excavations under Saint Peter's basilica. This archaeological work began in secret in 1939, and was made public a decade later.[13] What has become clear is that the present basilica was built on the remnants of the early fourth-century basilica of the Emperor Constantine the Great, which was demolished in the late fifteenth century. The fourth-century church had been built above a Roman cemetery that was on the lower side of the Vatican hill. Below the cemetery, on level ground, was the Circus of Nero. The assumption is that this is where Saint Peter was martyred during the Neronian persecution. It is reasonable that, *if* he had been martyred there, and *if* his body was recovered, it would have been buried in the nearby cemetery. Certainly the archaeological evidence is that there was a modest Christian monument built in the cemetery between the years 160 and 170.

Clearly, Constantine (d. 337) had no doubt that this was the tomb of Peter, for he built his basilica right in the middle of the cemetery, which he had to close. In doing this he broke Roman law—and offended Roman sensibility—by destroying many of the graves. Roman graves were actually mausoleums, constructed above ground. Constantine had to build the basilica into the side of the Vatican hill. All of this indicates that the emperor wanted to place his church on a specific site— the place where he thought the tomb of Saint Peter was situated. However, not all of the graves were destroyed because Constantine filled in much of the area with rubble. The key area in the excavations is the apostolic memorial abutting a second-century red wall. Claims have been made (most notably by Pope Paul VI) that bones found near this monument are actually those of Peter.

However, the optimistic assessments that argued that the actual grave of the apostle had been found[14] are now widely criticized. Daniel W. O'Connor, who examined all the literary, liturgical, and archaeological evidence, reaches conclusions that, while cautious and minimalist, probably still reflect the present state of the question:

> In summary, it appears *more plausible than not* that: (1) Peter did reside in Rome at some time during his lifetime, most probably near the end of his life. (2) He was martyred there as a member of the Christian religion. (3) He was remembered in the traditions of the church and in the erection of a simple monument near the place where he died. (4) His body was never recovered for burial by the Christian group which later, when relics became of great importance for apologetic reasons, came to believe that what originally had marked the general area of his death also indicated the precise placement of his grave.[15]

This minimalist assessment, however, must be placed within the context of the constant and very early tradition that Peter and Paul were in Rome at the end of their lives, that they were the foundation upon which the Roman church was built, and that they both were martyred in the Neronian persecution.

Where does this leave us theologically?

This confronts us with three theological questions: In what sense was Peter the 'founder' of the Roman church? If Peter was not the first Bishop of Rome, who was? And what about the question of papal—or episcopal—succession in Rome?

To take the question of 'founder' first, Peter was not the first preacher, nor was he the literal founder of the church in Rome, in the sense of being the first Christian there. Clearly there was a Christian community in the capital well before his arrival; the Roman church was probably established between the years 40 and 45. However, the word 'founder' does not have to be taken in a crudely literal sense. Since Cullmann there has been a broad scholarly recognition of the centrality of Peter as the head of the apostles in the early Church. If he was the bedrock upon which the Church was built, then his presence in a particular place could lead the local community there to see him, by extension, as the foundation upon which their church was established. The ancients did not have a literalist and modern historical mindset. Just as they often ascribed anonymous writings to a famous personage, there is no reason why they would not adopt an important person like Peter as the founder of their particular community. It was not only his presence, but especially his martyrdom, that gave to the capital city of the empire a dignity and importance that no other church had. The 'rock' upon which the apostolic group was founded had finally died for his Lord in the city that was the foundation of the empire.

Models of leadership in the early Church

To fit Peter into his proper context we need to understand how the early Church worked. In the earliest period the 'local church' was neither the parish nor the diocese in our sense. It really meant a regular community meeting in a large house or hall, or, during persecution, in the catacombs. The leader of this celebration gradually became identified with what we would call a bishop. In the early period this leader might be the owner of the house, and there is good evidence that some of these were women.[16] In some of the larger cities of the Roman Empire there were probably a couple of communities with similar structures operating side by side. For instance, this is probably true of Rome.

Until the emergence of modern critical studies, and a careful study of the history of the early Church over the last two centuries, it was assumed that the ministerial model of bishop, priest, and deacon could be found in the later writings of the New Testament. Nowadays it is clear that this is not the case. The notion of the bishop as sole head of a local church came into general use in the Church only by about 175. Prior to that, the situation was much more fluid. Different forms of Church leadership developed in different places. Some cities, such as Antioch, seemingly developed an episcopate much earlier than others. Even in the New Testament itself, as we have seen, there was real tension between a stable local church like that under the control of James in Jerusalem, and a traveling flying-squad of apostles and missionaries working principally with Gentiles, along the lines set up by Paul.

Even the word *episcopos* (bishop or overseer) was not clearly distinguished from *presbyteros* (elder) in early Christian usage. The term presbyter is a continuation of the Jewish notion of elders and is used right from the most primitive period of the Church. The word *episcopos* comes later in the New Testament. Bishops had a practical role: they came to be seen as the liturgical, jurisdictional, and, eventually, doctrinal leaders of the community. The terms presbyter and bishop are not necessarily incompatible: sometimes you find them applied to the same person. It was only in the second century that they came to be seen as denoting separate roles. The linking of the term priest to the role of presbyter came only from around the late-second century onwards.

To understand the leadership of the early Church, several things need to be noted about the New Testament and sub-apostolic patterns of ministry.[17] Firstly, ministries were both diverse and evolving; there were no hard-and-fast ways of ministerial operation. Secondly, there was no strict demarcation of functions; that is, nothing was specifically reserved to one precise group. Thirdly, the foundation of ministry was charism or call; it was the spirit of God that gave gifts to each individual to be used to build up the Church. Finally, the New Testament nowhere raises any obstacles against the ministry of women; in fact, they were very prominent in the work of the early Church, including the role of leadership in worship and community life. The only conclusion that we can draw from these observations is that no present-day Church order can appeal directly to the New Testament, or even to sub-apostolic times, to justify contemporary ecclesiastical structures. Thus the present Catholic bishop–priest–deacon model of ministry cannot be said to be apostolically normative. From this we can draw the conclusion that offices in the Church, including the papal office, are the result of a long evolution. They are not static and therefore can continue to develop. What we have now is not normative forever.

Given this context, and the importance of Peter in the New Testament Church, the Roman Christians would have had no problem recognizing his leadership. But we need to remember that he was only in Rome for a brief period. If he arrived in Rome after 58 and was martyred in around 64, his total residence in the capital cannot be more than six years. It is

Peter's martyrdom during Nero's persecution and his burial in the city that was most significant for later history. What about his successors?

From house church to episcopal rule in Rome

The problem that we have today is that we do not take the evidence of the past at its face value. We read history backwards by trying to find the origins, or at least traces, of what we have today, in past structures. This has been particularly true of Catholic apologists for the papacy. They look for signs of a monarchical bishop in Rome, presiding in solitary power, at the very beginning of the tradition. But the evidence we have does not fit with our contemporary expectations. For instance, we are used to lists of Roman bishops going back to Peter, who is immediately followed by Linus, Cletus (or Anancletus), Clement, and so on. But we know nothing of the two immediate successors of Peter. Both Tertullian (*c.* 160–*c.* 225) and Saint Jerome (*c.* 342–420) say that Peter ordained Clement as his successor. Where does this leave Linus and Cletus? Despite the fact that in *The Oxford Dictionary of Popes* Kelly gives estimated dates for their papacies, these cannot be taken as accurate.[18] The papal lists were drawn up a good deal later—the earliest being that of Saint Hegesippus (*c.* 160), who wrote five books of memoirs of which only fragments are preserved in Eusebius' *Ecclesiastical History*.[19] These later catalogers read back a monarchical episcopate into the early Roman community, when it did not exist there.

What we do know of Roman Christianity at the end of the first century suggests that it was made up of a number of 'house churches,' meetings for the eucharist held in a large house, each with its own community and led by a presbyter/episcopos. Possibly Linus, Cletus, and Clement (and others) were more or less contemporary with each other, and were leaders of different house churches in Rome. Perhaps they even exercised a type of 'collegial papacy'! We have no real way of knowing the nature of their relationship. The evidence seems to be that Rome was rather late in developing a monarchical episcopate compared, for instance, to Antioch.

We have some evidence of Clement of Rome through his extant *Letter to the Corinthians*, which is dated around 96.[20] We know little about the author, but reading the *Letter* you have the sense of a man who admires Roman order, which he wants to see applied to the Church. He distinguishes the leaders of worship from the *laikos*—the laity, the first time this distinction appears in Christian writing.[21] He emphasizes Church unity, order, and the apostolic succession of bishops and deacons.[22] The *Letter* seems to suggest a sense of Roman responsibility for the other churches. However, we cannot conclude from this that the Roman church was already a unified community governed by a single bishop, with a primacy of doctrinal jurisdiction. Clement nowhere says that he is the 'bishop' of Rome and the feel of the letter is that it is really one church exercising a kind of fraternal correction of another. We do not know the consequences of the letter and whether the Corinthian church took it seriously. The most that can be said is that Clement was a presbyter/episcopos of a Roman community speaking on behalf of all the Roman communities. Kelly concludes:

> While Clement's position as a leading presbyter and spokesman of the Christian community at Rome is assured, his letter suggests that the monarchical episcopate had not yet emerged there, and it is therefore impossible to form any precise conception of his constitutional role.[23]

Certainly the fact that the Roman church exercised some type of significant influence in the early Church is attested by a second major source in the first decade of the second century. Ignatius (*c.* 35–*c.* 107) was possibly either the second or third bishop of Antioch after Peter, and it is clear that the episcopate had emerged there earlier than elsewhere. There are seven extant and authentic letters from Ignatius written while he was on the way to Rome for martyrdom. It is clear from several of these letters that the episcopate had spread in Asia Minor, probably due to the influence of Antioch. Also, the letters offer evidence that Ignatius, like Clement, thought that his responsibility was wider than the territory of the church of Antioch. As a successor of the apostles he felt himself not only to be responsible for the fixed territory of his own church, but to be part of a collegiality that comprises all bishops. There is no clear assertion of Roman primacy in the *Letter to the Romans*, but there are passages that indicate that the Roman church had a special role among all the Christian communities.[24]

The opening passage is very deferential. He twice uses the word 'presidency' to refer to the Roman church. This was to evolve into the notion that Rome held the presidency of charity, the presidency of the 'koinonia,' the communion of the Church. Ignatius tells the Roman church: 'Ye were the instructors of others.'[25] Again, this is a brief, passing reference to the potential emergence of the church of Rome as a latter-day norm of orthodoxy. But, as always, it must be read within the context of its own time and it is certainly no second-century warrant for the present papal magisterium.

The development of 'early Catholicism'

Certainly the early, fluid situation evolved into a more settled structure reasonably quickly. The Protestant scholar Ernst Käsemann says that the earliest biblical forms of Church structure consolidated into what he calls 'primitive Catholicism.' He says that this is coterminous with the decline in eschatological expectation among Christians.[26] While he accepts the legitimacy of this development, he still emphasizes a disjunction between the earliest pattern and that which developed by the middle of the second century. Although Käsemann consistently underestimates the 'Catholic' elements that can be discerned in the New Testament itself, he is fundamentally right about the 'Catholicizing' process in the second century. The freewheeling, creative, and unstructured approach characteristic of the foundation period was replaced by a set pattern of life and belief. Roles were sorted out. Worship became more stylized and regular. The wandering apostles (such as Paul) disappeared, and preaching and evangelization settled down into a set form. The tradition of belief became important. By the middle of the second century a level of standardization had appeared. The definition of Christian belief came more and more under the influence of 'elders,' or community presiders.

As a result, the question of the succession of these elders became important. So the Church began to compile lists of bishops in order to trace apostolic authority. Robert B. Eno

emphasizes that this was especially true of the church of
Rome.[27] But, this having been said, it also needs to be
emphasized that the early Church was still a community of
communities and it was characterized by equality; it was not
hierarchical in the sense that has dominated Catholic thinking
since the early Middle Ages.

Those who look only for hierarchical patterns in the early
Church emphasize the emerging role of episcopal leadership.
But there was also a parallel group to the bishops in the
evolution of the tradition: these exercised the function of
didaskalia—teaching. The teachers instructed new converts in
the faith, strengthened the baptized by an ongoing interpretation of the meaning of belief, and explained the tradition
in relationship to the surrounding culture. In other words, these
teachers slowly became theologians. There was even a school of
theologians in the late-second century in Alexandria, located
around Clement and Origen.

All of this shows how the evolution of the papacy is
embedded in the process of the broader theological development of ministerial practice in the early Church. The apostles
did not hand over to the Church a fully formed model for the
exercise of authority in the community.

Developments in the second century

By the latter half of the second century, we can confidently say
that the Church order familiar to us today was gradually emerging. The practice of Asia Minor had spread, and the model of a
local bishop was close to becoming the norm. The bishop was the
principal celebrant of the liturgy, and his participation in
the apostolic succession—the line of bishops reaching back to
the apostles—ensured the local church's doctrinal orthodoxy.
The practical affairs of the church were in the hands of deacons,
and the presbyterate, or college of elders, was the body that
advised the bishop. The presbyters had begun the process of
evolution that would eventually lead in the fourth century to
the emergence of the priesthood as we know it.[28]

By the mid-second century the monarchical episcopate had
probably just spread to Rome, but exactly when we cannot say.
But it seems to have been in existence there when Saint
Irenaeus (*c.* 130–*c.* 200) of Lyons made his famous reference to

the Roman church in the *Adversus Haereses*.[29] But Denis Minns warns that 'there are hints in [Irenaeus'] writings that he was familiar with the more collegial form of church government evident in the New Testament and other early Christian sources.'[30] Minns says that bishops may not have been established in every church with which Irenaeus was familiar, but 'its introduction was not long to be delayed, and, indeed, the logic of the argument for apostolic succession required it.'[31] To sort out apostolic authority, Irenaeus actually listed the succession of bishops in Rome.[32] We do not have the original Greek of the *Adversus Haereses* and the Latin translation of the rest of this passage is very contentious. Minns cuts through the debate by saying:

> Irenaeus was badly served by his translator … he spoke not of the pre-eminent authority of the church of Rome but of its more excellent origin. It was distinguished from other churches of apostolic foundation by the fact that it was founded by two Apostles, and by Peter and Paul, the most glorious of them, at that. It was for this reason that Irenaeus chose to give the succession list of the Roman church.[33]

This list begins with Linus. Contrary to later tradition, Irenaeus does not say that Peter was first bishop, but that Peter and Paul as equals provided the apostolic foundation upon which Linus and his successors built. Pope Eleutherius (*c.* 174–189) is the last Roman bishop in the list of Irenaeus. With him we enter into a historical succession of bishops. This is not to suggest that his predecessors, beginning with Linus, did not exist. It is simply to say that we are not sure of their exact historical role and function in the Roman church.

Eleutherius' successor, Victor I (189–198) was the most important pope of the second century. He unsuccessfully tried to force the churches of Asia Minor to celebrate Easter on the Sunday following the Jewish Passover. He clearly thought that he had the right to interfere with the internal liturgical arrangements of other churches. Also, throughout the latter part of the second century a number of important Christian thinkers, both orthodox and heretical, visited Rome. Among them was Irenaeus himself, Polycarp (from Smyrna), Justin Martyr, and Hegesippus from Jerusalem. They came not because the city was an intellectual or theological center, but more likely because of the influence of the Roman church and its reputation for orthodoxy.

The papacy in the third and fourth centuries

It is clear that Rome under Pope Victor was already taking itself very seriously. Whether other churches took the Roman bishop's claims to heart, especially in the East, is another matter. If there was an escalation in papal claims in the second century there was a corresponding decline in the influence of the popes in the third century. In fact, the churches of the East largely ignored Rome and it was in the East that the greatest number of Christians were concentrated. Here they had their own dioceses of apostolic origin. In contrast, the North African churches looked to Rome for leadership, but there were limitations even to their tolerance of Roman interference. In the West, where the Bishop of Rome's influence would have been strong, large churches were few and far between: Rome, central and southern Italy, Naples, Lyons and the area around Marseilles had reasonable concentrations of Christians. Central and northern Gaul, Britain, Germany, and Pannonia were hardly affected by Christianity at all.

The position of Rome was probably weakened by the election of two antipopes[34] in the third century—Hippolytus (217–235) and Novatian (251–258). Both were intransigent rigorists. While there is doubt among contemporary scholars as to whether Hippolytus actually set himself up as an antipope, he was certainly a bitter critic of both Popes Zephyrinus (198/9–217) and Callistus I (217–222). Hippolytus is also important because of his *Apostolic Tradition*, a liturgical book that describes the sacramental worship of the Roman church. Novatian was contemporaneous with the persecution by the Emperor Decius (249–251), probably the worst and most extensive of the all the Roman persecutions.[35] Many Christians lapsed during this brief but very trying time for the community. Novatian was bitterly disappointed when he was not elected Bishop of Rome in March 251. Like others (such as Hippolytus) he opposed the readmission to the community of Christians who had apostatized during persecution, and he used this as a way of attacking the new pope, Cornelius (251–253). His schism spread quickly as a kind of parallel church in both East and West, holding the strict view that there was no forgiveness for serious sin committed after baptism. The Novatian schism persisted for several centuries.

The persecution of Decius was especially violent in North Africa. While some Christians made a stand and died as martyrs, the majority knuckled under and lapsed. Others went into hiding. The persecution was brief, for Decius was killed in June 251 in a campaign against the Goths. One of those who went into hiding was Cyprian, the bishop of Carthage.[36] This caused some surprise in the wider Church and he was often on the defensive about it, but it did not stop him discussing, in his book *De lapsis*, the problem of what to do about those who had offered pagan sacrifice. Cyprian held the view that the *lapsi* ought to be received back into the Church after due penance. But, as we have seen, this was not universally acceptable, especially to rigorists like Novatian, who wrote to Carthage accusing Cyprian of being a hireling who had abandoned the flock, unlike Pope Fabian (236–250) in Rome, who had been martyred. This led to a correspondence between Cyprian and Pope Cornelius. They agreed on a moderate policy in receiving the *lapsi* back into the Church.

Indeed, Cyprian and Cornelius agreed on many things. But Cyprian was no papal 'yes man,' as his relationship with Pope Stephen I (254–257) showed. The focus of Cyprian's theology was the unity of the local church, and his major work is *De Catholicae ecclesiae unitate*, written in 251.[37] He also emphasized the unity of the bishops throughout the world; one way to achieve this was by frequent episcopal meetings in councils and synods. (I will refer to his notion of the *cathedra Petri* in the next chapter (p. 163).)

Cyprian was himself martyred in 258 in the persecution of the Emperor Valerian (253–260). But in the period from about 260 until the persecution of Diocletian the Great (284–305)— the persecution began in 303—there is a lacuna in the Church history sources. Historical sources for the Roman bishops from Dionysius (260–268) to Miltiades (311–314) are almost non-existent. Possibly the reason for this is the severity of Diocletian's persecution and the successful attempts by this emperor to destroy the books and records of the Church.[38] The growth in the number of Christians, especially in the East, and their permeation of all classes of society, including the imperial household itself (Diocletian's wife Prisca and his daughter Valeria were probably Christians) and the army, clearly frightened the pagans, especially fanatics like Diocletian's co-emperor, Galerius.

At first Diocletian was tolerant of Christians. But under the influence of Galerius he began a purgation of the army between 297 and 301. The persecution became general in 303. It was applied in stages: firstly churches and Christian books were destroyed. Secondly, a capital sentence for bishops was introduced. Finally, everyone everywhere had to participate publicly in the civil cult and offer sacrifice to the gods. The persecution was particularly severe in the East. We know that the archives of the Roman church were taken and destroyed. The Roman bishop, Pope Marcellinus (296–c. 304), handed over the Bible and the sacred books, and also apparently, with several of his presbyters, offered incense to the gods. It was a sad end to the first stage of papal history.

But a whole new period for the Church was on the horizon. For in the years 312 to 313, Constantine adopted the Christian God as his God, but he also seized power as emperor.

Practical, modern conclusions from the primordial period

The importance and the normative value of the earliest period of Church history is derived from the fact that the essential lineaments of Church structure and operation can be discerned there. So what practical conclusions can Catholicism draw from the early period that will be of help to our contemporary situation?

Firstly, I want to focus on the person of Peter himself. There is a lot about him in the New Testament and from this material the profile of what is needed in a Church leader can be drawn. From Matthew's Gospel the image of Peter emerges of a scarred, sinful man who has committed the worst sin in the early Church: he was guilty of apostasy and the betrayal of Christ. Even before this, he had been called 'Satan' and a 'stumbling block' by Jesus. He was the very antithesis of a superstar. He was the humble, repentant man whose leadership could be trusted precisely because his failures were so well known. The early Church was very aware of the dangers of power and clericalism. Peter could never have an inflated opinion of himself because of his public sin and failure.

Peter seems to have taken an inclusive stance. In the disputes with Paul he saw it as his duty to try to hold the Church together. At the Jerusalem council he does not pontificate alone about the question of Jewish practices and Gentile Christians. He decides in concert with the other elders. He does not then try to impose those decisions, but attempts to lead people toward their acceptance. This is why Paul is so impatient with him and casts Peter in the role of weak-kneed compromiser in his letter to the Galatians (2:11–14). The disagreement was over ritual impurity and the use of gentile food at the eucharistic table. Paul says Peter 'used to eat with the Gentiles' until 'certain people came from James' in Jerusalem. But then Peter drew back 'and kept himself separate for fear of the circumcision faction.' As a result, Paul opposed Peter 'to his face, because he stood self-condemned.' Clearly, we only have Paul's version of this event, and a passionate and probably partisan version it is. A whole other interpretation might be that Peter was trying to keep the peace between the stodgy and conservative James in Jerusalem and the fire-eating Paul in Antioch. To use Paul's own words in 1 Corinthians, Peter was trying to be *omnia omnibus*—'all things to all people, that I might by all means save some' (9:22). In other words, he saw it as the role of the leader to allow and even encourage diversity. This is the kind of truly catholic, universal attitude that Catholicism needs to rediscover. Peter perhaps understood better than Paul that unity is not uniformity.

Peter's actions illustrate that the New Testament norm of leadership is significantly different from that of the political world. He lived out the advice given by Jesus to the apostles:

> Jesus called them to him and said, "You know that the rulers of the Gentiles lord it over them, and their great ones are tyrants over them. It will not be so among you; but whoever wishes to be great among you must be your servant, and whoever wishes to be first among you must be your slave; just as the Son of Man came not to be served but to serve ..." (Matthew 20:25–28)

In the light of this text, the Church's constant struggle ought to have been to avoid political models of power and to have exercised a form of servant leadership. In this context the absolute monarchy model of papacy is totally deficient and the notion of pope as oracle and superstar is repugnant.

The Petrine text is clear that the leadership of the Church was conferred on Peter and it is also demonstrable that there was a strong early tradition of identifying the bishops of Rome with Peter (and sometimes Peter and Paul). The pope was traditionally seen as the Vicar of Peter. The use of the term 'Vicar of Christ' is a very late development and only became current with Pope Innocent III (1198–1216). In fact, as Tillard points out, the notion of Petrine succession is far more significant than is generally recognized today.[39] He argues that there is an almost sacramental sense in which Peter lives on in the see of Rome. Just as the Word of scripture and the sacraments makes present now the saving power of God, so authority continues to reside in the Roman church and is realised in a particular way in each of its bishops.[40] In other words, Peter has 'vicars in the see of Rome rather than successors.' This is important, for it adds even further weight to the significance of the profile of Peter that emerges from the New Testament. The figure of Peter and his attitudes become normative for our time.

So, in the light of all this, what type of pope does the Church need today? Firstly, it needs a person whose humanity has been formed through suffering, pain, sin, and reconciliation, whose attitudes have been shaped more by experience of the Church and Christian living than by ideology or a sense of self-importance and destiny. The pope certainly needs to be a leader, but in the true Christian sense. This means someone who is focused outward toward the stimulation and support of the abilities and gifts of others, rather than inward through a conviction of a 'messianic' mission to dominate the Church and its ministry in order to 'save' it from itself. This does not mean that the pope should not make decisions, but they need to be made collegially, with others who are sensitive to the complexities involved. The Church desperately needs a pope who will build bridges both within the Church and outside of it—but especially within it. At present in the centralized, papalist hierarchical structure so many people of good will feel that they are marginalized, their gifts unrecognized, their services unwanted. Fundamentally, the Church needs popes who move away from the ideology of power toward a ministry of service. If the popes are the Vicars of Peter, they need to be more like their patron.

Secondly, what can we draw from the post-Petrine period of the early Church? The first thing that emerges is the sheer complexity of the development of office and ministry in the early Church. All ministerial offices, including the papacy and the episcopate, are the result of a long development and no present-day Church order can appeal directly to the New Testament. From this we can conclude that what we have now is not necessarily normative forever. The offices of pope, bishop, priest, and deacon will remain, but their form and function will change. This is the creative element of tradition. We transform what has been handed on to us according to our contemporary needs.

The presidency of charity: a model for the future?

An important development in the period between sub-apostolic times and the advent of Constantine is the sense of the Church as a community of communities, and the evolution of a notion of the Bishop of Rome exercising a presidency of charity in the Church. The term originates in the letter of Ignatius of Antioch (*c.* 35–*c.* 107) to the Romans. In praising the church of Rome he says that it holds 'the presidency of love.'[41] This text is often used by pro-papalist apologists to cite support for papal primacy in immediate sub-apostolic times. But this is a mis-reading of the text. In the earliest period, and for a long time after it, the primary ecclesiological model was local, and the prime expression of that local church was the community gathered in charity around the bishop celebrating the eucharist. The Greek word for love is *agape* and this word is the key to the meaning of the text of Ignatius. Just as the eucharist was the central focus and bond of the local church, so a eucharistic nexus holds all the disparate local churches together in unity.

In his letter to the Romans Ignatius speaks of the presidency of the *agape*—the eucharist. He is clearly saying that the churches form a eucharistic union that is founded in charity.[42] The Roman church presides over that eucharistic concord—it holds the presidency of charity. The Orthodox church historian, Nicholas Afanassief, writes:

> Because a local church was by nature identical with the concord of all the churches in love, an image came naturally to Ignatius' mind: he pictured the local churches grouped, as it were, in a eucharistic assembly, with every church in its special place, and the church of Rome in the chair, sitting in the 'first place' [the presidency]. So, says Ignatius, the church of Rome indeed has the priority in the whole company of churches united in concord.[43]

This does not mean that Afanassief accepts Roman primacy in the modern sense. He is simply saying that Rome played a pivotal role in the communion of the early Church. This may well be a clue for the ecumenical Church of the future.

A closely connected idea is expressed in the Latin word *communio*. This is a key to understanding the ecclesiology of the early Church.[44] 'Communion' is the word used to denote both the local and the universal Church, which is conceived of as a communion of communions. The eucharistic overtones here are absolutely clear and participation in eucharistic communion is the external sign of this union with the Church. The sinner was debarred from eucharistic communion and thus from the Church; this is what excommunication literally means, and how it was applied in the early Church. Christian travelers carried a letter or passport of communion—a *tessora*—issued by one's local bishop. This opened up for the visitor free lodging and hospitality as well as access to the eucharist. These passports were checked against a list of the principal churches with which the local church was in communion. The two norms by which the orthodoxy of a local church could be established were a link between the local bishop and the episcopate as a whole, and a real communal relationship with the oldest churches, especially Rome. Rome usually held the first place in the lists; if you were in communion with Rome, you were in communion with the Catholic Church.

In the early Church this all made sense because the Christian communities were small groups within a reasonably small city. People knew each other. So faith was lived out primarily in the local community, and only secondarily and remotely in the universal Church. A universalist ecclesiology made sense only in terms of the Church as a communion of local communions. But from about the twelfth century onward the emphasis in theology, canon law, and even historiography had shifted away from the local toward the universal Church and to a centralized papal authority. In contrast to the Orthodox churches, which still have a strong sense of cultural and national identity (so that we speak of the Greek Orthodox Church, the Russian Orthodox Church, and so on), the local Catholic churches have scarcely had a chance to develop a sense of themselves as specific cultural and national entities, let alone as local communities. Unlike the New Testament, the emphasis in Catholicism today is still very much on a universalist ecclesiology. While retaining the strengths of its universalism, the Catholic Church urgently needs to begin the development of a much greater sense of local cultural identity; it needs to become indigenized wherever it exists. Here I am not referring to ethnocentrism, nor to chauvinistic nationalism. But localism does imply an expression of the Church in and through local cultural forms.

Among some Catholics today there is nostalgia for 'community' in the sense that the local church or parish ought to provide the primary group for personal adhesion and fulfillment. But this by no means represents the desire of the majority. Many are still repelled at the thought of the possible development of a narcissistic, sectarian in-group. But *communio* does not imply community in the sense that people live in each other's pockets and provide a primary source of personal adhesion. Different people will belong to the local communion at different levels and in various ways. For some, their church will be their basic human community; for others, a sense of belonging will be expressed in terms of worship and symbol; and for still others it will provide a cultural and intellectual home. But whatever community means to individuals, the emphasis will be on the full assumption of responsibility for ministry at the local level.

How does the focus on communion and presidency of charity help us today? It does two things: it shifts the emphasis from a Rome-centered ecclesiology to an emphasis on the local church.

And it transfers the focus from a notion of unity centered on papal power to one centered on the eucharist. Many writers have stressed the need for the development of the local church and have suggested methodologies as to how the local church can develop. I am not going to detail that material here, except to mention an element that is often forgotten: the importance of a sense of history of the Catholic Church in particular cultures in developing a consciousness of local church. These local histories have begun to appear only fairly recently, but the situation is now quickly changing, especially in the Western world. Most English-speaking Catholic communities have good general histories, as well as many studies of particular persons, issues, and events. In the United States there are fine histories of the local church by John Tracy Ellis and James Hennesey.[45] In Ireland, where Catholicism is deeply embedded in the culture, there are many general histories and particular studies, but I refer especially to the recent work of Patrick Corish.[46] The English Catholic community also has several good general histories, especially the writings of John Bossy and Derek Holmes.[47] The Catholic Church in Australia probably has the most extensive historiography of all English-speaking countries. Patrick O'Farrell's *The Catholic Church and Community in Australia* is especially noteworthy.[48] All of these books encourage a sense of the Church community in relationship to a specific culture and nation. It nurtures deeply the sense of a spirit of local *communio*.

More important in the context of this chapter is the notion of the presidency of charity. It offers a whole new model for the papacy, or, more accurately, the relationship of the pope to the rest of the Church. It would also revive the notion of servant leadership, in which the ministerial task of the pope would be to encourage the growth of subsidiarity through which the local church would assume more responsibility for living out the faith in its own area. It would be part of the gradual abandonment of the monarchical and bureaucratic centralism that at present characterizes Roman attitudes. How then would the presidency of charity work?

It would begin to look at the Church from the bottom up, not the top down. Here the primary group is the communion of local communities that make up the diocese. But large dioceses can be very impersonal and people have no sense of belonging, because they never see the bishop. The statistics bring this home: in December 1993 (the most recent statistics available), there were 2435 archdioceses and dioceses worldwide, plus 232 other ecclesiastical circumscriptions.[49] In order to get some sense of belonging to a local church, the number of dioceses and bishops would need to be tripled or even quadrupled. In 1993 there were around 964 million Catholics worldwide. Thus in round figures, even if there were 10 000 dioceses, this would still mean approximately 96 000 people per diocese. If the local diocese is the fundamental unit of communion, the broader national church would be presided over by a metropolitan archbishop, and it would find its expression in a national conference that might well be an expansion of the present episcopal conference. A common national approach to evangelization, ethics, canon law, and clergy discipline could be decided by such a conference.

National conferences could find a broader expression in regional conferences that could correspond to a new set of geographical patriarchates. Here major issues of common concern could be discussed, debated, and decided. Only issues that affected the unity of the whole Church need be referred to the highest level—the papacy—which would hold the whole communion together. As I shall argue later, regular general Councils would be the prime expression of the universal Church. This kind of structure would have the advantage of deciding issues at the lowest possible level, according to the principle of subsidiarity, and, through interlocking levels of communion, give expression to the Church's unity. In this more communal Church, the pope would need *caritas* (charity) rather than *potestas* (power).

The ancient hymn expresses this succinctly: *Ubi caritas et amor, Deus ibi est*—where there is charity and love, there the love of God abides.

1 Quoted in Butler, *Council*, p. 355. See also Hasler, p. 91.
2 John Henry Newman, *On Consulting the Laity in Matters of Doctrine*, ed. by John Coulson, London: Collins, 1961. See also Webster T. Patterson, *Newman: Pioneer for the Layman*, Washington: Corpus, 1968.
3 John P. Meier, *Matthew*, Wilmington: Michael Glazier, 1980. p. 335.
4 Ibid., pp. xi–xii. See also Raymond E. Brown and John P. Meier, *Antioch and Rome:*

New Testament Cradles of Catholic Christianity, New York: Paulist, 1983, pp. 12–72.

5 Meier in Brown and Meier, p. 70.

6 Meier, p. 180.

7 Ibid., p. 181.

8 Oscar Cullmann, *Peter: Disciple, Apostle, Martyr*, Philadelphia: Westminster, 1953. Originally published in German in 1952.

9 Ibid., p. 226.

10 Tillard, *Bishop of Rome*, p. 96.

11 Gunther Bornkamm, *Paul*, London: Hodder and Stoughton, 1971, p. 40.

12 Brown and Meier, p. 98. See also Raymond E. Brown et al., *Peter in the New Testament*, New York: Paulist, 1973.

13 Jocelyn Toynbee and John Ward Perkins, *The Shrine of St. Peter and the Vatican Excavations*, New York: Pantheon, 1957. See also Umberto M. Fasola, *Traces on Stone: Peter and Paul in Rome*, Rome: Vision Editrice, 1980.

14 Such as J. E. Walsh, *The Bones of Saint Peter*, New York: Doubleday, 1982.

15 Daniel Wm. O'Connor, *Peter in Rome: The Literary, Liturgical, and Archaeological Evidence*, New York: Columbia University Press, 1969. p. 209. My emphasis.

16 Karen Jo Torjesen, *When Women Were Priests*, San Francisco: HarperSanFrancisco, 1993, passim, but especially pp. 76–82.

17 Edward Schillebeeckx, *The Church with a Human Face: A New and Expanded Theology of Ministry*, New York: Crossroad, 1990. pp. 40–123.

18 Kelly, pp. 6–8.

19 See Eusebius, *The History of the Church from Christ to Constantine*, English trans. G. A. Williamson, London: Penguin, 1989. pp. 79–80, 82–3. For Hegesippus see p. 373.

20 For a translation see J. B. Lightfoot, *The Apostolic Fathers*, ed. by J. R. Harmer, Grand Rapids: Baker Book House, 1974, pp. 13–41.

21 *1 Clement*, 40, in ibid., p. 30.

22 *1 Clement*, 42, in ibid., p. 31.

23 Kelly, p. 8.

24 For a translation see Lightfoot, pp. 75–9.

25 Ignatius, *To the Romans*, 3, in Lightfoot, p. 76.

26 Ernst Käsemann, *New Testament Questions of Today*, London: SCM, 1969, p. 237.

27 Robert B. Eno, *The Rise of the Papacy*, Wilmington: Michael Glazier, 1990, p. 23.

28 Kenan B. Osborne, *Priesthood: A History of the Ordained Ministry in the Roman Catholic Church*, New York: Paulist Press, 1988. See especially pp. 89–129 and 130–60.

29 For Irenaeus see Denis Minns, *Irenaeus*, London: Geoffrey Chapman, 1994.

30 Ibid., p. 121.

31 Ibid., p. 122.

32 *Adversus haereses*, III, 3. Quoted in Michael Winter, *St. Peter and the Popes*, London: Darton, Longman and Todd, 1960, p. 126.

33 Minns, p. 121.

34 Officially, an antipope is a person who is elected pope in opposition to the one who has been elected according to canon law. However, any study of the history of the papacy recalls the saying that 'history is written by the winners' and the roles of pope and antipope can be interchangeable!

35 See Marta Sordi, *The Christians and the Roman Empire*, London: Groom Helm, 1983, pp. 100–7. See also Eusebius, VI, 43–5, English trans. pp. 214–18.

36 Eno, pp. 57–65.

37 Cyprian, *The Unity of the Catholic Church*, trans. by Maurice Bevenot in the *Ancient Christian Writers* series, vol. 25, Westminster: Newman Press, 1957, pp. 43–67.

38 Eusebius describes the persecution in Chapter 8 of his *History*. See also Sordi, pp. 122–32.

39 Tillard, *Bishop of Rome*, pp. 96–101.

40 Ibid., p. 97.

41 Lightfoot translation, p. 76.

42 Nicholas Afanassief in John Meyendorff (ed.), *The Primacy of Peter: Essays in Ecclesiology and the Early Church*, Crestwood: St Vladimir's Seminary Press, 1992, pp. 126–8.

43 Afanassief in Meyendorff, p. 127.

44 Ludwig Hertling, *Communio: Church and Papacy in Early Christianity*, Chicago: Loyola University Press, 1972, pp. 15–76. See also Jerome Hamer, *The Church is a Communion*, London: Geoffrey Chapman, 1964, pp. 159–68.

45 John Tracy Ellis, *American Catholicism*, Chicago: University of Chicago Press, 1956. James Hennesey, *American Catholics: A History of the Roman Catholic Community in the United States*, New York: Oxford University Press, 1981.

46 Patrick Corish, *The Irish Catholic Experience: A Historical Survey*, Dublin: Gill and Macmillan, 1985.

47 John Bossy, *The English Catholic Community 1570–1850*, London: Burns & Oates, 1975. Derek Holmes, *More Roman than Rome: English Catholicism in the Nineteenth Century*, Shepherdstown: Patmos Press, 1978.

48 First published as *The Catholic Church and Community in Australia: A History*, Melbourne: Thomas Nelson, 1977, and most recently in a third revised edition as *The Catholic Church and Community in Australia: An Australian History*, Sydney: New South Wales University Press, 1992.

49 Felician A. Foy and Rose M. Avato (eds), 1996 *Catholic Almanac*, Huntington: Our Sunday Visitor, 1996, p. 368.

CHAPTER 6

The problem
of primacy

An ecumenical problem: the pope as "owner" of the Church

Primacy, rather than infallibility, is the real ecumenical problem facing the Church today. The idea of primacy, as spelled out at Vatican I, is simply unacceptable to the Orthodox, Anglican, and Protestant churches. The Council gave the pope the *tota plenitudo potestatis*, the utter fullness of supreme power, not only in governing the Church but also in faith and morals, without any limitation from bishops, synods, or local communities. For the Orthodox this notion of primacy is heresy, and for Protestants, with their emphasis on the local community, it is meaningless. This was recognized by Cuthbert Butler in his 1930 history of Vatican I:

> I cannot help thinking that the matter of primacy ... in reality presents much greater difficulties to non-Catholics of all kinds, much greater obstacles to that united Christendom ... that is ... the dream and object of prayers and strivings of countless men of good will.[1]

There is a sense in which Hans Küng led the discussion of papalism astray in 1970, when he focused on infallibility as the key issue affecting the question of authority in the Church. Despite the apparent conflation of the ordinary and infallible magisteria by Cardinal Josef Ratzinger, and even by Pope John Paul II himself, Vatican I hedged in infallibility with severe restrictions. The pope can define infallibly only after he has ascertained that what he teaches is already held by the vast majority of bishops and the faithful, and that it is clearly part of the traditional belief of the Church. Certainly *Pastor Aeternus* says that the definitions of the pope do not require 'the consent of the Church' (*non autem ex consensu Ecclesiae*). However, this does not mean that the pope does not need to check the belief of the Church, or that he can make up doctrine as he goes along. The phrase was added to *Pastor Aeternus* at the last minute to exclude explicitly the Gallican position, which maintained that papal infallibility became operative only when the Church accepted what the pope proposed. But the phrase has been misinterpreted to mean that somehow the pope is able to define doctrines almost according to whim and without a detailed and exhaustive process of consultation. Vatican I makes it clear that it is not easy to exercise infallibility!

But the Council was far less exhaustive in its treatment of primacy. There was no dispute at Vatican I that the Bishop of Rome traditionally held the first place in the Church. But the problem is the way in which this reality was defined at the Council. *Pastor Aeternus'* treatment of primacy ignored the role of the bishops and all the other ministerial functions of the Church. This imbalance was exacerbated by the terms used by Vatican I to describe the pope's primatial power: it was said to have full, supreme, ordinary, and immediate jurisdiction. The word jurisdiction comes from the tradition of Roman law, and refers to authority to govern the Church and the ability to demand obedience. Each of the other four words has a specific meaning. The pope's power is *tota*—full, complete. There is no limit to it. Everyone in the Church is subject to it, his judgments are final, and he cannot be judged by anyone, even by an ecumenical council. 'Ordinary' has a quite specific legal meaning; it means that his power is not delegated. By the very fact of being pope he has the fullness of power. The word immediate also has a specific canonical implication. This refers to the fact that the pope does not have to go through an intermediary—such as a bishop—but can deal with everything and everyone directly. He can ignore the local episcopate.

The minority bishops at Vatican I pointed to the danger of using these canonical terms in the definition.[2] They warned that such legalistic words implied that bishops were mere vicars or delegates of the pope. As a consequence of this, their own immediate and ordinary jurisdiction to govern their dioceses was overshadowed and lost in the emphasis on papal power. What has happened subsequently is exactly as they predicted.

This emphasis on papal power was an extraordinary inversion of the Church's long tradition of a balance existing between the authority of the pope, the bishops, and ecumenical councils. It was also symptomatic of the distorted ecclesiology promoted by ultramontanism. This disjunction with tradition needs to be stressed because the present emphasis in Catholicism on papalism is the direct result of the definition of primacy in *Pastor Aeternus*. A disjunction was introduced by Vatican I into the tradition of ecclesiological governance that was to have practical results throughout the twentieth century. Certainly the medieval popes had made extraordinary claims, but it is only in the modern world that these claims have been realized.

Primus inter pares—*primacy in the first millennium*

I have mentioned the traditional balance of ecclesial governance between pope, bishops, and councils. The original position of the Bishop of Rome was that he was 'the first among equals' [*primus inter pares*]. The 'equals' were, of course, the other bishops who share with the pope succession from the apostles and the right to govern the Church. In the early Church, bishops had a strong sense not just of governing their own dioceses, but also of caring for the rest of the Church. The letters of Ignatius of Antioch are full of this concern for the good of the whole community. Cyprian of Carthage's somewhat convoluted notion of the *cathedra Petri* contains a similar idea: all bishops sit in the chair of Peter, and it is their sharing in this that constitutes the unity of the Church. He certainly recognizes that the Bishop of Rome, above all, sits in this *cathedra*, but he never places Rome over and against the rest of the Church. Rome, for him, was the *ecclesia principalis unde unitas sacerdotalis exorta est*—'the principal church from which the priestly [episcopal] unity arose.'[3] In other words, Rome is the core of the unity that constitutes the whole Church. The Roman bishop is *primus*—president—of the communion of the Church; he does not stand in isolated splendor.

As we have seen, even in the first three centuries there was an ebb and flow in the claims made by the Roman bishops. The papacy entered the fourth century with the unfortunate apostasy of Pope Marcellinus (296–304) in the persecution of Diocletian. Kelly argues that there is no doubt about his failure, despite the claim of the *Liber Pontificalis* (a series of contemporary biographies of the early popes) that Marcellinus repented a few days later and was martyred.[4] After the grant of toleration to the Church by Constantine in 312, things still did not go well for the Roman bishops. The Emperor's conviction of a divine mission, reinforced by the sheer force of his personality, meant that the pope was pushed into the background. This was reinforced by the fact that Pope Silvester I (314–335) was not a strong personality and did not attend the councils called by Constantine.

The first of these was the Council of Arles (314), which accepted Roman decisions about both the Donatists and the date of Easter. The pope was not consulted, but there was a recognition at Arles that the Roman date was normative. Pope Silvester was asked to inform all the bishops of the West about the decisions. Pierre Batiffol writes that:

> The council justified its recourse [to the pope] by saying that the Bishop of Rome *majores dioceses tenet*, an obscure expression that seemed to indicate that it was the task of the pope to keep in touch with the entire Western Church and to ensure its unity of discipline.[5]

This is a recognition of primacy, even if in a somewhat backhanded way. At the ecumenical Council of Nicaea (325), the pope's two priest-representatives signed the acts of the Council immediately after the imperial representative, Hosius of Cordova, in recognition of Silvester's position.[6]

By the end of the fourth century things had changed radically and the popes had attained considerable influence in Italy, and, to a lesser extent, in the Western Church. In this period the *claims* made by the bishops of Rome were considerable. But it remained to be seen to what extent these claims were accepted by the wider Church. This ecclesiastical centralization reflected increasing political centralization in the fourth century. Despite appearances, the Roman Empire prior to Diocletian's reforms was very decentralized. For the first three centuries the Church followed this localized model. However, Diocletian achieved a real centralization of administrative power, and this was reinforced by Constantine.

The acceptance of papal claims varied from region to region. This variation in acceptance was based on the pre-existing zones of influence that had been gradually developing for several centuries. These zones were based on major churches of apostolic origin. Pierre Batiffol drew attention to this fact in his book *Cathedra Petri*. His notion of varying grades of papal power in different zones helps us to make sense out of the complex situation that evolved in the fourth and fifth centuries.[7] Batiffol himself cites canon six of the Council of Nicaea, which distinguishes three zones of influence, centering on three apostolic churches—Alexandria, Rome, and Antioch. This canon states:

> The ancient customs of Egypt, Libya, and Pentapolis shall be maintained, according to which the bishop of Alexandria has authority over all these places, since a similar custom exists with reference to the bishop of Rome. Similarly in Antioch and the other provinces the prerogatives of the churches are to be preserved ... If anyone is made a bishop without the consent of the metropolitan, this great synod determines that such a one shall not be a bishop.[8]

Added to the churches of apostolic foundation is, of course, the see of Constantinople, whose patriarch became increasingly important as the bishop of the new capital.

In the Italian zone the Bishop of Rome had a role of special supervision, and he exercised considerable influence over the bishops of the *regiones suburbicariae* (the suburbicarian region—the dioceses immediately around Rome). The influence of the papacy also extended to whole of the present-day Italian peninsula south and east of the northern borders of Tuscany and Umbria, as well as Sardinia, Corsica, and Sicily. There were many small dioceses in this area with bishops either consecrated or confirmed by the pope. There was a Roman council once a year.

The second zone comprised the West. This was made up of the whole of the Western empire—northern Italy, Gaul, Spain, Germany, Britain, western North Africa, and Illyricum (present-day Croatia, Bosnia, Serbia, and Slovenia).

Christianity was very much an urban religion and only slowly spread to the countryside. In the West, papal influence and power gradually increased and there was a clear recognition in the Western Church that Rome was the only apostolic see in that part of the empire. As a result, with the almost complete collapse of Roman civil power in the early fifth century, the popes gradually became independent in the West. In contrast, in the Eastern empire the activities of the Bishop of Constantinople were constantly scrutinized and limited by the imperial palace.

Damasus I (366–384) to Gelasius I (492–496)

Papal primatial claims escalated from the time of Damasus I (366–384). He gained the papacy in a disputed election, by using a gang of thugs to beat up and kill the supporters of his opponent, Ursinus. According to the pagan historian Ammianus Marcellinus, one hundred and thirty-seven people were killed in or near the church of Santa Maria in Trastevere. He then called in the city prefect to support him, thus setting a precedent that was to become an unfortunate characteristic of many papal elections over the centuries.[9] The entry in the *Liber Pontificalis* on Damasus is rather brief, even though the first of the compilers of the *Liber* incorrectly attributed the composition of the chronicle to Damasus, probably because he was the reorganizer of the papal archives.[10] The *Liber* says that, as pope, he was maliciously accused of adultery, but that he was exonerated.[11] Before his election he had been seen as something of a 'ladies' man'; he was called a *matronarum auriscalpius*, 'a ladies' ear-scratcher'! No doubt his confrontational style earned him a lot of enemies. Throughout his episcopate, Damasus was challenged by the supporters of Ursinus, who waged a continuous guerilla war against him. This led the pagan prefect of Rome, Vettius Agorius Praetextatus, to comment that Christians had an odd way of showing charity to each other!

From Damasus onwards the claims of the papacy to primacy, especially with regard to the Western Church, increased. Damasus was the first to appeal directly to the Petrine text in Matthew to support his position, and he claimed that his power came not from the Church, but from the fact that he was Saint Peter's successor. His letter *Ad Gallos Episcopos* (*To the Bishops of*

Gaul), is a reply to a series of questions about ecclesiastical discipline. It is clear from the letter that Damasus claims a primacy that was, in fact, recognized by many of the other Western bishops.

Two important figures of the later fourth century, Ambrose and Jerome, were cautious supporters of the primacy of Rome. Saint Ambrose, Bishop of Milan (374–397), is one of the great figures of the century. A civil administrator and a layman when elected to the bishopric, he quickly emerged as the greatest Western bishop of the century. During his episcopate, Milan was the capital of the Western empire and it became a metropolitan see. There is a real sense in which Ambrose overshadowed both Damasus and his successor, Pope Siricius (384–399). Ambrose argued for the independence of the spiritual power from the temporal, a theory that was taken up strongly in the Middle Ages. He says clearly in his *Sermon against Auxentius*: 'The emperor is part of the Church, not someone above it.'[12] His excommunication of the emperor Theodosius I (379–395), over the massacre of several thousand people in the circus at Thessalonica in 390, showed Ambrose's willingness to speak out against the civil power. Theodosius' repentance speaks well for the power of the Milanese bishop.

There is a sense in which Ambrose is the ideal Western bishop of the fourth century: he was cultured, intelligent, level-headed, and quite able to deal with the imperial court. Unlike Damasus, who wrote unfortunate jingles about dead popes and inscribed them on tombs in the catacombs, Ambrose was a poet who wrote fine Latin verse. He was also well versed in theological literature and was famous as a preacher. His influence on the conversion of Augustine was pivotal. It is clear that he honored the Roman see and saw it as the center of the communion of the Church and the touchstone of its belief. But he maintained his independence from Rome and differed with its bishop on occasions. He may well be a good example of the type of attitude that the Church needs to take to the pope at the present time.

With Saint Jerome we have a different approach to the position of the Bishop of Rome. As well as being a consummate biblical translator, much admired by Erasmus, Jerome was an unstable, violent character, a trait which was demonstrated especially in his vicious intellectual attacks on opponents, and in the grossness of his comments on marriage and sexuality. But in his excellent biography, Jean Steinmann denies that Jerome was a sexual masochist.[13] For a brief time Jerome was in Rome (382–385), and while there he acted as a kind of 'secretary' to Pope Damasus. He was probably the only Christian man in Rome who could actually read Hebrew: 'In those days, anyone who knew Hebrew was regarded with the awe which is reserved today for the authority on Sanskrit or Tibetan.'[14] The pope encouraged Jerome with his translation of Origen into Latin, and asked him to revise the defective Latin translation of the Gospels in use in Rome; the liturgical language in the city was now Latin rather than Greek. In his spare time Jerome taught a group of rich Roman women biblical exegesis, and introduced them to the monastic and virginal life.

Prior to his coming to Rome, Jerome fawned on the Roman bishop.[15] He was a strong supporter of the primacy, and he saw the Roman church as the center of the Church's universal communion and the possessor of the orthodox faith. At the time of the death of Damasus (11 December 384), Jerome even thought he might be elected pope. He was bitterly disappointed, and after three years in Rome he was forced to leave due to vicious recriminations with some of the Roman clergy. After that he wrote little more on the Roman see's prestige or importance. This is not to suggest that he changed his views on the primacy of Rome. It is simply to say that ultimately he would come down somewhere close to Ambrose in his understanding of the role of the Roman bishop.

Pope Siricius (394–399) was deeply conscious of his dignity as a successor of Saint Peter. He never hesitated to give directions to Western bishops; in fact, he was the first pope to issue decretals, or papal letters responding to specific questions, and it was his view that these responses had the force of law. Responding to a series of questions from Bishop Himerius of Tarragona (Spain), Siricius identified himself with Saint Peter: 'We carry the burdens of all who are oppressed; also, the apostle Peter carries them in us, he who protects and guards us as the heir of his office.'[16] There are a number of surviving letters from this pope, both to the entire Gallic episcopate and to individual bishops. It is hard to assess the influence of these papal letters. Siricius goes further than Damasus, in that he makes *new* laws; Damasus had satisfied himself with proclaiming and interpreting the existing Church law. But the influence of Siricius was overshadowed to a large extent by that of Ambrose, and the much more powerful and attractive personality of the Milanese bishop meant that the extent of the pope's influence has to be assessed within this context.

The year of Jerome's arrival in Rome saw the Emperor Gratian (367–383) take the momentous step of finally separating the Roman state from paganism; he disestablished the vestal virgins and removed the altar of victory from the senate. The toleration granted by Constantine was fast disappearing and the last stronghold of paganism in Rome, the conservative senatorial class, represented by the aristocrat Symmachus, had lost the long battle against Christianity. There is a sense in which the Petrine ideology of the papacy was a response to the pagan argument that *Roma aeterna* was safe as long as the gods were worshiped properly. The pagan aristocrats saw Christianity as an upstart and radical religion that endangered the state. The sack of Rome by Alaric in 410 seemed to confirm their worst fears.

The next pope of significance was Leo I (440–461). He is one of two popes accorded the title 'the great.' According to the *Liber Pontificalis*, Leo I was born in Tuscany.[17] He was a deacon in Rome from about 422 onwards, and he gained both theological and curial experience working for the Church. Leo's life and papacy spans some of the worst years of the collapse of the Roman Empire in the West. The barbarian tribal alliance of Vandals, Suebi, and Alans had crossed the frozen Rhine near Mainz on the last day of 406.[18] Northern Gaul was quickly overrun. The Vandals speedily pushed on through Gaul and Spain, crossing the Straits of Gibraltar in 429, eventually reaching Carthage in North Africa. Britain was abandoned by Roman troops in 407, and the Emperor Honorius bluntly told the Britons that they were on their own in 410. This was not the first time the Roman frontiers had collapsed, but the crossing of the Rhine led to a general invasion of the northern and eastern Rhine and Danube frontiers. The break in the defense line in 406 was clearly permanent. In response to the invasions, most Christians tended to identify strongly with the idea of imperial Rome. By now there was a conviction among Christians that the empire was a providential vehicle for the spread of the Catholic faith. It was thought that if Rome fell, the end of the world would follow.

The unthinkable happened when Rome was sacked by Alaric's Visigoths in 410. He had actually laid siege to the city on and off from the end of 408. He gained entry to the impregnable fortress only through someone opening the Salerian Gates on 24 August 410. The city was sacked for three days. The event shocked the whole Roman world; it seemed like the arrival of the apocalypse.

We do not know if Leo was in the city at the time of the Visigothic sacking, but he was present in Rome as pope in 452, when he confronted Attila and the Huns who had invaded Italy. They had moved across Europe from the steppes north of the Caspian, invaded the Eastern empire, and crossed the Rhine in 451. As the representative of the city, Leo went out to meet them and persuaded them to withdraw with a bribe and promises of an imperial grant. He was seen by the thankful inhabitants as the *papa*—the father of the city. He had been elected Bishop of Rome in September 440 by the Roman clergy and people while he was in Gaul. In outlook and attitude he was conservatively Roman and did not really understand the new barbarian world that was emerging around him. But he did see the papacy as a stabilizing element in the chaos facing the Western Church, and he certainly had a high view of its role in the wider Church. Clearly, stability was needed: Rome was again sacked, this time by the Vandals under Gaiseric, who invaded the city from their stronghold in North Africa in 455. But Pope Leo's leadership of the delegation to pacify and deflect Attila indicates that the papacy was playing an increasingly important role in the government of the city. This role inevitably increased with the complete collapse of the Western empire and the defeat of the last emperor, Romulus Augustulus (475–476), in Ravenna by Odoacer (476–493), and with the later establishment of the Ostrogothic kingdom by Theodoric (493–526).

Leo envisaged the Bishop of Rome as having authority over, and responsibility for, the whole Church. He argued that it was through the presence of Peter and Paul that Rome had truly become the *caput mundi*, the 'head of the world.' He held that the fidelity of Christ's commitment to Peter is eternal, and that this found its contemporary realization in the actions of the Bishop of Rome. Peter lived on in the Roman bishop.[19]

This notion, of Peter living on in his diocese, highlights the importance of papal succession. Succession gave the papacy a stability that had major practical consequences in a world that was falling apart. Leo also made important decisions regarding the Eastern Church; we will look at these in detail later, when we consider the relationship of Rome to the East.

Gelasius I (492–496) was probably the first pope to be called the 'vicar of Christ.' Like Leo, he had to deal with all the consequences of another barbarian incursion into Italy led by the Ostrogoth Theodoric, who had conquered Odoacer in Ravenna. He was successful in dealing with Theodoric, who went on to establish a cultured and civilized kingdom in Italy. Gelasius is important in two areas in the Church: firstly, his high pretensions regarding the papacy, and secondly, his theory of the relationship between Church and state.

Gelasius was determined to make the Church independent of both the Eastern emperor and the new leaders of the Western barbarian kingdoms. He taught that there are two separate spheres, Church and state. The Church is superior to the state and the bishop to the emperor, because the Church is responsible for the emperor's eternal salvation. Gelasius enunciates his position bluntly in his letter *Duo quippe sunt* to the Eastern emperor, Anastasius I, in 494:

> For there are two powers, august emperor, by which this world is principally ruled: the sacred authority of the pontiff and the regal power. Of these, the power of the priests is more important for they have to answer for the kings of men in the divine tribunal.[20]

Contained in this passage are the seeds of later conflict, for the papacy is clearly claiming to be responsible for the behavior of kings. The claim is based on the premise that the spiritual is superior to the temporal. Gelasius uses his 'Gelasian theory' to reinforce papal supremacy even in the Eastern empire. He asserts the superiority of the priesthood over the faithful, and emphasizes the particular power granted by God to the Roman see. This is the most far-reaching claim that any pope had made to this point; Gelasius claimed that he held the same position in the Church as the emperor in the state, and that the Church was superior to the state.

The popes had come a long way in the one hundred and eighty years since Constantine. By the time of Gelasius, the popes had defeated the powerful conservatives who had supported paganism and they had achieved the Christianization of Rome. They had expelled the heretical communities and their bishops from the city. They had imposed the Latin language to standardize Church worship. They had won considerable influence over the civil administration of Rome.

But outside Rome there were real limits to the acceptance of papal jurisdiction. The popes had considerable influence in suburbicarian Italy, especially through the Roman synod. In the wider regions of the West, real papal influence is hard to assess and was probably rather limited. Most historians have concluded that by the time of Gelasius I, the papacy as we know it was more or less established. The popes certainly did make claims, but the evidence is that the Church did not, in practice, generally accept those claims. Often enough the reason for this is very mundane: external circumstances, such as the gradual collapse of centralized power in the West after 406, meant that Rome was out of contact—or could only make sporadic contact with difficulty—with many parts of the empire, even in the West. But what the popes had achieved was the creation of a theoretical basis for later claims.

In an interesting analysis of papal letters and decretals for the period of Gelasius I, Bernhard Schimmelpfennig shows that the pope's main area of influence was suburbicarian Italy. Beyond that there was only intermittent correspondence.[21] Schimmelpfenning also points out that 'the mental horizon [of the Roman bishops] was extremely limited.'

This is revealed in that product of the papal curia, the *Liber Pontificalis*, where papal acts are usually described in terms of ordinations of deacons and priests, consecrations of local bishops, church construction, and the acquisition of pious objects for worship. It is a parochial focus, and it gives a clue to the attitudes prevalent in the papal curia. In a sense, the writers of the *Liber Pontificalis* were right; the popes were primarily bishops of Rome and it was in the city that their energy should have been focused. With the exception of popes like Damasus, Siricius, Leo, and Gelasius, who had sketched out the *theoretical* basis of papal claims, most of the other bishops of Rome in these two centuries seem to have been more circumscribed in their activities. But by claiming the same power in the East as they claimed in the West, the popes were laying the foundation for the schism that would divide the Church permanently.

Roman primacy and the churches of the East

In this section I want to review the relationship between the bishops of Rome and the Eastern Church during the fourth and fifth centuries. This was the great period of Christological controversy. The geopolitical context of these disputes is of pivotal importance. Constantine shifted the center of the empire from Rome to Byzantium, which, as a result of his massive building program, quickly emerged as the 'new Rome'—Constantinople. A gradual politico-cultural separation began to emerge between the two parts of the empire. The Church reflected this division, but the gradual drift toward ecclesiastical separation between East and West went deeper. There were clear differences of language and attitude (Greek versus Latin). The genius of the Eastern Church was mainly speculative, while the West tended to be more practical. As a result, the East was late in developing an ecclesiology, and it tended to accept the prevailing 'caesaro-papism' (that is, a Church controlled by and subsumed to the priorities of the state). The Roman Church, at the same time, was developing an ecclesiology and laying the foundations for a kind of 'papo-caesarism' that would emerge in the medieval period. The relatively quick collapse of the empire in the West created something of a cultural vacuum into which the Church was able to move; the Church in the East became increasingly tied to Byzantine culture and power structures. The separation between East and West was also deepened by the growing claims of the bishops of Constantinople. With the exception of Leo I, *none* of the popes of this period were prominent theologians and the papacy was not strongly represented at any of the ecumenical councils of the period, except Chalcedon (451).

When Constantine established the new imperial capital at Constantinople in 330, the bishop of the 'New Rome' had a significant role, although his position was constantly challenged by the older sees of apostolic origin. Gradually, Constantinople came to be seen as second after Rome. This was made clear at the First Council of Constantinople (381): 'Because it is the new Rome, the bishop of Constantinople is to enjoy the privileges of honour after the bishop of Rome.'[22] However, the upstart see did not have an easy ride, and there was a long struggle for supremacy, and for theological dominance, between Antioch, Alexandria, and Constantinople. The Council of Chalcedon (451) attempted to deal with the doctrinal and disciplinary issues that arose as part of this rivalry.[23] The immediate cause of Chalcedon was the confused teaching of the monk Eutyches. His monophysite teaching conflated the divine and human natures of Christ. This was the only ancient council at which the papacy played a major role, for Pope Leo I had a good knowledge of both Eastern and Western theology.

Leo was actually opposed to the holding of the Council. Louis Duschesne says that the bishops of the West 'were more disturbed about Attila than about Eutyches [and] had every possible reason for staying at home.'[24] However, the pope was prepared to fall in with the imperial government and the leader of Leo's legates at the council was Paschasinus, Bishop of Lilybaeum on the west coast of Sicily (the present day Marsala). The papal legates did not preside, but they were given a place of honor to the right of the imperial delegates.[25]

Having declared that the 'orthodox doctrines' had come down to the Council through the 'Blessed Cyril' (of Alexandria), as well as from 'the Letter [*Tome*] of the primate of greatest and older Rome, the most blessed and most saintly Archbishop Leo ... because it is in agreement with great Peter's confession,' the Council substantially accepted Leo's *Tome* with respectful approval and used it as the basis for the statement of its faith.[26] Leo's teaching clearly emerges in the Council's *Definitio*. Chalcedon was also concerned with disciplinary measures regulating ecclesiastical order, monastic life, and the laity. One of the most important canons, number 28, reaffirmed the granting of patriarchal and metropolitan rights to the see of

Constantinople, on the grounds that it, like Rome, was an imperial city. Pope Leo at first refused to sign the Council's proceedings, and even when he did in March 453, he declared Canon 28 invalid because he claimed that it was a contradiction of the teaching of the Council of Nicaea on patriarchal sees.

Chalcedon did not settle the dispute about the relationship of nature and person in Christ and the monophysite influence continued. The protests of Pope Simplicius (468–483) were ignored by the Eastern Church and Pope Felix III (483–492) excommunicated Acacius, the Patriarch of Constantinople, because of his support for pro-monophysite bishops. This was the beginning of a schism between Rome and Constantinople that lasted until 519. It was an ominous sign of what was eventually to become a permanent reality. With the exception of Leo I and Gelasius I, most of the Roman bishops of the period were not theologians in the Eastern sense. Given the seemingly never-ending Eastern theological disputes, one is tempted to say 'Thank goodness'! The Western genius was much more practical. The bishops of Rome were forced to be realistic in the face of the almost complete disintegration of ordered political life around them. However, one can exaggerate their influence in cultural and civic life in the period up to the eighth century. They were certainly important, but their remit was not necessarily normative; they were respected but not always obeyed. It was really only in the late-eleventh century that they successfully and consistently projected their authority beyond Italy into the rest of Western Europe. By then the schism with the Eastern Church was complete.

What conclusions for the Church can we draw from the first millennium?

What ecclesiological sense can we make out of the first millennium for our own time? There is no doubt that the pope has always had a leadership role in Christian history. The one thing that is clear from the earliest period onwards is that the recognizable symbol of leadership in the Church has always been somehow linked to the Roman church and its bishop. The nature of the relationship between the Roman bishop and the wider Church takes different forms in different periods. The actual influence of Rome in the Church also varies from period to period. History does not throw up one normative model of the papacy. It has had a variegated relationship with the Church over the centuries. The Bishop of Rome's leadership is founded in the fact that he is the bishop of *Rome*. His leadership is not a personal charismatic gift, but it is essentially linked to the church and diocese of that city and to succession from Saint Peter. The two cannot be divorced; they are interdependent.

From fairly early on in Church history, the primacy of Rome was accepted by the Church. Here we must be careful, for the word primacy comes to us loaded with the specific theological content injected into the word by Vatican I. The word is originally derived from *primus*, meaning first, and this implies that there are others. Traditionally, the Bishop of Rome was *primus inter pares*, the first among *equal* local bishops. During the first millennium, this is how the Roman church and its bishop were viewed. Despite all the tensions, especially with the Eastern Church, Rome was seen as the touchstone of orthodoxy and the center of the Church's communion. It was not until the fourth and fifth centuries that a Petrine theology was applied by the popes themselves to the papacy. But in the first millennium this was not developed in terms of direct doctrinal authority, or coercive power over the other local churches, except in the immediate sphere of Roman influence in the dioceses immediately around Rome. Certainly the pope was seen as patriarch of the West and it was accepted that this was his sphere of influence.

However, this patriarchal role did not mean dominance over the churches of the West, nor did it imply direct authority over local decisions. Even in central Italy itself, papal power was exercised synodally—through the Roman synod. If Rome had wanted direct control over the other Western churches, the conditions of Europe in the long period of chaos after the fall of the Western empire would have made it impossible. The simple fact is that local synods were the most characteristic form of Church government in the first millennium. Most bishops were elected locally, approved by their metropolitan, and acted largely independently of Rome. In other words, the Church was decentralized and the principle of subsidiarity was respected.

But, at the same time, it was always recognized that communion with the Bishop of Rome was the touchstone of orthodox, apostolic faith. And Rome itself recognized that it should interfere only in *major* issues and that the nature of its remit differed in different parts of the Church.[27] This could well provide a model for a more collegial Church of the future. Typical of the attitude to the papacy in the first millennium was that of Ambrose of Milan. While he held a high view of Rome's primatial role and viewed the Roman bishop as the touchstone of the Church's orthodoxy, he maintained his episcopal independence and did not hesitate to differ with the papacy when he saw fit. And, theologically and personally, Ambrose overshadowed the popes of his time.

Those historians and theologians who have argued for the emergence of a clear articulation of papal primacy and doctrinal authority in the period between Damascus I and Leo I see strong evidence to support their view in the claims made by the popes of the period. In this, pro-papal historians are probably right: the popes certainly *claimed* a doctrinal and disciplinary jurisdiction based on their sharing in the Petrine office. But there are two elements that are generally neglected by such historians. First, there is the doctrinal principle of reception. This involves the acceptance, by bishops and the faithful, of doctrinal and ethical teaching and of disciplinary decrees. In the final analysis, a papal teaching must be received by the Church. It is in this area of reception that care must be taken regarding the claims of the popes from the fourth century onward. Bishops, councils, synods, theologians, and even the imperial authority all had major parts to play in discerning Christian belief and the Church's teaching. The popes could make claims but their claims had to be accepted and received. This was particularly true in the Eastern Church. Rome's remit in the judgment of disciplinary matters was limited largely to suburbicarian Italy and, to a much lesser extent, the West. The authority and influence of the Eastern patriarchates—Antioch, Alexandria, Constantinople, and even Jerusalem—were pretty much normative in their own areas. It is significant that on as important a theological point as the date of Easter, the East simply did not accept Rome's position.

So we can safely say that in the first millennium Rome claimed a theoretical primacy based on the Petrine texts, but that often the pope's real power was limited to central Italy. A strong, influential pope may have been able to influence the Church in the West, but Roman primacy was increasingly severely restricted in the East. The theoretical leadership of Rome was never questioned, but the real, practical decisions were almost always taken at a local or regional level.

From the Middle Ages to the present day

A major shift occurred in the understanding of papal primacy after the much-needed reform of the Church at the turn of the first Christian millennium. From about the time of Gregory VII (1073–1085) onwards, the emphasis shifted in the Western Church from the Bishop of Rome providing a service of leadership in the Church and a focus for its unity, to an increasing emphasis on papal power. If, in general terms, the Greek word *diaconia* (service) characterized papal leadership in the first millennium, the Latin word *potestas* (power) characterized the papacy in the second. There is a significant shift from a Petrine theology of leadership to a papal ideology of power.

Further, the medieval emphasis on the hierarchy of being created an intellectual ambience in which everything was arranged in an ascending/descending order of importance. Thus in ecclesiology there was a shift from an emphasis on community leadership to a focus on hierarchical office. The Church had been slowly developing in a hierarchical direction throughout the first millennium, but this is not where the emphasis was laid. The primary focus was on leadership as service. But a change occurs around the beginning of the second millennium as feudal concepts begin to permeate the European cultural ambience. The medieval emphasis on a hierarchically structured set of interrelationships became more exaggerated as the Middle Ages progressed. But in the medieval Church and feudalism there was also a corresponding stress on the *mutual* responsibilities inherent in hierarchical relationships.

Medieval society had a sense of the need to balance power relationships, local autonomy was emphasized, and there was a firm notion of the role of the commune or local corporation to counterbalance excessive centralization. Thus the power of the popes was balanced by synods, councils, bishops, the college of cardinals, universities, and the politico-religious power of the Holy Roman Emperor.

In the sixteenth and seventeenth centuries, with the final breakdown of feudalism and the emergence of absolute monarchies, the sense of mutual interdependence and co-responsibility was lost and a more dictatorial approach to government emerged. This is reflected in the monarchical model of papacy developed by Saint Robert Bellarmine and those who followed him. At the same time there was a decline in the idea of synodal government in the Catholic Church. The authority of the bishops and the wider community was weakened, and by the nineteenth century the episcopalism inherent in Gallicanism and Febronianism had been swept away. The centralized power of the papacy stood alone. This was a new phenomenon.

Another striking characteristic of medieval thought about the Church is that it is dominated by legalistic rather than theological categories. The whole medieval debate about the Church centers on the origin and legal scope of papal power. The Middle Ages were characterized by a very weak ecclesiology. Without a developed theology of the Church, primacy eventually became coterminous with the extent of papal power and its ability to impact on events in both the civil and ecclesiastical spheres. This led to the long and ultimately destructive struggles between the German emperors and the papacy. The papacy finally achieved a pyrrhic victory over the Holy Roman Empire, but only at the price of a loss of prestige and the secularization of the office of pope. Theories of papal power reached ludicrous lengths in the claims of Boniface VIII (1294–1303), as we shall see later in this chapter (pp. 182–6).

Throughout the struggle with the Empire, and in the period following, canonical theories of papal power continued to develop in an extreme direction. This was highlighted by the claims of Pope Innocent III (1198–1216), and continued under Pope Gregory IX (1227–1241), when papal decretals were collected from the previous century. These decretals had been influenced, in turn, by earlier canonists. This collection of papal decretals now became the source for further commentary. So the modern habit of popes commenting on their predecessors, and even their own encyclicals and letters, has a long history. The problem is that this methodology has an inbuilt intellectual incestuousness that leads ultimately not to development, but to stultification. This is precisely what happened to medieval canonical thought.

Until the thirteenth century, there was a clear recognition by canonists that both papal and imperial power was bestowed by God; the struggle was about which of the two was superior within the context of Christian society. But in the thirteenth century, a new school of canonists arose: the decretalists. The greatest of them was Pope Innocent IV (1243–1254). He was more of a hierocrat that Innocent III, but he did leave some room for legitimate political power. His younger decretalist successor was Cardinal Henri de Suse (d. 1271)—known as Hostiensis. He conceded that there were two authorities on earth, but that the temporal was completely subject to the spiritual:

> Therefore, in the order of greatness, there is only one head, namely the pope. There ought to be only one as our head, one lord of spiritualities and temporalities, because 'the earth and the fullness therefore' [sic] belong to him who committed all things to Peter.[28]

It was Boniface VIII who attempted to apply this idea to the reality of political life.

Innocent III (and some of his predecessors) had claimed for the pope the *plenitudo potestatis*—the fullness of authority and power. In the thirteenth century, the fullness of authority became synonymous in canonical thought with primacy. As J. A. Watt has pointed out, two historical sources come together to inject meaning into the term *plenitudo potestatis*.[29] The canonists tied together the authority granted by Christ to Peter in the Petrine text, with the notion of imperial power that had come into canon law from Roman law, the study of which had been revived in this period. So increasingly, in practice, the popes imitated imperial power.[30] By the time of Innocent III, the term *plenitudo potestatis* denoted papal sovereignty.[31] Thus sovereignty and primacy came to denote the same thing. As this developed, the papacy claimed that it was the source of all power—spiritual and temporal.

The problem is that this development lacks any theological content. In it the primacy is described in *legal terms*. It is split off from the theological definition of the Church and it has no sense of other ministries. Papo-centrism dominated the high Middle Ages (and nineteenth and twentieth centuries), because of an underdeveloped, even primitive ecclesiology. The power and role of the leader was defined before there was a rounded and evolved notion of the body that was being led. Certainly, this was the result of historical circumstances, but it was also the result of a papal bid for power. The consequence is that we still have to deal with an exaggerated notion of papalism in the Church.

This same tendency is also seen in the growth of the legal notion that *Papa est iudex ordinarius omnium* (the pope is the ordinary judge of everyone in the Church). The term *iudex ordinarius* again comes from Roman law. It was argued that if the pope was the *iudex ordinarius*, and held the *plenitudo potestatis*, then there was no limit to his jurisdiction.

> The ... formula *iudex ordinarius omnium* had its birth in the general context of the jurisdictional omnicompetence of the pope over the whole hierarchy, [and] was therefore associated with the plenitude of power and had particular reference to the principle that appeals might be made immediately to the pope, with intervening, subordinate jurisdictions by-passed.[32]

But, while the theory of *plenitudo potestatis* has survived in the Church, the days of the medieval universal papal monarchy were quickly drawing to a close in the fourteenth century.

In the forty years between the death of Innocent IV in 1254 and the election of Boniface VIII, there were twelve popes, often with long delays between elections. These delays were caused by political pressure on the cardinals and deep divisions among themselves. The Second Council of Lyons tried to bring stability by passing a detailed decree on papal elections.[33] The decree gave the cardinals ten days to come together for the conclave. If they had not elected a pope within three days, a graduated fast was to be imposed on them. This was not immediately successful, for the longest breaks between popes occurred immediately after the Council!

These long breaks, and the resulting instability, eventually led to the incident of Celestine V (1294). He is the only pope who certainly resigned, although, as Patrick Granfield points out, there are debates about nine possible papal resignations.[34] Pope Celestine is instructive on several scores: he shows that saints—he had been a hermit before election—are not necessarily the best popes, and, in the light of the suggestion of modern popes resigning at a predetermined age, it poses the question of what to do with a resigned pope. The whole period highlights the fact that the Church still does not have a mechanism to deal with heretical, unsuitable, or insane popes.

Celestine V was elected in July 1294 after a vacancy in the papacy of two years and three months. He quickly fell under the influence of his royal protector, Charles II, who insisted that he live in Naples. As pope, Celestine was incompetent and was easily influenced by both the king and the ambitious Cardinal Benedetto Caetani. Under royal influence he appointed twelve new cardinals, seven of whom were Frenchmen. By November it was clear even to Celestine himself that resignation was the only way out, and, advised by Caetani, he abdicated.

Boniface VIII (1294–1303) and Unam sanctam

A fortnight later Caetani himself was elected as Boniface VIII. (Celestine was arrested, escaped back to the mountains, was recaptured, and died in confinement in 1296.) Boniface had came to the papacy in circumstances that were at the very least dubious. There was no clear precedent for a resignation, and Boniface's enemies were later to say the election was invalid. Because he made such extreme claims, Boniface is worth studying in some detail. He takes papalism to its logical conclusion.

After his election, Boniface quickly got down to work. He seemed to thrive on conflict, and his years as pope were characterized by impulsive interference in international affairs, with an obvious lack of success. Centralized national monarchy was on the rise in Europe. This was not to occur without enormous opposition from feudal barons and urban and communal movements jealously guarding their hard-won liberties against the kings. We should not overestimate the centralization of these medieval kingdoms, but the lineaments of the modern state could be discerned in them. Kings, especially in England and France, struggled to maintain their positions and to fight each other. To achieve this they needed two things: a doctrine to support the legitimacy and independence of their emerging states, and money through taxation to make this a reality. It was Saint Thomas Aquinas (1225–1274) who provided them with their ideology. And the kings saw the Church as a source of money through taxation.

Following Aristotle and natural law theory, Aquinas argued that the state was rooted in the social nature of humankind. This is the opposite of what the popes were claiming. Aquinas suggested that authority arises from the very nature of the state itself.[35] Therefore God intended government and human society; the common good demands that someone must give this process a sense of direction 'because human beings are naturally social animals ... The social life of the many would not be possible unless someone presided over it to look after the common good.'[36] Aquinas considered that the best form of government was limited monarchy. This clearly stands in contrast to the hierarchical, papal view whereby *potestas* descends from God through Peter to Peter's successor, and thus down the hierarchical ladder, just like the great chain of being itself.[37] Aquinas held that Church and state should work together, but he is clear that secular power is not derived from the pope or the Church, but from the natural law itself. This explains why on this and a number of other questions he was considered suspect by his contemporaries.

The most extreme pro-papalist of the period was Aegidius Romanus (Giles of Rome), one of Aquinas' teachers. His *De Summi Pontificis potestate* provides the foundation for the bull *Unam sanctam*. Giles argued from the intrinsic superiority of the spiritual over the material. For Giles, the lordship of the pope was beyond anyone's judgment, and he held that it was implicit in the order of the universe. He argued that theoretically the pope was the owner of all material goods in the world: because souls were spiritual, they were governed by the pope; bodies were subject to souls; material goods existed to serve the needs of the body; *ergo*, all material goods were subject to the pope!

The aggressive Boniface VIII held these extreme hierocratic views and this led to his conflict with Philip IV (1268–1314) of

France. At one stage the pope boasted that he was as much emperor as pope! In the bull *Asculta fili* (December 1301), Boniface referred to himself as he 'who holds the place on earth of Him who alone is lord and master.'[38] This was followed by the bull *Unam sanctam* (18 November 1302). The bull states the most extreme hierocratic position: the pope argued categorically that the temporal is completely subject to the spiritual. In the Church, Boniface argued, 'there is one body and one head, not two heads as if it were a monster.'[39] That head is firstly identified with Christ, then with Peter, and then his successor. Basing himself on the text 'Feed my sheep' (John 21:17), Boniface maintained that everyone is subject to the papacy because Christ 'committed to [Peter] all his sheep.' The pope writes that whoever resists the spiritual power 'resists the ordination of God.' Thus the concept of *plenitudo potestatis* in *Unam sanctam* is stated in the extreme form. He concludes the bull with the extraordinary claim: 'Consequently we declare, state, define, and pronounce that it is altogether necessary to salvation for every human creature to be subject to the Roman Pontiff.'[40]

Philip's reply was a personal attack on Boniface, including denunciation for homosexual misconduct. The pope was also called a heretic and usurper. A demand was raised for a general council to depose him. Boniface was seized at Anagni on 7 September 1303, by Philip's minister, Guillaume de Nogaret, and Sciarra, head of the powerful Colonna family, who demanded that he resign.[41] He refused to accept their demands and was rescued by the citizens of the town. It is said that one of the Colonna thugs bashed him, but he does not seem to have been injured. But Boniface was deeply shaken and he died in Rome on 12 October. He was succeeded ten days later by Benedict XI (1303–1304). His successor, Clement V (1305–1314), took the papacy to Avignon.

What are we to make today of Boniface's papacy, and of the extreme papal claims that he enunciated? As pope, he was a disaster. His arrogance and lack of judgment led directly to the Avignon papacy, which, in turn, led straight to the great Western schism. His total failure to read what was happening in the contemporary political life of Europe, and his extreme clericalism enhanced the secularizing tendencies already operative in the French (and later the English) monarchy. But it was his theology that was most outrageous. The extreme teaching of *Unam sanctam* cannot be justified by any biblical or traditional standard. So what is the doctrinal significance and binding force of *Unam sanctam*? Given that parts of it are clearly time-conditioned, how is it to be reconciled with modern papal teaching authority? Is it, for instance, infallible? Or is it only 'ordinary magisterium'? If it is neither of these, what is it?

The Catholic ecumenist George Tavard argues that most late-medieval theologians considered that 'the doctrines of *Unam sanctam* were not received by the Church as authoritative.'[42] Reception is one of the necessary norms for the truth of a doctrine. Some other modern theologians, such as Yves Congar and M. D. Chenu, seem to suggest that what is of permanent value in *Unam sanctam* is that all political action is subject to the ethical demands of the gospel. However, this generalizing tendency hardly does justice to the precise specifics of Boniface VIII. Other theologians hold that only the final sentence is a dogmatic definition. The rest is merely the odd papal claims of the thirteenth century. But, as Tavard correctly asks, how can this last sentence of *Unam sanctam* be divorced from the body of the text?[43] The whole text has a specific meaning of which the last sentence is merely a pointed summary.

Clearly it is not an 'infallible definition' in the modern meaning of the term, but if it is not infallible what is its doctrinal status? If, as Pope Pius XII (1939–1958) says, Boniface VIII's teaching was a 'medieval conception ... conditioned by its time,' surely the same norm can be applied to the teaching of Pius XII himself?[44] This is the nub of the problem: When and how does doctrinal teaching, clearly intended by the enunciating pope to be universally binding, become 'conditioned by its time'? What are we to make *doctrinally* of Boniface's claims, even if they come from the fourteenth century? The simple fact is that this problem has never really been dealt with either by Vatican I or by modern ecclesiology. But by bypassing these historical problems the Church renders suspect all of today's papal claims.

In the early Middle Ages, a distinction was made between the earthly, militant Church and the triumphant, heavenly Church, with an emphasis on the latter as the truest realization of the Church. Because of this distinction, early medieval theologians did not stress the Church's institutional aspect, which was seen as imperfect. But in the later Middle Ages the theological emphasis shifted in an institutional direction. As Yves Congar wrote, the Church became:

> machinery of hierarchical mediation, of the powers and primacy of the Roman see, in a word, a 'hierarchology.' On the other hand, the two terms between which that mediation comes, the Holy Spirit on the one side, the faithful people ... on the other, were kept out of ecclesiological consideration.[45]

In different modalities, this emphasis has continued right through until our own time. It is not an oversimplification to say that in the second millennium of the Christian era, the primacy of service has gradually become the primacy of power to control and mediate.

Papal control through appeals and faculties

Part of the reason why Rome gained so much power from the medieval period onwards was because litigants in local disputes often appealed over the heads of their bishops to the pope. The highest and final court of appeal is always the most powerful. As a result of these appeals and the process of centralization, a whole series of specific and extraordinary permissions were gradually reserved to Rome. Having lost the power to deal with these issues, local bishops were given dispensations and faculties to operate in these matters via papal letters that were issued through the apostolic chancery. As time went on, Roman bureaucrats further constricted the power of bishops to govern their dioceses by forcing them to refer more and more issues to Rome. As the Church expanded into the New World, Urban VIII (1623–1644) had the Inquisition and the Congregation of Propaganda draw up lists of the most frequently requested dispensations. Various lists were prepared according to local needs and distance from Rome. Faculties covering these issues were granted to bishops at the time of their appointment, and they were renewed on a five- or ten-yearly basis. These lists were revised again by Benedict XV in 1920, and were issued to bishops as either quinquennial or decennial faculties through either the Consistorial Congregation or Propaganda. There was a further reform in 1963 by Paul VI.

Originally these permissions were to do with major pastoral issues, such as marriage or the rights of bishops over exempt religious orders. But by the nineteenth century, they became more and more specific and dealt with trivial matters such as dispensations from the Lenten fast, or allowing nuns to wash altar linen. Thus bishops lost the power to govern their own dioceses in a whole range of issues both important and trivial. These faculties suggested that they were merely papal delegates, granted power by the papal curia to operate.

But the question has to be asked: Why do bishops need 'faculties' at all? The notion of Rome as a final court of appeal is both traditional and reasonable, but there seem to be no theological grounds to justify bishops being in such dependence on the Roman curia that they need permission to operate in their own dioceses. Most of the important pastoral issues covered by such faculties should be in the hands of national and regional episcopal conferences. Paul VI, in *Pastorale munus* (30 November 1963), did try to break down the previously absurd centralization, and many petty restrictions were swept away, but the granting of faculties is still part of the Roman system. Subsidiarity surely demands that decisions that can be taken at a local level ought not to be referred upward. The whole thing is part of the seemingly endless centralization that has characterized the papacy over the last eight hundred years. This centralization needs to be radically rethought.

Vatican II and the rediscovery of episcopal collegiality

In some ways that rethinking began at Vatican II. If the role of bishops had been simply ignored at Vatican I, it became one of the most fought-over issues at Vatican II. In theory, at least, Vatican II rediscovered the episcopal *pares* (equals) among whom the pope was *primus*. There was considerable drama over this issue at the Council. The first text on collegiality is contained in chapter three of *Lumen Gentium*. There had been ongoing and, at times, devious opposition throughout the

Council to the idea of collegiality from a determined minority of bishops, including many in the Roman curia.[46] The core of the problem was that collegiality was seen as impinging on papal primacy, even though there was already a heavy emphasis on the Vatican I doctrine in the text of *Lumen Gentium*. The minority correctly foresaw that if the office of bishop was taken seriously, the influence of the Roman curia would be seriously threatened.

Paul VI tried to bring the opponents of collegiality onside by extraordinary concessions, including issuing on 16 November 1964 an Explanatory Note (*Nota explicativia praevia*) setting out the sense in which collegiality was to be understood in *Lumen Gentium*.[47] The key issue emphasized by the pope was that the exercise of collegiality depended completely on the permission of the pope. The *Nota*, which is written in extraordinarily convoluted language, fundamentally relativizes the power of the bishops 'so that the full power of the Roman Pontiff will not be placed in contention.'[48] The *Nota* perpetuates the distinction, which originates in the medieval period, between the ministerial authority that a bishop receives in his ordination and the exercise of that authority that can come about only through juridical permission from Rome.

The word 'collegiality' is never actually used in the documents of Vatican II, but the idea is certainly contained in both *Lumen Gentium* and the Decree on the Pastoral Office of Bishops (*Christus Dominus*). The view of the Council is the traditional one: the bishops form a college with the pope, and assume with him responsibility for the whole Church. But, as in so many of the documents of Vatican II, the teaching is compromised by an extraordinary emphasis in the texts on the papal primacy. It reflects the papalist fear of anything that remotely questioned the *plenitudo potestatis*. There is a sense in which *Christus Dominus* is a far more open document than *Lumen Gentium*. It refers to the long tradition of bishops getting together in synods and councils to confront common problems and to promote the proclamation of the gospel. It goes on to recommend the re-establishment of local and national episcopal conferences, and it states (n. 36) that the Council:

> expresses its earnest hope that these admirable institutions— synods and councils—may flourish with renewed vigor so that the

growth of religion and the maintenance of discipline ... may increasingly be more effectively provided for in accordance with the needs of the times.[49]

As I have already mentioned, a number of these episcopal conferences—such as the Dutch, Italian, United States, and Brazilian Bishops' Conferences, as well as the pan-continental Latin-American Bishops' Conference (CELAM)—were, especially in the 1970s and 1980s, very creative bodies in developing common ecclesial approaches to issues that concerned their own regions. This is because they had a sufficient number of pastorally minded bishops able to take these conferences along with them. But this has now collapsed to a considerable extent, especially in the important conferences, as the bishops appointed by John Paul II develop a critical mass within local episcopates. Several hierarchies—such as those in Austria and the Netherlands, and, to a lesser extent, the United States— have been subverted by the appointments of reactionary bishops, many of them seemingly lacking any pastoral sense. A couple of these appointments have been disastrous.

In terms of sheer numbers, the establishment of bishops' conferences since Vatican II has been successful. In 1992, as well as the Synod of Bishops, there were just over one hundred episcopal conferences in the Western Church, fourteen synods or episcopal conferences in the Eastern Catholic Church, several pan-African bishops' conferences, the Federation of Asian Bishops' Conferences, the Council of Episcopal Conferences of Europe, CELAM, and the Episcopal Secretariat of Central America and Panama.[50] While these conferences and synods have varied widely in their success in assuming responsibility for the local church, their very existence has led to major concerns in Rome.

We have already mentioned the nobbling of the Synod of Bishops by its complete dependence on Roman *fiat*. Its secretariat is at present presided over by Cardinal Jan Schotte. Established by Paul VI in 1965 to try to involve the bishops of the world—in the words of the *Code of Canon Law* (can. 342)— in fostering 'a closer unity between the Roman Pontiff and the bishops,' and assisting him 'with their counsel in safeguarding and increasing faith and morals,' the Synod has become a complete fiasco in terms of collegiality, especially since the advent of John Paul II. Paul VI intermittently tried to encourage the Synod, but he was always ambivalent about it. The canons governing the Synod in the *Code of Canon Law* tie it up hand and foot, and it has absolutely no independence. This is clear from Canon 343: it says that while the bishops can discuss a predetermined agenda, they are unable to resolve or determine issues unless the pope grants them deliberate power and, even then, he has to ratify their decisions. In other words, it is a completely nobbled gathering. It is even left to the pope to write and distribute the conclusions reached in the process.

For instance, the so-called 'Extraordinary Synod' summoned by John Paul II in 1985, despite a lot of good work by many bishops, ended up simply reflecting the papal line on issues such as liberation theology and the status of local bishops' conferences.[51] Peter Hebblethwaite commented that wise bishops at the 1985 Synod knew that:

> While one may be allowed to make fine speeches about collegiality and the Church as a mystery, the gritty reality of Church life depends upon who has control of the institutions—the nomination of bishops, the license to teach theology, the proposal of models of holiness. The Synod of Bishops has been caught up in this process of institutional control which is concerned with *who may speak*, who is allowed to have a voice. Quite simply, this Synod lost its voice.[52]

This is the essence of the problem: it is clear that those who do not toe the official line will simply be given no voice. Clearly, the world Synod of Bishops has already been subverted by Rome and is now largely a rubber stamp for the curial line. In fact, Hebblethwaite claims that the final text for the 1985 Synod had been prepared in advance![53] This may or may not be true, but there is no doubt that the pope and Cardinal Ratzinger knew exactly where they wanted the Synod to go, and controlled proceedings from beginning to end.

No one with real knowledge of the Church now takes these synods seriously; they probably never did. But if the Synod of Bishops actually set its own agenda and freely reached and published its own conclusions, it might become a useful balance to papalism. It still exists as a recoverable entity, but in the Wojtyla papacy it exists merely as a rubber stamp and a clear symptom of the disease of papal absolutism.

Similar attempts have been made to reign in episcopal conferences. In a comprehensive essay, Joseph Komonchak has outlined the theological debate concerning the teaching and ministerial authority of bishops' conferences.[54] He notes that two world Synods of Bishops were devoted to episcopal conferences—1969 and 1985. The key issues that emerged were the threat that such conferences pose to the authority of the individual bishop, on the one hand, and to the authority of the pope, on the other. There have been warnings also that episcopal conferences would lead to the revival of nationalism in the Church. Several major theologians—Henri de Lubac, Hans Urs von Balthasar, Jerome Hamer, and Josef Ratzinger— have attacked the teaching role of such conferences. Ratzinger was quite blunt in 1985: 'We must not forget that the episcopal conferences have no theological basis, they do not belong to the indispensable structure of the Church as willed by Christ; they have only a practical, concrete function.'[55] I have always been intrigued by people who thought that they knew exactly what Christ 'willed' for the Church! The notion that Jesus had the Church all worked out in his head, down to the distinction between the papacy, national episcopal conferences, the curia, and general councils, and even the distinction between the ordinary magisterium and the infallible magisterium, has always struck me as nonsense. The theologians who talk like this seem to inhabit a world that has no relationship to either history or contemporary reality. All of these things are so obviously the result of development over many centuries that it hardly needs mentioning; that is unless your reality is pre-determined by your ideology.

This was, of course, not always Ratzinger's view. In 1965 he was a strong supporter of episcopal conferences.[56] He later referred to such conferences as a fundamental part of the Church's structure and as a 'normal pattern of orderly life in the Church.'[57] But by the time of the 1985 *Ratzinger Report*, it was the role of the individual bishop that he stressed as he downgraded the importance and significance of the episcopal conference. Komonchak points out that Ratzinger has also left behind his early ideas about the development of new patriarchical regions, each embracing a number of episcopal conferences, with their own legislative power and structural forms.[58] This earlier vision has much in common with the notion of the presidency of charity, a eucharistic communion that makes up the Body of Christ. Ratzinger now sees this as a romantic vision of the Church, and the only legitimate exercise of collegiality that he recognizes is the universal collegiality given expression through a general council. Otherwise episcopal conferences have only a very limited role.

Clearly a national conference does not have the same authority as a general council, but it might well be better equipped to make practical and theological decisions that impinge on the local scene than pope, curia, or council. For this is the primary role of a national episcopal conference: to assume responsibility for the local scene, and to encourage local leadership so that a genuine sense of the local church will begin to emerge. The national bishops' conference should take primary responsibility for the development of local liturgy and catechetics, and the appointment and ordination of bishops. It should also address regional ethical and social issues and the function of local marriage customs in relationship to the sacrament of matrimony, and determine the lifestyle and training of the local clergy, as well as assessing who should be ordained and the nature of clerical commitment. It is the responsibility of the local bishops to interact with national governments. This role should be assumed only in extraordinary circumstances by papal nuncios or Rome. All other issues should be dealt with on the local level in accordance with the principle of subsidiarity. It is hard to see any reason why Rome should even be consulted on these issues; at most, the papacy should simply function as a court of appeal, and as a way of measuring the customs of the local church against the universal Church.

The habit of the local episcopal conference making decisions about the local church is, as we have seen, a very traditional way of operating. This was the way Western Church operated for the first thousand years of its history. So the shift in emphasis from a universalist to a local ecclesiology would not be an innovation, but a return to an older tradition.

But to achieve this the bishops will have to find more courage in their dealings with Rome than they have hitherto shown. This is the bind that contemporary Catholicism is in: it badly needs strong leadership, but as long as the pope appoints bishops it is unlikely that anyone who would assume real responsibility for the local church will be appointed. Of course, there are exceptions, and there will always be unusual bishops, such as Archbishop Oscar Romero, who change radically after appointment. But generally only safe, cautious types will be appointed. So there is a need to find another way to appoint bishops. Again, tradition does not fail us: we can do what they did for the first thousand years—the local church needs to take back the right to elect them! This can be done via a local consultative process, and election by a synod representing clergy and people. The *Proposed Constitution of the Catholic Church*, which I will examine a little later, sets out in detail how this could be achieved.

A democratic Catholic Church

One of the most tiresome repetitions of those who want to retain the papal monarchy is the phrase 'the Church is not a democracy.' Most people surrender defeated as soon as this is said, because they think that it is a fact. But the phrase is actually incorrect: there is a true sense in which the Church *is* a democracy, a rule of the people. In fact, a democratic model is much closer to New Testament forms of the Church, and even to later traditions of ecclesiology, than is the bureaucratic, absolute, divine-right papal monarchy. The historical fact is that absolute monarchy only saw the light of day in the late fifteenth and early sixteenth centuries, although much earlier popes, such as Innocent III and Boniface VIII, claimed a universal jurisdiction and power. No one is suggesting that the full panoply of representative democracy, replete with political parties, be imported into the Church. But a democratic approach has strong connections with a communitarian model of Church government. There is also a close relationship between democracy and the theological notion of the *consensus fidelium*.[59]

There are many historical examples of this democratic approach to Church government. The early Church emphasized the equality of all disciples of Jesus and the word church (*ekklesia*) connoted an assembly of equal and fully participating citizens.[60] Eugene C. Bianchi and John Beal have argued that the ecclesiological and canonical traditions of the Western Church contain democratic elements that have been, in Karl Rahner's sense, 'forgotten.'[61] We need to recover these traditions in order to develop alternative structures of Church government. Bianchi refers to a number of examples in the Church's tradition where what we would call democratic structures were developed. The early Church is a clear example: the Pauline communities have been characterized by Wayne Meeks as 'intense spiritual families' and the Lucan communities were characterized by 'communal rules of village solidarity.'[62] Both these approaches implied strong egalitarian and democratic tendencies. Another example is fourth-century Arianism: this movement is seen increasingly by scholars as a democratic, egalitarian approach to Church government.[63] The Gallic church in the fifth century generally recognized Roman leadership, but it looked to its own councils to decide disputed questions. The authority of the pope in fifth-century Gaul seems to have been minimal. The community life of Pachomian monasticism in Egypt stressed a kind of democratic brotherhood, rather than the vertical authority of the Benedictine abbot (who was nevertheless *elected* by the community), and a similar democratic and elective structure operated among the medieval Franciscans and Dominicans. While Thomas Aquinas supported the papal-episcopal model of Church government, for him the *congregatio fidelium* (the whole people of God) is the theological essence of the Church on earth. Conciliarism offers a developed model of Church government that draws inspiration especially from Italian notions of the commune, a form of municipal government in which the people's power was vested in elected officials.

In the nineteenth century, it was significant that Catholicism flourished especially in countries like the United States, Canada, and Australia, where democratic forms of government influenced the way in which the Church operated. Here the Church did not lose the migrant working class.[64] Democratic notions such as collegiality, freedom of conscience, the recognition of churches with more synodal structures, and an emphasis on human rights were all part of the teaching of

Vatican II. But all these emphases still remain in the domain of theory; when is the Catholic Church going to make these a reality in her own government and structure? When is the Church going to take her own teaching seriously?

A constitution for the Church?

Democracy needs a constitution. There have been several attempts to develop a constitution for the Church in the past, the most recent of which was the proposal put forward by Paul VI in 1965 for a *lex ecclesiae fundamentalis*. There was widespread concern from both liberals and conservatives about the nature of this constitution, and the proposal was finally dropped. But, elements of it did go into the revision of the *Code of Canon Law*. Recently, a group of Catholics in the United States, associated with Professor Leonard Swidler of Temple University in Philadelphia, and sponsored by the Association of the Rights of Catholics in the Church (ARCC), have actually drawn up *A Proposed Constitution of the Catholic Church*.[65] This is a very useful foundation for discussion about an ecclesial constitution.

The proposed *Constitution* can be divided into two parts: the first deals with the rights of Catholics and it generally follows the ARCC *Charter of Rights*.[66] But the most interesting part of the *Constitution* concerns structures of governance. It reiterates the principle of subsidiarity, now well established in Catholic social thought, that all decisions be made at the lowest possible level. The *Constitution* calls for the establishment of representative councils at every level of the Church—parish, diocese, national, and international—each with its own body of governing regulations. On the national and international levels, the *Constitution* calls for two 'Houses': a House of Bishops, and a House of Clergy and Laity. The national councils would elect delegates who would meet every ten years for a general council. This council would 'function as the main decision-making body of the Universal Church,' and it would 'bear ultimate responsibility for passing the laws governing the Universal Church and setting policy concerning worship, education, social outreach, administration, finances.'

All Church leaders must be elected 'in a manner which will give a serious representative voice to all those who are to be led by them.' This is an echo of Pope Leo the Great. Clergy and laity should be involved in the election of the parish pastor, the bishop, and the pope. Pastors would be electable for five years (renewable once), and the pope and bishops would be electable for a ten-year non-renewable term. In this proposal, the pope would be elected by delegates selected by national councils in proportion to the number of registered Catholics in each nation. One-third of these papal electors would be bishops, one-third priests, and one-third laity. The *Constitution* emphasizes the need for a separation of powers, and it says that 'a system of diocesan, provincial, national, and international tribunals shall be established which shall serve as courts of first instance, each with designated courts of appeal.' These courts will deal with disputes, contentions, and crimes against the rights of Catholics. The first process is that of conciliation and arbitration, but where this fails the Church tribunals can adjudicate.

The *Constitution* outlined by Swidler and the ARCC is comprehensive and radical. Its great strength is that it gives expression to the notion of the Church as a communion, and in the process it sidesteps some of the complex problems involved in the relationships of pope and bishops. As an exercise in imagining the possible future structure of the Church it is very useful, for we need to develop new models of ecclesiastical governance. It could well serve as a basis for the development of a genuine constitution for the Church, in keeping with the needs of the coming decades. It will appeal especially to Catholics from a democratic tradition. It is difficult to know how those who experience other forms of government would react, but cross-cultural perspectives are becoming increasingly important in Church life.

The *Constitution* models what has to happen for change to occur. We need to imagine what the Church could be like, to think through in practical terms how a more communal Church might operate. If this is not done, the danger is despair: there is no model toward which we can move. We need to activate the potential of the tradition to plan for the future.

It is very useful to have a democratically oriented *Constitution* already prepared for the Church. But how would this *Constitution* be discussed and implemented? How would it be applied to the Church? The best way would be through a general council. This leads us to that final vexed question.

1 Butler, *Council*, p. 330.

2 Ibid., pp. 332–4.

3 Cyprian, *Epistola*, LIX, 16. My translation.

4 Kelly, pp. 24–5. For an English trans. of the *Liber Pontificalis* see Raymond Davis, *The Book of Pontiffs*, Liverpool: Liverpool University Press, 2 vols, 1989 and 1992.

5 Pierre Batiffol, *Cathedra Petri: Etudes d'Histoire ancienne de l'Eglise*, Paris: Editions du Cerf, 1938, p. 51. My translation. The Latin phrase literally means 'holds the major dioceses.'

6 Tanner, vol. 1, p. 2.

7 Batiffol, pp. 41–59.

8 Tanner, vol. 1, pp. 8–9.

9 Ammianus Marcellinus, *Res Gestae*, XXVII, 3.

10 *Liber Pontificalis*, trans. by Davis, vol. 1, p. 1.

11 Ibid., vol. 1, p. 29.

12 Jacques Paul Migne, *Patrologicae cursus completus: Series Latina*, Paris: Garnier, 1844–1891, vol. 16, p. 1018. My translation.

13 Jean Steinmann, *Saint Jerome*, London: Geoffrey Chapman, 1959, pp. 355–6.

14 Ibid., p. 114.

15 Jerome, *Letter* XV, 2.

16 Siricius, *Directa ad decessorem* (10 February 385), author's translation.

17 *Liber Pontificalis*, 47, trans. by Davis, vol. 1, p. 37.

18 See Arther Ferrill, *The Fall of the Roman Empire: The Military Explanation*, London: Thames and Hudson, 1983, pp. 83–116. For the barbarian tribes see Hans-Joachim Diesner, *The Great Migration: The Movement of Peoples Across Europe, AD 300–700*, London: Orbis Publishing, 1982.

19 Leo, *Third Sermon on the Anniversary of his Consecration*.

20 Quoted in C. Kirch and L. Ueding, *Enchiridion fontium historiae ecclesiasticae antiquae*. 8th ed., Fribourg: Herder, 1960, p. 959. My translation.

21 Bernhard Schimmelpfenning, *The Papacy*, New York: Columbia University Press, 1992, p. 50.

22 Tanner, vol. 1, p. 32.

23 Aloys Grillmeier, *Christ in Christian Tradition: From the Apostolic Age to Chalcedon (451)*, London: A. R. Mowbray, 1965, pp. 453–95. R. V. Sellers, *The Council of Chalcedon: A Historical and Doctrinal Survey*, London: SPCK, 1961.

24 Louis Duchesne, vol. 3, p. 297.

25 Sellers, pp. 103–4.

26 Tanner, vol. 1, p. 85. Fundamentally, the *Tome* was the letter sent by Leo I to Flavian of Constantinople in 449. For its text see Barry, vol. 1, pp. 97–102.

27 Thomas J. Reese (ed.), *Episcopal Conferences: Historical, Canonical, and Theological Studies*, Washington: Georgetown University Press, 1989. See especially pp. 25–58.

28 Hostiensis, *On Decretals*, 4.17.13, quoted in Brian Tierney, *The Crisis of Church and State 1050–1300*, Englewood Cliffs: Prentice-Hall, 1964, p. 156.

29 J. A. Watt, *The Theory of Papal Monarchy in the Thirteenth Century: The Contribution of the Canonists*, London: Burns & Oates, 1965, p. 79.

30 Ibid.

31 Ibid, p. 81.

32 Ibid, p. 95.

33 Tanner, vol. 1, pp. 314–18.

34 Granfield, *Papacy in Transition*, pp. 152–7.

35 Frederick Copleston, *A History of Philosophy*, New York: Doubleday/Image, 1983, vol. 2, pp. 412–22. See also Tierney, *Church and State*, pp. 165–71.

36 Thomas Aquinas, *Summa Theologica*, I, Q 96, A 4. My translation.

37 Francis Oakley, 'Celestial Hierarchies Revisited: Walter Ullmann's Vision of Medieval Politics,' *Past and Present*, 60 (1973), pp. 6–10.

38 Quoted in Tierney, *Church and State*, pp. 185–6.

39 Boniface VIII, *Unam sanctam*, in Barry, vol. 1, p. 466.

40 *Unam sanctam*, quoted in ibid., p. 467.

41 T. S. R. Boase, *Boniface VIII*, London: Constable and Company, 1933, pp. 341–351.

42 George Tavard in Paul C. Empie and T. Austin Murphy (eds), *Papal Primacy and the Universal Church*, Minneapolis: Augsburg, 1974, p. 113. See also pp. 105–19.

43 Ibid., pp. 116–17.

44 Pius XII (7 September 1955) quoted in ibid., p. 115.

45 Yves Congar, *Lay People in the Church*, London: Geoffrey Chapman, 1957, p. 39.

46 Rynne, *Third Session*, p. 52.

47 Ibid., pp. 240–54. For the text of the *Nota* see pp. 347–50.

48 *Nota*, quoted in ibid., p. 349.

49 Flannery, *Documents of Vatican II*, p. 586.

50 *Annuario Pontificio*, 1992, pp. 1061–82.

51 For a positive assessment see Xavier Rynne, *John Paul's Extraordinary Synod: A Collegial Achievement*, Wilmington: Michael Glazier, 1986. For a less sanguine approach see Peter Hebblethwaite, *Synod Extraordinary: The Inside Story of the Rome Synod, November–December 1985*, London: Darton, Longman and Todd, 1986.

52 Hebblethwaite, *Synod*, p. 140. My emphasis.

53 Ibid., pp. 136–9.

54 Joseph A. Komonchak, 'Introduction: Episcopal Conferences Under Criticism,' in Reese, pp. 1–22.

55 Josef Ratzinger with Vittorio Messori, *The Ratzinger Report: An Exclusive Interview on the State of the Church*, San Francisco: Ignatius Press, 1985, p. 59.

56 Josef Ratzinger, 'The Pastoral Implications of Episcopal Collegiality,' *Concilium*, I, Glenrock: Paulist Press, 1965.

57 Quoted by Komonchak in Reese, p. 14.

58 Komonchak in Reese, p. 15.

59 Leonard Swidler, '*Demo-kratia*, the Rule of the People of God, or *Consensus fidelium*,' in Swidler and Fransen, pp. 226–43.

60 Elizabeth Schüssler Fiorenza, 'A Discipleship of Equals,' in Eugene C. Bianchi and Rosemary Radford Ruether (eds), *A Democratic Catholic Church: The Reconstruction of Roman Catholicism*, New York: Crossroad, 1992, p. 19.

61 Eugene C. Bianchi, 'A Democratic Church,' in ibid., pp. 34–51, and John Beal, 'Toward a Democratic Church,' in ibid, pp. 52–79. Karl Rahner, 'Forgotten Truths Concerning the Sacrament of Penance,' *Theological Investigations*, Baltimore: Helicon Press, 1963, vol. 2, pp. 135–6.

62 Wayne D. Meeks, *The First Urban Christians*, New Haven: Yale University Press, 1983, p. 89. Bianchi in Bianchi and Ruether, p. 37.

63 Bianchi in Bianchi and Ruether, p. 38.

64 Ibid., p. 47.

65 I have worked from a version dated 6 November 1995.

66 Leonard Swidler and Herbert O'Brien (eds), *A Catholic Bill of Rights*, Kansas City: Sheed and Ward, 1988, pp. 1–6.

CHAPTER 7

The need for a new general council

The need for a council

This book has focused on the problems and distortions that papalism poses for the Church, and it has suggested some ways of dealing with these. But the best way for the Church to come to grips with high papalism is through a general council. Rome has usually been very wary of councils. For, as Vatican II showed, they have a way of getting out of control. It is in the interest of those who want to maintain papalism not to have a council. Certainly, a council would be a most unlikely eventuality during the papacy of John Paul II. It is clear that the pope is the best person to call a council, and in subsequent papacies there is no reason why this should not be a possibility. We never know when another pope in the style of John XXIII will be elected; the serendipity of the Spirit is a characteristic of Church history. While the modern separation of Church and state is most desirable it does mean that there is no powerful secular authority ready to assume the responsibility of summoning a council on behalf of the Church. Nowadays there is no emperor, like Sigismund at Constance in 1414, to summon, organize, and protect the gathering. Nor would one place much hope in the Synod of Bishops as it is presently constituted.

However, there are other possible groups that might bring pressure to bear: a combination of national episcopal conferences could have a potentially powerful influence, especially if supported by a groundswell from the grassroots. Bishops and people acting in concert might well be the most desirable way to put pressure on Rome for the pope to call a council. This concerted support from a widespread and influential group in the Church would certainly be a more representative way than a mere summons from a pope acting alone. The time has come for grassroots pressure to begin to influence important movements in the Church, in preference to arbitrary decisions from the top. A council is the only place where different voices can be heard on the international level, different views articulated, different priorities debated. Genuine collegiality, which now ought to be extended beyond bishops to include priests and people, needs a genuine opportunity to work, and it is above all when the Church gathers in council that this can happen. An important way of breaking down over-centralization is to have regular general councils. The Church needs to take seriously the decree *Frequens* of the Council of Constance (1414–1418).

What we need first is a *general* rather than an *ecumenical* council. This distinction is very useful here. A general council (like the councils of this millennium) represents the Western Roman Catholic Church; an ecumenical council is much broader, and includes representatives of all Christians. If there were regular decennial general councils these could gradually move toward a universal and truly ecumenical council. This would happen with the increasingly full participation of the Orthodox, Protestants, and Anglicans. In fact, a genuine reform of the papacy could open the way to the ecumenical Christian Church of the future.

A series of councils, with increasing participation by the other churches, would seem to be the best way to heal the divisions of Christianity. The role of the papacy would have to be one of the key issues resolved in the movement toward inter-Christian reconciliation. Agreed statements between Catholics and other Christians have generally shown that many churches would be willing to recognize a strictly limited model of papal primacy and the notion of the pope as the president of charity at the heart of the communion of churches. Thus the traditional function of the papacy in the early Church would be revived. No one is happy with the present dictatorial approach of the papacy, except those who derive power or comfort from it: curalists, assorted hierarchs, and fear-filled reactionary Catholics. This is why the Catholic Church has to deal with the problematic notions of primacy, infallibility, and magisterium before the ground for negotiations with the other Christian churches can be laid out. In fact, the goal of mutual acceptance of the Christian churches and eventual full intercommunion could provide the primary spur for Catholics to reform the distortions of power and authority operative in the contemporary papacy.

Clearly the aim will be the reunion of Christendom, but not in the sense of one church entering into corporate union with another. To move in this direction would be to run the risk of the largest church (Western Roman Catholicism) swallowing up many of the others. We need to maintain the richness and diversity of the Christian traditions. What is really called for is a mutual recognition of each other's traditions, ministries, and structures, and, on the basis of that, an entry into full inter-communion. In this scenario all the churches would remain corporate entities—the Orthodox in their several varieties, the Anglicans, the Lutherans, the United Methodists, Presby-terians, Baptists, and so on would retain their integrity, but there would be full recognition of each other as legitimate Christian churches. Many Protestants, especially members of the non-episcopal, congregationally based churches, might well have difficulties with episcopal forms of governance. But this does not mean that the negotiation should not be attempted. However, it will only make sense if Catholics are willing to tackle the distortions involved in high papalism.

But this is jumping ahead. The Roman Catholic Church already has enough crises to keep any council busy for many sessions. Most of the problems would be practical and disci-plinary, such as the crisis in the priesthood and ministry, and the increasingly complex ethical issues facing contemporary society. There are also deep-seated theological issues to be confronted as Western society rethinks at a very profound level its underpinning meaning structures and a whole new, post-communist world order emerges. So, added to the problem of the governance of the Catholic Church itself, there is much to challenge a conciliar gathering.

But the last thing we need is *Vatican Council III*. The next council should be held as far away from Rome as possible. It should not be in Italy and not even in Europe. Europe is no longer the pivot of the world, which now focuses on regions like the Americas, Asia, Africa, and the Pacific. Among these peoples there has been a strong call for the 'inculturation' of faith and theology; that is, that Christianity express itself in and through the various indigenous cultures. This approach received papal encouragement in the 1975 papal letter of Paul VI *Evangelii nuntiandi* (*Evangelization in the Modern World*).

Recently among a number of European theologians there has considerable concern about the translation of faith and theology into local cultural expressions and forms. Despite the fact that the large majority of Catholics now live outside Europe, some remain convinced that the theology of Catholicism is still best expressed in terms of European culture and philosophy. Apparently some Europeans think that having made the transition from its original Judeo-Christian matrix, Christianity found its perfect and only possible expression in and through the culture of Europe. Here again we encounter the *a*historical ideology that so characterizes the approach of many conservative theologians and Catholics. Such people seem to lack any historical sense or knowledge of a wider world. The Eurocentric model of the Church was bluntly expressed by the eccentric English writer Hilaire Belloc (1870–1953), who maintained that 'Europe is the Church, and the Church is Europe.'[1] If this is the case, God help the rest of us, given the state of the Church in most European countries!

But there is one practical issue that is important to note in this: the different political-cultural backgrounds of continental Europeans and those of us from the Anglo-American tradition. As the ecumenically experienced Anglican Bishop Mark Santer comments, 'English and American ideas about how to do business are not the same as those of Italians or Germans or Poles.'[2] This is important to remember, and, as Santer also points out, these contrasts will become exacerbated as the churches become more embedded in the different cultures of the world. This is already a major problem for Catholicism. It is not just the Anglo-American and European world that the Church has to deal with; it is also the cultures of Latin America,

Africa, Asia, and the Pacific. As Santer says: 'Sorting out what is of theology and what is of culture is a most delicate task.' What is acceptable ethical and social behavior in some cultures is not in others.

This, of course, reinforces the need for a much more diversified cultural approach to canonical and legal structures, as well as to worship and catechetics. This is where the proposal to establish regional patriarchates makes a lot of sense. These differences of approach are already important in intra-church negotiations. They need to be kept in mind as the Church tackles the difficult issue of becoming a truly world Church.

Moreover, to tie the Catholic tradition to European culture, rich as it is, is to distort the essence of Catholicism. The very word catholic implies universality, and is derived from the Greek *kath'holu*, which means 'universal,' 'according to the whole,' or 'on the whole.' So in order to assert symbolically the universalism of Catholicism the time has come for a decisive step: the next general council should be held outside Europe.

There is another good reason for this. Just as both the councils of Constance and Trent were specifically held outside the Papal States to avoid the influence of the papal government, so it is important for the next council to be held well away from the Vatican to avoid the activities of the curia. The people who act as hosts always have a big influence on any agenda. The outer limits of Roman centralism were reached when the synods of the Dutch and African churches were recently held in Rome. There was only one reason for this: so that the Vatican could control the agenda, the process, and the outcome. A general council for which there was worldwide preparation and which was held outside of Europe would have a chance of setting its own agenda. It would not have to spend so much of its energy dealing with the agenda of the papacy. The organization of any forthcoming council would need to be in the hands of a separate and independent body, elected and funded by the world's bishops and a broad cross-section of Catholics. There is no justification in tradition for the Vatican bureaucrats to be involved in organizing councils. They exist to serve the papal government, not, as they seemingly imagine, to control the universal Church.

What norms can be developed to work out where the general council should be held? The place should have a significant Catholic presence. It should represent the shift of the center of the majority of the Catholic population to the New World. Yet a feeling of the wide religious diversity of the contemporary world would also need to be present. This means that an exclusively Catholic atmosphere would probably be counterproductive. With the ready availability of simultaneous translation, the language of the council should not be Latin; the council should include all of the major contemporary languages. The most numerically predominant and widely spoken languages of the Church are Spanish and English. A shift away from Latin would be seen as symptomatic of the transition of the Church from the old world to the new. Documents should be published in at least Spanish and English.

Within this context there are several geographical possibilities. We have already eliminated Europe from the potential places for the council. If Africa were chosen, Nairobi (Kenya), Kampala (Uganda), Lagos (Nigeria), and Harare (Zimbabwe) would all be possible locations. Equatorial Africa has the big advantage of being the crossroads between Christianity and Islam, and of being the newest growth area of Catholicism. Its difficulty may well be its political instability, although in terms of Church history this would be nothing new in the background to councils. In North America, Toronto should be considered. The United States would be eliminated by its solo superpower status. If Central America were chosen, Mexico City, Puebla, or Guadalajara would be possibilities, and in South America the choice would seem to be between Lima (Peru), Sao Paulo (Brazil), or Quito (Ecuador). One of the difficulties with the whole of Latin America is that, despite the inroads of North American fundamentalist Protestantism, it is still a strongly traditional Catholic region. Its advantage is that it has the largest concentration of Catholic populations in the world. In Asia, Manila would clearly be the best choice. The Philippines would suit because it is a Catholic country that is struggling with all the issues of poverty, environmental degradation, and development, and it is surrounded by neighbors representing the other great religions of Asia. It is on the Pacific rim, which is expected to be the center of the world by early in the twenty-first century.

The council should be representative of the whole Church. As well as pope and bishops, there should also be present representative laypeople, religious women and men, and priests. There are ample precedents for their attendance. As already noted, most of the early ecumenical councils were actually called by the emperors, as were several medieval councils. Constance and Basel set a model for a more wide-spread presence of laity, religious, and clergy. If they were in attendance there is no reason why they should not have an active voice and vote. As I have already argued, reception by the whole Church is part of the process of establishing the veracity of Church teaching. A more broadly based conciliar vote would symbolize this. As Newman argued, the belief of the laity must to be taken into account in the development of doctrine. The presence of a broad cross-section of people would vividly illustrate the willingness of the Church to embrace a more communal approach to ecclesiology. There would also need to be other Christian churches present from the start, with some form of deliberative as well as consultative voice. If the council was ultimately directed toward reunion this would be essential.

Am I recommending conciliarism?

From what I have written there will certainly be some Catholics who accuse me of conciliarism. What is conciliarism? It can have several meanings. Fundamentally, it is an opinion enunciated by a group of medieval canonists who argued that a general council is the highest authority in the Church and is ultimately superior to a pope. At the heart of conciliarism is the attempt to limit papal power and demand greater accountability from the pope. There are variations on the conciliar theme: sometimes the council was seen as representing the whole Church and called together in Christ. There were strong 'democratic' and communal elements in the evolution of conciliarist themes. Conciliarism of the late medieval period needs to be seen within its historical setting. It evolved within the context of fears of the possibility of a heretical, schismatic, or even mad pope, such as Urban VI (1378–1389). The context of the great Western schism—at one stage there were three claimants to the papacy—gave conciliarism its greatest impetus.

In the technical sense, the word conciliarism refers to the idea that a council is the highest authority in the Church and is superior to a pope. This tradition lasted until the nineteenth century and many Catholics still held to a conciliar position at the time of the Reformation. Saint Thomas More, for instance, is often put forward by ultramontane Catholics as an apologist for the papacy against the schism of Henry VIII. This is incorrect. He was in fact a champion of the unity of the Church, and he held that a general council could decide about the role and function of the pope in the Church. 'In his polemical works, More had steadily maintained that a general council could not err—a claim he never once made for the papacy.'[3] For More, a general council was the only way to solve the divisions that were growing ever-wider in the Church of the sixteenth century. The conciliar tradition survived in a compromised form in the Gallican theory, and was probably held in a pure form at Vatican I by several of the bishops.

Am I advocating conciliarism? I would certainly admit that I lean strongly in that direction in the light of the present papalist dominance of the Church. My position would be viewed by some Catholics as doctrinally untenable. However, a more careful look at the historical development of conciliarism shows not only that it is a complex movement capable of several interpretations, but also that the doctrinal status of the decrees of the Council of Constance (1414–1418) are far more legitimate than papalist apologists or Vatican I suggested. In fact, Vatican I completely failed to deal with the key decrees of Constance. It is important to see this council in its historical context. It is from this context that I argue that there is a legitimate form of conciliarism.

The historical context of conciliarism

Conciliarism's historical roots lie in the late-medieval attempt to limit papal power and the desire for greater accountability from the papacy. Also inherent in the theory was the notion that a general council represented the whole Church, and that it was not merely a gathering of autonomous local bishops. The churchmen facing the constitutional crisis of the Western schism drew on the canonical tradition that assisted them most in dealing with the crisis. It is ironic that it does not seem to have been noticed at Constance, but the idea that the council represented the whole Church also implicitly questioned the notion of a local, petty episcopal dictator as much as it clearly challenged the idea of a papal monarch. Conciliarism is rooted not only in the communal traditions of the Italian city-states and the universities, but also in the other late-medieval expressions of a broader franchise, the parliament in England, the cortes in Spain, and the parlement in France. These were to be swept away in the sixteenth century in France under Francis I (1494–1547), and Spain under Ferdinand V (1474–1516) and Isabella (1474–1504), and sidelined in England by absolute monarchs like Henry VIII (1509–1547).

The great Western schism (which effectively lasted from 1378 until 1415) began immediately after the return of the papacy from Avignon to Rome. In April 1378, Pope Urban VI (1378–1389) was elected in riotous and controversial circumstances in Rome. Serious questions were soon being asked about his justifiable attempts to reform the college of cardinals, his violent temper, and his sanity. By September the cardinals had decamped from Rome and declared that they were not free in Urban's election, and, having declared the papacy vacant, proceeded to elect Clement VII (1378–1394), who retreated to Avignon. Europe was almost equally split between the two popes.

What are we to make of the election of Urban? There is a fair consensus among modern historians that the predominantly French college of cardinals elected Urban 'under duress.'[4] Further doubts are raised by his obvious mental instability, which became worse throughout his papacy. According to canon law the election of a person of unsound mind was illegal. The historian K. A. Finke, who has looked closely at the issues, thinks that 'the election of Urban VI was neither absolutely valid nor absolutely invalid, and that most contemporaries, including those most intimately concerned in the events, were in a state of invincible ignorance.'[5] Therefore, after 1378 there were two doubtful popes.

In one sense the cardinals had staged a *coup d'état*. To see their revolt against Urban in broader perspective it is necessary to backtrack a little, to Avignon. Here the cardinals had come to see themselves as a corporation, and even a kind of senate around the pope. The notion gained ground that if the cardinals elected the pope, he was bound by their advice and assent in granting privileges. Some thought that his relationship to them was the same as a bishop to his cathedral chapter. Most of the French cardinals of Avignon were secular aristocrats whose accomplishments were modest and whose interests and expectations were those of their class. They were the princes of the Church, and the pope was responsible to them.

Any attempt to reform the cardinals met with resistance. One of them told Urban VI to his face that if he diminished their honor they would do their best to diminish his.[6] Some canonists argued that the *ecclesia Romana* was constituted by pope and cardinals, and one could not act without the other. The pope's *plenitudo potestatis* was increasingly limited by the need to consult with the cardinals. They also shared in the wealth of the papacy, and this, together with the electoral influence that came from their remaining a small group, made them anxious to limit the number who could be appointed to the college. With the election of Urban VI they were faced with the problem of a possibly insane pope. They responded by asserting that if they elected an unsuitable pope they had the power to annul that election. What they could not have foreseen was how intractable and extended the schism was to become. To try to deal with the impasse that resulted from the schism, theologians and canonists developed the theory of conciliarism.

The canonical background to concilarism

Concilarism is the term used to cover the variety of theories put forward to solve the problem of the schism. All of them involved the holding of a general council and they asserted in some form or other the superiority of a council over the pope.[7] The concilarist position was different from that of the oligarchic cardinals. They simply sought a dominant role for themselves in the government of the Church. They did not favor the doctrine of conciliar authority, which was more 'democratic' in tendency. However, both positions were actually:

> offshoots of the same canonistic tradition and that is why when the conflicting interests of both parties were submerged in a common desire for unity, they could be blended without incongruity into a coherent system of church government.[8]

A key element in the conciliar theory was the concept of an ecclesiastical corporation.[9] This notion is rooted in canonical discussion of the relationship between local bishops and their cathedral chapters. A chapter was made up of senior priests (canons) of the diocese, and local bishops in the Middle Ages were usually elected by the chapter. However, the ongoing centralizing tendencies of the medieval popes, especially the Avignon popes, tended to limit this right. In the thirteenth century, chapters increasingly formed themselves into corporations for protection, and by the beginning of the fourteenth century the canons had acquired considerable power, especially during an episcopal vacancy. The notion gained ground that bishops acted as agents of the chapter with a derivative, limited authority. Tierney perceptively comments that in the theological background to this, there is a broad Catholic notion that the Church is more than the hierarchy.[10]

The next step was the application of the concept of an ecclesial corporation to the universal Church. The key person in making this transition was Cardinal Hostiensis, who applied the notion of corporation law to the papacy. As a cardinal he promoted the theory of the intimate relationship between pope and cardinals—*tanquam sibi inviscerati* (literally 'as though they [the cardinals] were "intergutted" to him').[11] In this view, the cardinals shared in the *plenitudo potestatis* of the papacy. But Hostiensis went further. He applied corporation law to the Roman clergy and people. He argued that if the entire group of cardinals was wiped out during a papal vacancy, then the Roman clergy and people could convoke a council to elect a pope and guide the Church. So in the broadest sense the whole Church could be considered as an ecclesiastical corporation in which all members shared in its authority. These ideas were picked up and developed by the conciliarists.

There are a couple of other theorists whose ideas formed part of the conciliarist background. Guillaume Durand (d. 1330), the Bishop of Mende, was certainly compromised by his attachment to Philip IV of France, his opposition to Boniface VIII, and his participation in the trial of the Templars. But at the Council of Vienne (1311), he strongly condemned the power of the papal chancery to dominate the Church and to overrule even archbishops. He was concerned to defend the traditional rights of bishops against pope and curia; he called for a definition of the primacy. The French Dominican, John of Paris, was another writer from the anti-Boniface VIII camp, but his *De potestate regia et papale* (*Concerning Papal and Regal Power*) was probably the most balanced study written at the time of the dispute between Philip and Boniface. He held that the Church could own property, but that ownership of Church goods was vested in the whole Christian community, and that the pope, far from being an overlord, administered the Church's property on behalf of the community. John was a follower of Thomas Aquinas, in that he believed that civil government originated in the social nature of humanity and that regal power ought to be limited by constitutional means. He applied the same norm to the Church: the pope is the servant of the community, and if he is deficient in his service he would be liable to rebuke and ultimately dismissal, preferably by a council, or, *in extremis*, by the cardinals. The council acts for the whole Church and no pope is immune from its judgment.

The greatest conciliar theorist and canonist was the Italian Cardinal Francesco Zabarella (1360–1417).[12] In his *Tractatus de Schismate* (1402–1408), he held that the whole of the mystical Body of Christ was a corporation and that a corporation can exercise jurisdiction even when there is no effective head. Schism, Zabarella argued, creates a quasi-vacancy in the papacy since neither claimant can govern the whole Church. In these circumstances the authority of the Church could and should be exercised by the *congregatio fidelium*. This was exercised through a general council. In a schismatic situation a council should be called forthwith—either by the popes themselves, by the cardinals, by the emperor or by other civil powers. Zabarella held that the convocation was actually secondary, for the council's authority came not from its convocation but from the whole *congregatio fidelium*. In fact, the extraordinary situation of a schism only reinforced the fact that ultimately the pope held the *plenitudo potestatis* only 'as a limited and derivative authority.'[13] In 1545, Zabarella's *De schismate* was placed on the *Index of Forbidden Books* because it asserted the supremacy of a council over the pope. Zabarella brings us to the conciliar period itself.

All of these ideas are extraordinarily suggestive for our own time. The medieval notion of the corporation found primary expression in the communes of the city-states of northern and central Italy, and in the quasi-democratic structures of the medieval universities. It is precisely because these late medieval thinkers were working from an ecclesiological notion of the Church as a whole, and were not purely focused on papal power, that they were able to see the pope as an integral part of the Church and not someone who stood above it as a kind of exempt monarch, not bound by its laws and its constitutive nature. Thus their view of the Church was more comprehensive and more inclusive of its constitutive parts. They had a lot in common with the inspiration of Vatican II.

The overture to the Council of Constance

The Roman pope Urban VI showed no interest in healing the schism and seemingly descended further into monomania and madness. The Papal States fell into anarchy. His cardinals were confronted with the problem of what to do with a pope who was clearly deranged. Some of them plotted to place him under a guardian, but he forestalled this, and in 1384 imprisoned and brutally tortured six of them. Shortly afterwards five others mysteriously disappeared. He died in Rome in 1389, possibly the victim of poisoning. The alternative pope, Clement VII (1378–1394) organized a curia in Avignon and appointed a genuinely international group of cardinals. He hoped that with the death of Urban he would be recognized by the Roman cardinals. But Urban's successor, Boniface IX (1389–1404), showed no willingness to compromise. He gradually regained control of the Papal States and he refused to negotiate with the newly elected Avignon pope, Benedict XIII (1394–1417).

Boniface was totally unscrupulous in his attempts to raise money. He sold church benefices and offices to the highest bidder, and he exploited the commercial possibility of the sale of indulgences. His successor, Innocent VII (1404–1406), was ineffective and continued the policy of refusing to negotiate with Benedict XIII. Innocent's successor, Gregory XII (1406–1415), was initially anxious to heal the schism. The Roman cardinals had taken an oath in the conclave that if elected they would abdicate if Benedict XIII of Avignon also did so. In May 1408, nine of Gregory XII's cardinals, convinced that their pope would never resign, abandoned him and made their way to Livorno to enter into negotiations with Benedict XIII. He proved as obdurate as Gregory and eventually the cardinals of both camps decided to bypass their popes and to call a Council at Pisa. It began on 25 March 1409. Eventually there were four patriarchs and twenty-four cardinals from both jurisdictions present, together with one hundred bishops, one hundred and seven abbots, the generals of the mendicant and other religious orders, plus canonists, theologians, and representatives of universities, cathedral chapters, and princes.

The Council of Pisa cited the two rival popes to appear, and when they failed to do so it deposed them after a careful legal process and declared them contumacious schismatics, perjurers, and obdurate heretics. The Council had applied the long-accepted norm that a pope could be deposed if he deviated from the faith. Today historians generally accept that the Council of Pisa was a legitimate council.[14] Thus the Council had the power to declare that the Holy See was vacant. This position, however, has never been accepted by papalist historians who have maintained the legitimacy of the Roman line. Interestingly, the recent collection of the *Decrees of the Ecumenical Councils* does not include Pisa, but does include the whole of Constance.[15]

The Council of Pisa then proceeded to elect Peter of Candia, a Franciscan, as Alexander V (1409–1410). The Council had probably already fatally weakened the positions of both Gregory and Benedict, but now there were three popes. Tragically, Pope Alexander died in Bologna the following year. He was succeeded by Baldassare Cossa, a completely worldly adventurer and libertine. He took the style John XXIII (1410–1415, d. 1419). He was elected quickly because the Pisan cardinals felt that his military experience would assist in the recapture of Rome and because he already had threatening military forces at his disposal. No doubt generous bribes also helped. It was a disastrous mistake. By his scandalous life he destroyed the efforts of Pisa to heal the schism.

The Council of Constance (1414–1418)

Between 1411 and 1413, John established himself in Rome, but he eventually had to flee and to appeal to the German King

Sigismund, who placed him under enormous pressure to call a council at Constance. The Council began on imperial territory on 5 November 1414 in the local cathedral. Franzen says that the Council was 'ecumenical from the start.'[16] Tanner's *Decrees* also accepts its ecumenicity from the beginning.[17] Older historians, such as Cuthbert Butler, argue that the Council only became 'ecumenical' from 4 July 1415, when the legate of Gregory XII staged a rereading of the bull of convocation.[18] Franzen comments that 'apart from Gregory and his supporters, no one in Constance took this [second convocation] seriously.'[19] The Council also made the same offer to the Avignon pope. This is important today because pro-papalists have continued to maintain the figment that this 'second convocation' somehow constituted the ecumenicity of Constance. Given that the all-important decree *Haec sancta*, declaring that the council was superior to the pope, had already been passed, the pro-Roman view tries to maintain that this decree was not part of the Council's *acta* and was thus not binding. However, Franzen shows that the doubtful election of 1378, the three-decade schism, and the fact that both Gregory XII and Benedict XIII had already been deposed at Pisa in 1409, made it clear that the Council considered that there was no legitimate pope.

The decree *Haec sancta* is the most important decision of Constance. Its language is direct and it is a clear expression of the communal ecclesial tradition that lies behind it. It was prepared by Zabarella.

> This holy synod legitimately assembled in the holy Spirit, constituting a general council and representing the catholic church militant, it has power immediately from Christ; and that everyone of whatever state or dignity, even papal, is bound to obey it in those matters which pertain to the faith, the eradiction of the said schism and the general reform of the said church of God in head and members.[20]

It is important to note that the decree does not directly assert the superiority of the council over the pope, but it needed to imply it in order to claim the power to dismiss all three papal claimants. The clear assertion of the superiority of council over pope comes slightly later at the Council of Basel. *Haec sancta* simply says the pope is bound to obey the Council. It makes three primary points: (1) the Council is 'legitimately assembled'; (2) that it 'represents the Catholic church' and; (3) that the Council has 'immediate power from Christ.' It is clear about its purpose: 'the eradication of the present schism' and the 'reform of God's church [in] head and members.'[21] As a result, 'everyone of whatever state or dignity, even papal, is bound to obey it in those matters which pertain to the faith, the eradication of the said schism, and the general reform of the ... church.'[22] The very directness of the language of *Haec sancta* conveyed the feeling of the need for direct action in a time of crisis.

Haec sancta also guaranteed the freedom of the Council, quashed the decrees and decisions of John XXIII, and commanded his curia to remain in Constance. The Council went on to declare on 9 October 1417, in the decree *Frequens*, that 'the frequent holding of general councils is a pre-eminent means of cultivating the Lord's patrimony.'[23] The time span is clearly nominated:

> The first shall follow in five years immediately after the end of this council, the second in seven years immediately after the end of the next council, and thereafter they are to be held every ten years forever. They are to be held in places which the supreme pontiff is bound to nominate and assign within a month before the end of each preceding council.[24]

Meanwhile on 4 July 1415, after 'convoking' the Council, Gregory XII authorized his envoy, Carlo Malatesta, to abdicate in his name. Benedict XIII refused to abdicate and he was tried and deposed on 26 July 1417. The Christian world was now united under a single authority—the Council of Constance.

The theological significance of Constance

What is the theological status of these assertions? The general consensus of modern historians would be that *Haec sancta* is a legitimate conciliar decree. As part of the canonical tradition it is juridical in emphasis, but it is rooted in ecclesiology and has 'permanent value' because it is the statement of a general council.[25] The decree was not a mere emergency measure. It can be compared to *Lumen Gentium* of Vatican II. As Luis Bermejo correctly comments, 'Both *Haec sancta* and *Lumen Gentium* are fundamental doctrinal decrees affecting the constitution of the Church, both proceed from a general council, but neither is a dogma of faith.'[26] There is a sense in which *Haec sancta* is far closer to the teaching of Vatican II than are the decrees of Vatican I. Constance reflected a communitarian and even more democratic model of the Church, was more collegial, and gave representation to a broad cross-section of the people of God. Vatican I's focus was narrowly hierarchical and simply did not take the evidence of Church history seriously. As the Church moves away from an emphasis on hierarchy and papalism toward a broader sense of itself as a universal communion of communities, Constance becomes more relevant than does Vatican I.

The claim that a council represents the Catholic Church and has immediate power from Christ is very significant for the modern Church. This shifts the emphasis away from the notion that somehow the papacy 'owns' the Church, that it is the sole source of all power and authority in the community. The medieval notion, originating in the period between Innocent III and Boniface VIII, that the pope is the source of all power in the Church and even in society itself, is a gross distortion of the much more traditional notion that authority finds its source in Christ, is diffused throughout the community, and that it finds its best representation in a more synodal approach to Church government and ecclesiology. *Haec sancta* correctly shifts the source of power away from the papacy to Christ, and asserts that this power is granted, especially in times of crisis or change, primarily to the Church meeting in council. In this context the pope can exercise his authority only as a member of the Church.

The pope in *the Church*

This focuses the essence of the issue for us today. The pope has authority only *as a member of the Church* and as an office-holder in it. The way in which papalist theories have placed the pope over and above the Church has led to doctrinal distortions and even heresy.[27]

Just as the model of the absolute monarch or dictator places the ruler not only above the state and its laws but above society

213

itself, so the papalist interpretations of primacy and infallibility
at Vatican I make the pope into some type of solo guru and
intermediary between God and the Church, with the Catholic
community as a passive recipient of papal oracles that are to be
received with 'full submission of mind and will.'

This view cannot be sustained any longer. The papalist
location of the pope as over and above the Church is a distortion
that is not in keeping with the mainstream tradition. Christ gives
authority to the whole Church, and just as the pope cannot teach
what is not held by the Church nor propose what is contrary to
the tradition, so he cannot exercise authority divorced from the
Church. Regular councils would be a way of restoring authority
to the Church community. Tillard says that even before a more
conciliar approach is realized at the macro level, it needs to
become a reality at the local level of the diocese and the parish.
This is beginning to happen in some places. But the problem is
that most Catholics have entirely lost a sense of themselves as
having any authority at all in the Church. Even those who took
on board renewal after Vatican II, and committed themselves to
the Church's ministry, have found that they had absolutely no
power and authority. They are entirely dependent on the whim
of various hierarchs. They usually experience this at the level of
the local priest, but the arbitrary nature of Church authority
reaches right up the line. This applies to religious and priests,
as much as it does to the laity. Almost all of those who have tried
to achieve change have had their fingers burned.

The central contemporary problem is the awkward and
unresolved corrosive disjunction between a vision of the Church
as a participative community and the reality of the Church as
a hierarchical power structure. As I pointed out a decade ago in
Mixed Blessings, the Church's most profound structural and
theological problem is the product of the ambivalence and
compromises built into Vatican II's *Lumen Gentium* itself.[28] The
tension that this creates for Catholics is considerable, as there
is a real dichotomy between what their internal vision of what
the Church should be comes to confront what they actually
experience at the level of the institution. The advent of the high
papalism of John Paul II has only exacerbated this tension. It is
now driving people out of the Church in droves.

This disjunction is not the only thing driving people out of the Church. Here we should not blind ourselves to the sheer corruption of power within the hierarchical institution. We have already seen something of this in the financial scandals of the Vatican. A. W. Richard Sipe quotes a recent conversation with an American bishop who said, 'The thing that pains me about the organization to which I belong is that it is rotten from the top down.'[29] One is tempted to respond: 'Welcome to the real world, bishop!' The context of the remark was clerical sexual abuse. Sipe has correctly related the Church's sexual problems to the issue of power. Power and authority, not sex, is the nub of the Church's contemporary problems. Abusive sexuality is a symptom. The abuse of power occurs most where it is most centralized—at the top of the hierarchy. It is far too large a problem for an individual to confront. It requires the attention of the whole Church.

That is why I have repeatedly said in this book that the Church has to move decisively away from an emphasis on the hierarchy and power, toward a more communal, even democratic model of the Church. It is basically a question of a shift of emphasis. The need for the development of a representative, democratic, conciliar, and synodal approach to Church government is urgent. It will need to begin to develop at the base level, but the urgency of the problem facing the Catholic Church cannot be exaggerated. While I am not confident that anything will happen as long as the papacy of John Paul II continues, that does not mean that Catholics should not prepare for the future. Tradition—*tradere*—as I said, means to hand *on to the coming generation*. The failure of Vatican II, Paul VI, and John Paul II to grasp the real issues facing the Church will be compounded if the present generation of mature and committed Catholics do not act to hand on the faith. Even if most of our episcopal leaders have failed us badly, this does not absolve us from our responsibility as ordinary Catholics. We need to pass on the tradition, to give to those who come after us the gift that we have received.

The main place where this can be done is in a council which represents the whole Church and which marshals the power and authority given to the Church by Christ. It is clear that renewal of the Church will not come from the hierarchy. Generally speaking, they are fear-filled and self-engrossed. That leaves the wider Church community. The time has come for us to seize the initiative.

But there is still a major theological question lurking behind all of this: Is it possible to reconcile the conciliarist teaching of Constance and the ultramontane teaching of Vatican I? While it is true that a healthy tension can exist between a conciliar and a papal view of the Church, the simple fact is that the two probably cannot be reconciled. The Church needs to face this disjunction. As Bermejo points out with his typical truthfulness: 'If two general councils cannot in all honesty be reconciled, which of the two prevails, the earlier or the later council?'[30] Bermejo says that we are not in a position to resolve this issue, but he does quote the Spanish Dominican Cardinal Juan de Torquemada (1388–1468),[31] a strongly pro-papal theologian who held that if councils cannot be reconciled the later one is to be rejected 'since the doctrine of the earlier one had already been adopted and received by the universal Church.'[32] Bermejo also says that the final criterion will be 'the supreme criterion of Scripture and that of the early apostolic tradition' as taught by the first seven ecumenical councils.[33] Within this context it is quite clear from our historical studies that Constance is far closer in its ecclesiology to the early Church than is Vatican I. So the contemporary Church is clearly faced with the possibility that the teachings of Vatican I might not be in accord with tradition. If that were the case serious questions would have to be asked about them.

Hope for the future

The most profoundly and uniquely Christian characteristic is not faith or love, but hope. And hope, as I said, is intimately linked with the creative imagination. Both contemporary Catholics and other modern Christians are challenged by their commitment to hope to imagine the shape of the ecumenical Church of the future. There is no doubt that the Christian Church has little future outside this ecumenical context. Clearly, the papacy will have a leadership role in this Church of the future. But for the papacy to be ecumenically acceptable the present papalist power structures will have to be largely jettisoned. So there is a sense in which we are probably at the end of the model of papacy as absolute monarch. One hopes there will be no more John Paul IIs.

In the short term, Catholics need to cultivate the virtue of hope, although certainly not the type promoted by the old-style Roman triumphalism. They need to have a sense that their community has an important future in helping people to attain a sense of meaning and to develop appropriate ethical, spiritual, and liturgical approaches to human existence. Part of the core of that hope is that, despite the vagaries of its history, the Church has survived for so long. The Church is a major component in the building of the culture to which all people of European origin belong. At the same time, the modern Church has come a long way already in integrating peoples of widely differing cultures into its ranks. For the first time it is now a universal Church in the full geographical sense. In the third world, the growth of Catholicism throughout this century has been extraordinary. It is clearly not dying, even if it faces quite serious problems, especially in the developed world.

I have placed considerable emphasis on history in this book. This is not only because history gives us a sense of cultural and religious continuity, and a feeling of being able to build on deep foundations, but also because it frees us. And freedom to shape the future is what is most needed in today's Church. This freedom will come primarily from the grassroots, from ordinary Catholic Christians. The higher one goes in the Church, the less liberty there is. Paradoxically the institution makes slaves of those to whom it seemingly grants most power. The future of the Church is not really in the hands of the pope or the bishops but in ours.

In this book, I have stressed that the first millennium of papal history was characterized by *diaconia* (service), and the second by *potestas* (power). What will be the key sustaining notion of the third? I would suggest that it will be participation. The popes of the third millennium will have to encourage Catholics from all levels of the Church to be a real part of the Church's ministry, to participate in its work. This will mean that the words of Jesus quoted at the beginning of this work (Matthew 20:25-28) will have to become a reality in the life of the Church: an opportunity will have to be provided for all

Catholics to serve. For popes to do this they will have to learn something of the humility that was typified by Jesus himself.

1 Hilaire Belloc, *Europe and the Faith*, London: Constable, 1921, p. 32.

2 Mark Santer, 'Bishop's Moves,' *Times Literary Supplement*, 21 March 1986, p. 313.

3 Richard Marius, *Thomas More: A Biography*, London: Collins, 1986, p. 458.

4 August Fransen, 'The Council of Constance: Present State of the Problem,' *Concilium*, 7, p. 19.

5 K. A. Fink quoted in ibid.

6 Quoted in Geoffrey Barraclough, *The Medieval Papacy*, London: Thames and Hudson, 1968, p. 158.

7 Brian Tierney, *Foundations of the Conciliar Theory: The Contribution of the Medieval Canonists from Gratian to the Great Schism*, Cambridge: Cambridge University Press, 1955, p. 5.

8 Ibid., p. 239.

9 Ibid., pp. 96–153.

10 Ibid., pp. 130–1.

11 Hostiensis quoted in ibid., p. 149. My own (inelegant) translation.

12 Ibid., pp. 220–37.

13 Ibid., p. 225.

14 Franzen, p. 22.

15 See Tanner, vol. 1, pp. 401–3, where the text jumps from Vienne to Constance.

16 Franzen, p. 23.

17 Tanner, vol. 1, p. 403.

18 Butler, *Vatican Council*, pp. 28–9.

19 Franzen, p. 23.

20 *Haec sancta*, in Tanner, vol 1, p. 409.

21 Ibid.

22 Ibid.

23 Ibid., p. 438.

24 Ibid., p. 439.

25 Bermejo, p. 278.

26 Ibid.

27 J. M. R. Tillard, 'The Primacy-Conciliarity Tension,' *Theology Digest*, 41:1 (Spring 1994), p. 41.

28 Collins, *Mixed Blessings*, pp. 53–6.

29 Sipe, *Sex, Priests, and Power*, p. 3.

30 Bermejo, p. 287.

31 Not to be confused with Tomas de Torquemada (1420–1498), the Spanish Grand Inquisitor.

32 Quoted by Bermejo, p. 288.

33 Bermejo, p. 289.

Bibliography

Alberigo, Giuseppe. 'Serving the Communion of Churches.' *Concilium*, 1979.
——. (ed.). *The Reception of Vatican II*. Washington: Catholic University of America Press, 1987.
Alberigo, Giuseppe and Joseph A. Komonchak (eds). *The History of Vatican II: Volume 1*. Maryknoll: Orbis and Leuven: Peeters, 1995.
Barraclough, Geoffrey. *The Medieval Papacy*. London: Thames and Hudson, 1968.
Barry, Colman J. (ed.). *Readings in Church History*. Three volumes. Westminster: Newman Press, 1960–1965.
Batiffol, Pierre. *Cathedra Petri: Etudes d'Histoire ancienne de l'Eglise*. Paris: Editions du Cerf, 1938.
Belloc, Hilaire. *Europe and the Faith*. London: Constable, 1921.
Bermejo, Luis. *Infallibility on Trial: Church, Conciliarity, and Communion*. Westminster: Christian Classics, 1992.
Bianchi, Eugene C., and Rosemary Radford Ruether (eds). *A Democratic Catholic Church: The Reconstruction of Roman Catholicism*. New York: Crossroad, 1992.
Blondel, Maurice. *Letter on Apologetics and History of Dogma*. Trans. and edited by Alexander Dru and Illtyd Trethowan, London: Harvill Press, 1964.
Boase, T. S. R. *Boniface VIII*. London: Constable and Company, 1933.
Bornkamm, Günther. *Paul*. Trans. by D. M. G. Stalker. London: Hodder and Stoughton, 1971.
Bossy, John. *The English Catholic Community 1570–1850*. London: Burns & Oates, 1975.
Boyle, John P. 'The Ordinary Magisterium.' *Heythrop Journal*, 20 (1979), pp. 380–98, and 21 (1980), pp. 14–29.
Brodrick, James. *Robert Bellarmine: Saint and Scholar*. London: Burns & Oates, 1961.
Brown, Raymond E. et al. *Peter in the New Testament*. New York: Paulist, 1973.
Brown, Raymond E., and John P. Meier. *Antioch and Rome: New Testament Cradles of Christianity*. New York: Paulist, 1983.
Bugnini, Annibale. *The Reform of the Liturgy 1948–1974*. Collegeville: Liturgical Press, 1990.
Butler, Cuthbert. *The Life and Times of Bishop Ullathorne 1806–1889*. Two volumes. London: Burns, Oates and Washbourne, 1926.
——. *The Vatican Council, 1869–1870*. London: Longmans Green, 1930.
Canon Law Society of America. *Code of Canon Law: Latin-English Edition*. Washington: Canon Law Society of America, 1983.
Chirico, Peter. *Infallibility: The Crossroads of Doctrine*. Wilmington: Michael Glazier, 1983.
Clark, Kenneth. *Civilization*. London: BBC/John Murray, 1969.
Collins, Paul. *Mixed Blessings: John Paul II and the Church of the Eighties*. Ringwood: Penguin, 1986.
——. 'Coming Clean.' *Eureka Street*, March 1996, pp. 32–5.
Congar, Yves. *Lay People in the Church: A Study for a Theology of the Laity*. London: Geoffrey Chapman, 1957.
Copleston, Frederick. *A History of Philosophy, Volume II: Mediaeval Philosophy, Augustine to Scotus*. New York: Doubleday/Image, 1983.
Coppa, Frank J. *Cardinal Giacomo Antonelli and Papal Politics in European Affairs*. Albany: State University of New York Press, 1990.
Corish, Patrick. *The Irish Catholic Experience: A Historical Survey*. Dublin: Gill and Macmillan, 1985.
Cornwell, John. *A Thief in the Night: The Mysterious Death of John Paul I*. London: Penguin, 1989.
Cullmann, Oscar. *Peter: Disciple, Apostle, Martyr*. Philadelphia: Westminster, 1953.
Cwiekowski, Frederick J. *The English Bishops and the First Vatican Council*. Louvain: Publications Universitaires de Louvain, 1971.
Cyprian. *The Unity of the Catholic Church*. Trans. by Maurice Bévenot. *Ancient Christian Writers* series. Westminster: Newman Press, 1957.
Dahm, Charles. *Power and Authority in the Catholic Church: Cardinal Cody in Chicago*. Notre Dame: University of Notre Dame Press, 1981.
Dansette, Adrien. *Religious History of Modern France*. Edinburgh-London: Nelson, 1961.
Davis, Charles. *A Question of Conscience*. London: Sheed and Ward, 1967.

Davis, Raymond. *The Book of Pontiffs*. Trans. of the Liber Pontificalis. Two volumes. Liverpool: Liverpool University Press, 1989, 1992.

DeFonzo, Luigi. *St. Peter's Banker: Michele Sindona*. New York: Franklin Watts, 1983.

Dentin, Pierre. *Les Privilèges des Papes devant l'écriture et l'histoire*. Paris: Les Editions du Cerf, 1995.

Diesner, Hans-Joachim. *The Great Migration: The Movement of Peoples Across Europe, AD 300–700*. London: Orbis Publishing, 1982.

Duchesne, Louis. *The Early History of the Church from its Foundation to the End of the Fifth Century*. Three volumes. London: John Murray, 1909–1924.

Duncan, Bruce. *The Church's Social Teaching: From Rerum Novarum to 1931*. Melbourne: Collins Dove, 1991.

Ellis, John Tracy. *American Catholicism*. Chicago: University of Chicago Press, 1956.

Empie, Paul C., and T. Austin Murphy. *Papal Primacy and the Universal Church*. Minneapolis: Augsburg, 1974.

Eno, Robert B. *The Rise of the Papacy*. Wilmington: Michael Glazier, 1990.

Eusebius. *The History of the Church from Christ to Constantine*. Trans. by G. A. Williamson. London: Penguin, 1989.

Fasola, Umberto M. *Traces on Stone: Peter and Paul in Rome*. Rome: Vision Editrice, 1980.

Ferrill, Arthur. *The Fall of the Roman Empire: The Military Explanation*. London: Thames and Hudson, 1983.

Fesquet, Henri. *The Drama of Vatican II: The Ecumenical Council June 1962–December 1965*. New York: Random House, 1967.

Flannery, Austin (ed.). *Vatican Council II: The Conciliar and Post Conciliar Documents*. Dublin: Dominican Publications, 1975.

———— (ed.). *Vatican II: More Post Conciliar Documents*. Grand Rapids: Eerdmans, 1982.

Ford, John T. 'Infallibility: A Review of Recent Studies.' *Theological Studies*, 40 (1979), pp. 273–305.

Foy, Felician A., and Rose M. Avato (eds). *1996 Catholic Almanac*, Hungtington: Our Sunday Visitor, 1996.

Fransen, August. 'The Council of Constance: Present State of the Problem.' *Concilium*, 7, p. 19.

Granfield, Patrick. *The Papacy in Transition*. Dublin: Gill and Macmillan, 1981.

————. *The Limits of the Papacy: Authority and Autonomy in the Church*. New York: Crossroad, 1990.

Grillmeier, Aloys. *Christ in Christian Tradition: From the Apostolic Age to Chalcedon (451)*. London: A. R. Mowbray, 1965.

Hales, E. E. Y. *Pio Nono: A Study in European Politics and Religion in the Nineteenth Century*. London: Eyre and Spottiswoode, 1954.

————. *Revolution and Papacy 1769–1846*. Notre Dame: University of Notre Dame Press, 1966.

Hamer, Jerome. *The Church is a Communion*. London: Geoffrey Chapman, 1964.

Hasler, August Bernhard. *How the Pope Became Infallible: Pius IX and the Politics of Persuasion*. New York: Doubleday, 1981.

Hebblethwaite, Peter. *The Year of Three Popes*. London: Collins, 1978.

————. *The New Inquisition? Schillebeeckx and Küng*. London: Collins/Fount, 1980.

————. *John XXIII: Pope of the Council*. London: Geoffrey Chapman, 1984.

————. *Synod Extraordinary: The Inside Story of the Rome Synod, November–December 1985*. London: Darton, Longman and Todd, 1986.

————. *Paul VI: The First Modern Pope*. London: HarperCollins, 1993.

Hennesey, James.. *American Catholics: A History of the Roman Catholic Community in the United States*. New York: Oxford University Press, 1981.

Hertling, Ludwig. *Communio: Church and Papacy in Early Christianity*. Chicago: Loyola University Press, 1972.

Holmes, Derek. *More Roman than Rome: English Catholicism in the Nineteenth Century*. Shepherdstown: Patmos Press, 1978.

Jedin, Herbert, and John J. Dolan (eds). *History of the Church: The Church in the Industrial Age*. Volume 9. New York: Crossroad, 1981.

————. *History of the Church: The Church in the Modern Age*. Volume 10. New York: Crossroad, 1981.

Kaiser, Robert Blair. *The Politics of Sex and Religion: A Case History in the Development of Doctrine 1962–1985*. Kansas City: Leaven Press, 1985.

Käsemann, Ernst. *New Testament Questions of Today*. London: SCM, 1969.

Kelly, J. N. D. *The Oxford Dictionary of Popes*. Oxford: Oxford University Press, 1986.

Kirch, C. and L. Ueding. *Enchiridion fontium historiae ecclesiasticae antiquae*. Fribourg: Herder, 1960.

Kselman, Thomas A. *Miracles and Prophecies in Nineteenth Century France*. New Brunswick: Rutgers University Press, 1983.

Küng, Hans. *The Council and Reunion*. London: Sheed and Ward, 1961.

———. *Structures of the Church*. New York: Nelson, 1964.

———. *Infallible? An Inquiry*. London: Collins, 1971

———. *Infallible? An Unresolved Inquiry*. London: SCM, 1994.

Küng, Hans, and Leonard Swidler (eds). *The Church in Anguish: Has the Vatican Betrayed Vatican II?* San Francisco: Harper and Row, 1986.

Lash, Nicholas. 'On Not Inventing Doctrine.' *The Tablet*, 2 December 1995.

van Lierde, Peter Canisius. *The Holy See at Work: How the Catholic Church is Governed*. London: Robert Hale, 1962.

Lightfoot, J. B. *The Apostolic Fathers*. Ed. by J. R. Hamer. Grand Rapids: Baker Book House, 1974.

Loisy, Alfred. *The Gospel and the Church*. London: Isbister, 1903. Reprinted by Fortress (Philadelphia), 1976.

McBrien, Richard. *Catholicism*. New edition. Melbourne: Collins Dove, 1994.

McClory, Robert. *Turning Point: The Inside Story of the Papal Birth Control Commission*. New York: Crossroad, 1995.

McManners, John. *The French Revolution and the Church*. New York: Harper and Row, 1968.

Marius, Richard. *Thomas More: A Biography*. London: Collins, 1986.

Meeks, Wayne D. *The First Urban Christians*. New Haven: Yale University Press, 1983.

Meier, John P. *Matthew*. Wilmington: Michael Glazier, 1980.

Meyendorff, John (ed.). *The Primacy of Peter: Essays in Ecclesiology and the Early Church*. Crestwood: St. Vladimir's Seminary Press, 1992.

Migne, Jacques Paul. *Patrologiae cursus completus: Series Latina*. Paris: Garnier, 1844–1891.

Minns, Denis. *Irenaeus*. London: Geoffrey Chapman, 1994.

Molony, John. *The Worker Question: A New Historical Perspective on Rerum Novarum*. Melbourne: Collins Dove, 1991.

Newman, John Henry. *On Consulting the Laity in Matters of Doctrine*. Ed. by John Coulson. London: Collins, 1961.

Oakley, Francis. 'Celestial Hierarchies Revisited: Walter Ullmann's Vision of Medieval Politics.' *Past and Present*, 60 (1973).

O'Connor, Daniel W. *Peter in Rome: The Literary, Liturgical, and Archaeological Evidence*. New York: Columbia University Press, 1969.

O'Farrell, Patrick. *The Catholic Church and Community in Australia: An Australian History*. Third revised edition. Sydney: New South Wales University Press, 1992.

Ormerod, Neil, and Ormerod, Thea. *When Ministers Sin: Sexual Abuse in the Churches*. Sydney: Millennium, 1995.

Osborne, Kenan B. *Priesthood: A History of the Ordained Ministry in the Roman Catholic Church*. New York: Paulist Press, 1988.

Patterson, Webster T. *Newman: Pioneer for the Layman*. Washington: Corpus, 1968.

Peters, W. H. *The Life of Benedict XV*. Milwaukee: Bruce, 1959.

Rahner, Karl. *Theological Investigations: Volume 2*. Baltimore: Helicon Press, 1963.

Ratzinger, Josef. 'The Pastoral Implications of Episcopal Collegiality.' *Concilium*, Glenrock: Paulist Press, 1965.

Ratzinger, Josef, with Vittorio Messori. *The Ratzinger Report: An Exclusive Interview on the State of the Church*. San Francisco: Ignatius, 1985.

Reese, Thomas J. (ed.). *Episcopal Conferences: Historical, Canonical, and Theological Studies*. Washington: Georgetown University Press, 1989.

Ritzer, Remegium, and Pirminum Serfin. *Hierarchia Catholica Medii et Recentioris Aevi*. Volume 3. Pavia: Il Messaggero di S. Antonio, 1978.

Bibliography

Rynne, Xavier. *Letters from Vatican City: Vatican Council II (First Session): Background and Debates*. London: Faber and Faber, 1963.

————. *The Second Session: The Debates and Decrees of Vatican II: September 29 to December 4, 1963*. London: Faber and Faber, 1964.

————. *The Third Session: Debates and Decrees of Vatican Council II: September 14 to November 21, 1964*. London: Faber and Faber, 1965.

————. *The Fourth Session: The Debates and Decrees of Vatican Council II: September 14 to December 8, 1965*. London: Faber and Faber, 1966.

————. *John Paul's Extraordinary Synod: A Collegial Achievement*. Wilmington: Michael Glazier, 1986.

Santer, Mark. 'Bishop's Moves.' *Times Literary Supplement*, 21 March 1986.

Schilleebeeckx, Edward. *The Church with a Human Face: A New and Expanded Theology of Ministry*. New York: Crossroad, 1990.

Schimmelpfenning, Bernhard. *The Papacy*. New York: Columbia University Press, 1992.

Schultenover, David G. *A View from Rome: On the Eve of the Modernist Crisis*. New York: Fordham University Press, 1993.

Sellers, R. V. *The Council of Chalcedon: A Historical and Doctrinal Survey*. London: SPCK, 1961.

Sipe, A. W. Richard. *A Secret World: Sexuality and the Search for Celibacy*. New York: Brunner/Mazel, 1990.

————. *Sex, Priests, and Power: Anatomy of a Crisis*. London: Cassell, 1995.

Smith, Denis Mack. *Italy: A Modern History*. Ann Arbor: University of Michigan Press, 1969.

Sordi, Marta. *The Christians and the Roman Empire*. London: Groom Helm, 1983.

Stacpoole, Alberic (ed.). *Vatican II by Those Who Were There*. London: Geoffrey Chapman, 1986.

Steinmann, Jean. *Saint Jerome*. London: Geoffrey Chapman, 1959.

Sullivan, Francis A. *Magisterium: Teaching Authority in the Catholic Church*. Dublin: Gill and Macmillan, 1983.

————. 'Guideposts from Catholic Tradition.' *America*, 9 December 1995.

Swidler, Leonard, and Piet F. Fransen (eds). *Authority in the Church and the Schillebeeckx Case*. New York: Crossroad, 1982.

Swidler, Leonard, and Herbert O'Brien (eds). *A Catholic Bill of Rights*. Kansas City: Sheed and Ward, 1988.

Szulc, Tad. *Pope John Paul II: The Biography*, New York: Scribner, 1995.

Tanner, Norman P. *Decrees of the Ecumenical Councils*. Two volumes. London: Sheed and Ward, 1990.

Tierney, Brian, *Foundations of the Conciliar Theory: The Contribution of the Medieval Canonists from Gratian to the Great Schism*. Cambridge: Cambridge University Press, 1955.

————. *The Crisis of Church and State 1050–1300*. Englewood Cliffs: Prentice-Hall, 1964.

————. *Origins of Papal Infallibility 1150–1350: A Study on the Concepts of Infallibility, Sovereignity and Tradition in the Middle Ages*. Leiden: E. J. Brill, 1972.

Tillard, J. M. R. *The Bishop of Rome*. Wilmington: Michael Glazier, 1983.

————. 'The Primacy-Conciliarity Tension.' *Theology Digest*, 41:1 (1994).

Torjesen, Karen Jo. *When Women Were Priests*. San Francisco: HarperSanFrancisco, 1993.

Toynbee, Jocelyn, and John Ward Perkins. *The Shrine of St. Peter and the Vatican Excavations*. New York: Pantheon, 1957.

Walsh, J. E. *The Bones of Saint Peter*. New York: Doubleday, 1982.

Walsh, Michael. *The Secret World of Opus Dei*. London: Grafton, 1989.

————. *John Paul II: A Biography*. London: HarperCollins, 1994.

Ward, Wilfred. *William George Ward and the Catholic Revival*. London: Macmillan, 1893.

Watt, John A. *The Theory of Papal Monarchy in the Thirteenth Century: The Contribution of the Canonists*, London: Burns & Oates, 1965.

West, Morris. 'One Man's Voice.' *Eureka Street*, August 1994, pp. 28–32.

Winter, Michael. *St. Peter and the Popes*. London: Darton, Longman and Todd, 1960.

Yallop, David. *In God's Name: An Investigation into the Murder of Pope John Paul I*. London: Corgi, 1985.

Zizola, Giancarlo. *The Utopia of John XXIII*. Maryknoll: Orbis, 1978.

————. 'Secretariats and Councils of the Roman Curia.' *Concilium: The Roman Curia and the Communion of Churches*. New York: Seabury Press, 1979.

Index

Index